J. M. COETZEE AND THE POLITICS OF STYLE

J. M. Coetzee's early novels confronted readers with a brute reality stripped of human relation and a prose repeatedly described as spare, stark, intense and lyrical. In this book, Jarad Zimbler explores the emergence of a style forged in Coetzee's engagement with the complexities of South African culture and politics. Tracking the development of this style across Coetzee's first eight novels, from *Dusklands* to *Disgrace*, Zimbler compares Coetzee's writing with that of South African authors such as Gordimer, Brink and La Guma, whilst re-examining the nature of Coetzee's indebtedness to modernism and postmodernism. In each case, he follows the threads of Coetzee's own writings on stylistics and rhetoric in order to fix on those techniques of language and narrative used to activate a 'politics of style'. In so doing, Zimbler challenges long-held beliefs about Coetzee's oeuvre, and about the ways in which contemporary literatures of the world are to be read and understood.

JARAD ZIMBLER was born in Johannesburg and is now a Lecturer in Modern English Literature at the University of Birmingham. He has published articles on book history, Pierre Bourdieu and postcolonial pedagogy, and is co-editor of *Crafts of World Literature: Field, Material and Translation*, a special issue of the *Journal of Commonwealth Literature*.

J. M. COETZEE AND THE POLITICS OF STYLE

JARAD ZIMBLER

University of Birmingham

CAMBRIDGE
UNIVERSITY PRESS

CAMBRIDGE
UNIVERSITY PRESS

32 Avenue of the Americas, New York NY 10013-2473, USA

Cambridge University Press is part of the University of Cambridge.

It furthers the University's mission by disseminating knowledge in the pursuit of
education, learning and research at the highest international levels of excellence.

www.cambridge.org
Information on this title: www.cambridge.org/9781107624597

© Jarad Zimbler 2014

First published 2014
First paperback edition 2015

A catalogue record for this publication is available from the British Library

Library of Congress Cataloguing in Publication data
Zimbler, Jarad, 1980–
J. M. Coetzee and the Politics of Style / Jarad Zimbler, University of Birmingham.
pages   cm
Includes bibliographical references and index.
ISBN 978-1-107-04625-2 (hardback)
1. Coetzee, J. M., 1940 – Criticism and interpretation.   I. Title.
PR9369.3.C58Z99   2014
823'.914–dc23   2013042667

ISBN 978-1-107-04625-2 Hardback
ISBN 978-1-107-62459-7 Paperback

Contents

Acknowledgements

I have been fortunate in my family, friends, teachers and colleagues, on whom I have relied for conversation, comfort and guidance. Whether they realize the full measure of what they have given, I am particularly grateful to: William Charrington, Jesse Copelyn, John Copelyn, Henry Dean, Priyamvada Gopal, Mary Jacobus, Simon Jarvis, Megan Jones, David Nowell-Smith, Edward Oates, Molly Oldfield, Ato Quayson, Esther Schwartz, Caryn Solomon, Joan Solomon, Louis Solomon, Alastair Sooke, Aleksandra Wasylkow, Simon Woods, Daniel Zimbler and Kelly Zimbler. To those who have read and commented on portions of the work, a special thanks: Corinne Abel, David Attwell, Elleke Boehmer, Rachel Bower, Alex Englander, Mark Knight, Robert MacFarlane, Nisha Manocha and Christopher Warnes; the two anonymous readers for Cambridge University Press, who were astute in their criticisms and helpful in their recommendations; and Allen Zimbler, for his meticulous scrutiny of several drafts. I am appreciative of assistance received from: Ernst Engelbrecht, Lesley Hart, Peter Randall and Ray Ryan; and of generous support provided by: the Arts and Humanities Research Council, Pembroke College, Cambridge, the Anglo-California Foundation, and Wolfson College, Oxford, to whose president, Hermione Lee, I am especially indebted for advice and encouragement. Finally, I wish to acknowledge Peter D. McDonald, for what he has made possible, and Ben Etherington, for his intellectual largesse. Above all, I thank Adrian Poole, who has been, in every respect, a model of good humour, generosity, sensitivity and care.

For permission to reproduce 'Hero and Bad Mother in Epic', I thank J. M. Coetzee. For permission to use Cecil Skotnes's 'Three Figures' (Private Collection, Basel, Switzerland), I thank Pippa Skotnes, John Skotnes and the work's owners.

Introduction

Emergence of a Prose Style

Upon its publication in 1986, *Foe* elicited a number of surprisingly hostile responses. While it was by no means universally decried, a general air of discontent clung to the novel, streaked through with the fug of not a little confusion. Many early readers, both in South Africa and abroad, found it bewildering, plodding and too encumbered by its literary debts.

In *The Times* of London, Nicholas Shakespeare wrote that *Foe* was Coetzee's 'most disappointing fiction to date'; Neill Darke, reviewer for a Cape newspaper, described it as 'pointless, incomprehensible and tiresome'; and, in the *New York Review of Books*, D. J. Enright compared *Foe* unfavourably with the novels of Daniel Defoe, alongside which, he suggested, 'Coetzee's revision' could only 'seem a static and anemic affair'. Yet the harshest of these judgements was tempered with appreciative remarks on the writing itself. Whilst Shakespeare conceded that the prose of Coetzee's novel remained 'that of a true craftsman, detached and granite grey, and chipping away to reveal a cold polished work', Darke reminded his readers that 'Coetzee has previously shown that he has a towering talent. His superbly structured prose is sparse, razor-sharp'. Even Enright acknowledged 'the elegance of the writing'.[1]

At least in one respect, then, those reviewers who patently disliked *Foe* found cause for agreement with readers for whom the quality of the writing was of a piece with the work as a whole. One such was Isabel Hofmeyr: 'The book itself', she observed, 'is very easy to read. Written in the lean, taut prose that won Coetzee the Booker Prize for his last novel, *Life & Times of Michael K*, the sentences are immaculately constructed. The words could not be simpler. Yet this limpid prose tells an endlessly complex story.' Heather Mackie, writing several months later, felt that *Foe* was 'another superbly crafted novel' composed 'with masterly skill in lean, taut prose of metronomic simplicity'; and Alexander Johnston

I

believed that, though *Foe* could be read on 'individual, social, parochial and universal levels', it yet retained 'its clean lines, and fluent straightforward narrative'.[2]

That reviewers who felt so differently about the novel nevertheless agreed that *Foe* was well written is certainly of interest, but not nearly as intriguing as the fact that they agreed also on what the novel was like, or at least chose descriptive words that often overlapped and coincided. For, whatever their differences, we find much in these reviews that is shared: an insistence on the simplicity of the writing; an experience of something imperturbable; an encounter with a prose that has nothing loose, baggy, soft or superfluous about it, but which is instead sparse, lean and taut. It is this semantic congruence that suggests something like a common experience of and response to *Foe*.

In examining the reviews of Coetzee's earlier novels – *Dusklands* (1974), *In the Heart of the Country* (1977), *Waiting for the Barbarians* (1980) and *Life & Times of Michael K* (1983) – it soon becomes apparent that the responses to *Foe* drew upon and consolidated a sense of Coetzee's prose style that had been more than a decade in the making. Certainly, the clarity and simplicity of Coetzee's writing had been remarked from the outset, in reviews which often juxtaposed these qualities with a force or intensity that likewise came to be regarded as characteristic.

In an early review, Peter Wilhelm described *Dusklands* as a 'stark and obsessional' work with a 'cerebral' style and a 'language' that 'seethes'. If this combination of cool detachment and brute force led Ursula Barnett to comment that the style of the novel was occasionally 'uneven', other reviewers were as impressed as Wilhelm with the manner in which the writing kept in tension such apparently contradictory qualities.[3] Frances Bowers, for one, praised the novel as a 'brilliantly told, dryly savage yet very moral tale' that was at once 'disturbing and beautifully written', and Peter Temple celebrated the 'lucid, compelling, intensely graphic prose' which produced scenes that had about them a 'frozen, cinematic quality'.[4] Later readers of *Dusklands* responded in like fashion. Nicholas Shakespeare, in his review of the 1982 British edition, compared Coetzee to a glasscutter whose 'pieces' were 'clear and sharp in exposition', but also, in certain moments, 'jagged and refracting'. For Victoria Glendinning, the two parts of *Dusklands* were likewise 'tight, hard adventure stories' and also 'dramatically alive, told in a quick, urgent voice', a voice that was 'harsh' and 'compelling'.[5]

Reviewers of Coetzee's subsequent novels were similarly impressed. One wrote that the prose of *In the Heart of the Country* was 'controlled but always expressive', creating a 'brooding, oppressive atmosphere' in a work that was 'relentless and chilling', and another praised the work's 'scenes of extraordinary intensity and delicacy' in which the 'vivid energy of the language' balanced 'the severity of the theme'.[6] In Lionel Abrahams's evocative description, Coetzee's second novel emerged 'as a thing of metallic presence which, however streaked with dust, blood, faeces and semen, gleams with the silvery brilliance of his style' and with a 'hard vividness', whilst Jaap Boekkooi suggested of *Waiting for the Barbarians* that its 'narrative may be cool and evocative as medieval stained glass, but the message is the wail, plea and cajole of a prophet like Jeremiah', giving rise to a 'bitter grapes-of-wrath quality' in a novel 'told with power, depth and compassion'.[7] Reviewers of *Life & Times of Michael K* again found evidence for the 'very simple, bleak' style of Coetzee's novels, their use of 'plain words' and 'simple language' to give voice to 'a deep compassion that boils up'.[8]

If there was thus continuity, there was also development, for reviewers now began to perceive, over and above the effects of simplicity, clarity and intensity, a mode of composition characterized by economy and precision and a basic style marked by 'originality of voice and a spare prose'.[9] Irving Howe, for example, who had found *In the Heart of the Country* somewhat 'overwrought', described *Waiting for the Barbarians* as a 'realistic fable, at once stark, exciting and economical', at the centre of which lay 'a setpiece of austere prose', whilst Dave Wightman observed of the novel that 'Each word' seemed to have been 'carefully and crisply chosen'.[10] Later reviewers came to much the same conclusions: *Life & Times of Michael K* was 'written throughout in a beautiful, spare, observant prose'; a prose that was 'clean, economical, often almost matter-of-fact'; the 'clean lines' and 'leanness' of the novel suggesting 'a restraint and rigour about the style'; suggesting, in fact, 'a gift for sparse, spare story-telling, in which there is not a wasted word or image'.[11]

In a few of the later reviews, the link between compositional economy and the effects of clarity and intensity was in fact made explicit. Anne Pogrund felt that one was 'immediately and uncomfortably involved' in the novel by its 'bare and intense' style of writing, the 'compact economy of prose, so simple, yet telling so much'; and Cynthia Ozick found 'the grain' of the novel's sentences so 'flat and austere, but also so purifying to the senses that one comes away feeling that one's eye has been sharpened, one's hearing vivified'. All of which Beryl Roberts captured most neatly: 'In lyrical but economic language, with each word shaped and honed to extract the maximum significance from every image, Coetzee depicts a terrifying world' and offers 'a stark depressing message' which is all 'beautifully delivered in polished prose'.[12]

The reviewers of *Foe* therefore had behind them a decade's worth of judgements, and an established consensus concerning the basic characteristics of Coetzee's style. The experiences of their predecessors were not identical, but they were very seldom, if ever, contradictory, at least where the writing itself was concerned.

It is true that reviewers of *Dusklands* and even *In the Heart of the Country* were less precise, but this is hardly surprising, since repetition is required to produce pattern and they lacked the benefit of retrospective distance afforded to later critics. Only over time did the simplicity of the writing come to be understood as the consequence of compositional economy, a process of paring down. On the other hand, the affective force of the novels was evident from the outset. Words such as *gripping*, *compelling*, *forbidding*, *disturbing* and *terrifying*, as well as *vivifying*, *exciting* and even *purifying*, register an often visceral experience, one which led to the use of both sensual and psychological descriptive terms: *hard*, *bitter* and *sharp* on the one hand, *intense*, *brooding* and *oppressive* on the other.

None of the minor variations should in any case obscure the remarkably uniform characterization of the *prose*, *writing*, *language*, *form*, *narrative*, *presentation* and *style* of Coetzee's novels. This uniformity suggests the existence of something like a stylistic substance common to each of these works, a substance that could be imaginatively related to glass and ice and metal and stone, and whose range of qualities found condensed expression in particularly evocative and oft-repeated words: *vivid*, to suggest both clarity and intensity; *taut* to intimate control, tension and concision; and *stark*, which seems to capture most powerfully, and all at once, the force, severity and economy that came to be associated with Coetzee's fictions.

Reading and Analysing

It is certainly possible that Coetzee's reviewers were responding to one another, rather than to the novels themselves, and that the similarities of their judgements were therefore produced by mutual influence. This suspicion cannot be dismissed out of hand: it would be naïve to imagine that reviewers are unaffected by their predecessors and by the marketing efforts of publishers. Particular adjectives may well proliferate because they are sanctioned by the blurb and, seemingly, the author himself.

For all that, reviewers remain free to disagree with one another, which they often do, both in their interpretations and estimations, and it is therefore of interest if they should use the very same words to describe an author's style. It is of greater interest still if these words vary while remaining semantically congruent, for in this we see evidence of a compulsion to display both critical acuity and verbal dexterity, two markers of the reviewer's own craft: trying to find exactly the right way of articulating what is most distinctive about a particular work, everything depends on the reviewer's insight and feeling for language, his or her capacity to produce the *mot juste*.

Applied to writing, words such as *vivid, taut* and *stark* are obviously difficult to substantiate. Plainly metaphorical, they indicate a struggle on the part of readers to give expression to apparently spontaneous intuitions, to experiences that are sensuous and yet surprisingly durable, the tone and texture of a novel often remaining with us long after we have forgotten the details of its plot. But if these words are therefore subjective and descriptive, they are also to some extent evaluative, and, moreover, imply a presumption of common if not universal assent. They are claims, in other words, about the work itself, and not simply the experience of the work.

That they are seldom treated as such by literary critics makes only more compelling the fact that Coetzee himself drew on similarly impressionistic characterizations in his PhD dissertation on Samuel Beckett. There, he observed: 'Writers on *Watt* have resorted to a number of curious metaphors to describe its style: the compulsive evacuation of the reason, the graph of a half-absent mind, counting, the turning out of the coins of logic from a die.' To Coetzee, the fact that 'four critics, stretched to using their metaphoric faculties, should have produced figures superficially so dissimilar yet fundamentally so alike' was an indication that there might well be 'some incessant, half-sleeping, computational quality to *Watt* accessible only to metaphor'. Indeed, this semantic overlap bolstered the intuition that 'behind the verbal habits of *Watt* ... lies a single principle, a central nervous flexion which causes the tics we see on the verbal surface'.[13]

The proposition that stylistic qualities are accessible only to metaphor is of course one that Coetzee's study attempted to disprove: far from lying beyond the reach of analysis, it hoped to show, those verbal tics and habits to which readers respond intuitively could be identified and explained, at least provisionally. As to whether this analysis would shed light on the meaning of the work, that is a question with which any study of style is necessarily concerned. Certainly, it will be the focus here, where the principal aim is not only to clarify how the bareness of Coetzee's prose is produced but also to explore its consequences for interpretation.

In pursuit of this aim, a certain privilege has been granted to the experience of readers, in respect of which the procedures of the present study may seem to converge with what has come to be known as reader-response theory. Yet, while the insights of such critics as Wolfgang Iser, Stanley Fish and Michael Riffaterre are clearly relevant, there are reasons to approach them with caution.[14]

To begin with, it is difficult to agree that the reading of a literary work is ever so cool, rational and attentive as that proposed by Iser, or so rooted in the step-by-step unfolding described in Fish's early work on affective stylistics. Furthermore, though it is clear that particular codes and assumptions will always delimit attempts at interpretation, Fish's later writings on interpretive communities seem to fall into an extreme relativism and to ignore both the inertia that limits the variability of social structures and the possibility that hermeneutic frameworks can be analysed, articulated and used reflexively. As for Riffaterre, his approach is especially problematic because it disregards the actual 'content' of readers' responses; presuming relevant only those moments at which readers are consciously arrested, he dismisses altogether the kind of judgements catalogued here, which tend to concern features that are pervasive.

As such, whatever its debts to reader-response theories, this study is in several respects more closely aligned with the expanding fields of sociolinguistics, pragmatics and narrative rhetoric, where it is taken for granted that one might imperceptibly sway one's auditors and readers by one's manner of speaking, and that the slightest nuances of verbal expression are capable of generating meaning at speeds that defy immediate explication of their functioning. If this is hardly more than classical rhetoricians presumed, the work of twentieth-century linguists and narratologists has more fruitfully enabled analysis of those aspects of a work that ground and incite readers' intuitions, those subterranean operations of syntax, lexis, prosody and narrative structure that intimately and often invisibly determine their particular impressions.

It is these impressions that precede or at the very least saturate interpretation, and to leave them out of account is to ignore what are often the most tangible and lasting effects of any work; it is to designate style as little more than adornment, superfluous to meaning. The argument pursued here is that, on the contrary, style is fundamentally important to the ways a novel mediates and knows the world, to what Theodor Adorno calls its 'truth content', and that it is therefore a mistake to respond – as many of us do – as if style were little more than the writer's calling card, or something to be savoured by connoisseurs.[15] To elucidate stylistic qualities, then, is not simply to appreciate them more fully, but to show what it is about the work that affects us and why this manner of being affected is important; it is to bring to consciousness what are otherwise intuitions without bearing.

This is not to imply, however, that 'non-analytical' reading is necessarily deficient. It would be as much a mistake to forego a surrender to the work as to leave off without some attempt to understand what emerges from that surrender. Were we to launch ourselves immediately into analysis we might find little to analyse, and certainly little more than the dusty remains of a carcase too hastily picked over. The analytical reading will less often be a first than a third, fourth or fifth reading.

As to whether it remains possible to surrender to the work once we have acquired the habits of analysis, it must certainly be acknowledged that the work itself becomes different once its linguistic and narrative details have been closely examined. Indeed, the ability to dissect the operations of language must in itself affect cursory readings of even the most prosaic texts. Yet, if the acquisition of linguistic and rhetorical knowledge inevitably alters our readerly responses, this need not extinguish our capacity to be swept up or even swept away, compelled to adjust ourselves to the rhythms and patterns of a language and thought that is not our own. This, at least, has been my own experience. For no matter how often I have read one of Coetzee's novels, no matter how intently I have scrutinized its linguistic and rhetorical workings, there remain moments in which I find myself subjected to the narrative, suddenly in its grip, bound inexorably to the world it has created. The task, then, is to explain this experience.

Form and Style

Clearly discernible in the reviews of Coetzee's early fictions – and especially in the negative reviews of *Foe* – is a commonplace distinction between what one says and how one says it, that is, between content and form. The host of difficulties to which this distinction gives rise can partly be set aside if we avoid thinking of the literary work as an entity with mutually exclusive component parts and view it instead as an object about which different kinds of questions can be put.

Thus, we might ask what a novel is about and answer by giving a paraphrase, involving a brief account of the central characters and a record of those events that are salient, or by speaking of the themes or ideas that seem most pertinent, or by referring to its subject matter. In each case, the work is addressed as a whole, and the sense of what is pertinent or salient is affected by the novel's language or narrative strategies. Such features might themselves be the focus of a different set of questions, those pertaining to form or technique, and here again there is no absolute division, because to ask how a story is told one must already have some provisional sense of what the story is.

One consequence of understanding form and content in this way is that questions of the how need not be limited to the features isolated by linguistics and rhetoric. On the contrary, once form is the focus, there are few aspects of a work that cannot be considered. Thus, while it is usual to associate story with the content of a novel, we might ask whether a given plot might not be framed by another kind of story, where, insofar as we speak less about the forms of a particular novel and more about different novel forms, we begin to broach the topic of genre (understood here simply as a convenient means of dividing the vast ground covered by such categories as *novel, short story* and *poem*). Of course, we might step back even further and ask whether a certain subject or theme might not have been otherwise communicated, and so treat the novel itself as a form of address, the features of which set it apart from other media and modes, whether of fiction or fact.

There is nothing unusual about this manner of conceiving form and content. Similar understandings have been elaborated elsewhere and for some time. In his 1948 essay 'Technique as Discovery', Mark Schorer insisted: 'When we speak of technique, then, we speak of nearly everything.'[16] However, since the moment of New Criticism, to which Schorer's essay belongs, the rise of linguistics and structuralism *has* encouraged the emergence of a more sophisticated conception of form than one that begins and ends with imagery and symbolism. Building on the work of the Russian Formalists and Prague School linguists, and further enabled by the Chomskyan and silicon revolutions, critics have become more willing to grapple in earnest with patterns of language use at the level of the clause and phrase, the phoneme and morpheme.

It is perhaps the consequence of these developments that, in the 1960s, when Coetzee's career as a literary critic began, talk had turned increasingly from *form* to *style*. For the most distinctive and elusive qualities of an author's writing seem more closely related to the minutiae of language than to a certain imagery or set of tropes. The study of style, in other words, is not merely the study of 'all the strategies of language that are used to shape prose and verse into expressions of thoughts and feeling', because what is missing from this definition, offered by the first editors of the flagship journal *Style*, is the concern with that which is characteristic of a particular work or author.[17] Style, then, is not simply form by another name, but form understood relationally, as a value within a field of values, and it is by explicitly addressing the relational character of literary practices – the way these practices are shaped and given meaning alongside and against one another – that stylistic and formal analysis might usefully be differentiated.[18]

Such an approach to style is in any case indicated by the nature of the judgements cited previously. For there can be no absolute standard on the basis of which to describe a work of fiction as *spare, stark, economic* or *lyrical*, and there is no particular arrangement of words and clauses – no particular form – that is inherently any of these things. On the contrary, when we use a word like *spare*, we immediately invoke a field of practices in which values are open to modification and redefinition. At the very least, we rely on a familiarity with the history of a particular genre or tradition and its constitutive range of characteristics, as well as with the judgements made about those characteristics, a familiarity, however vague, developed over the course of primary, secondary and tertiary education and through a lifetime's reading, whether casual or critical, which enables even the non-specialist to appreciate and adjudicate on an author's style.

This relational dimension is further apparent in the two understandings of style delineated by Coetzee in his PhD dissertation: style as defined by Bernard Bloch in terms of the statistical distribution of lexical and syntactical variables peculiar to a given work, or to the works of a given author; and style as apparently conceived by Beckett, a form related to a content, a set of techniques chosen in view of a particular subject matter. For, whatever their differences, these understandings implicitly share the sense of style as that peculiar combination of factors by which an author comes to be known, indeed, comes to be identifiable.

With regard to Bloch's definition, it is worth noting that Coetzee's stated aim was to demonstrate that, though new analytical methods promised a science of literature, statistical information would seldom add much of value to an understanding of literary works, and that, even if the study of style were strictly axiomatic, it could only be incorporated in literary interpretation by some intuitive leap. These insights remain salutary, but what proves most helpful in Coetzee's preference for the conception of style he finds in Beckett is that it sheds further light on the term's meaning. For, in speaking of the relation of form to content, one speaks not only of the work's unity and coherence, but also of the extent to which its various elements are so related that they produce an impression of necessity, such that the work appears as if it were an organic whole. Here it is worth noting that though we associate style with terms as vague as *writing*, *prose* and *language*, our judgements of a novel are inevitably related not to particular features treated in isolation, but to the way these features coalesce.

The notion that style is a function of the relation between parts is of further interest because it entails the evaluative dimension of stylistic analysis. It is precisely because a work might sometimes fail to produce the aforementioned impression of necessity that we can speak of the success or failure of a given moment or a given work. And if we might question whether particular techniques – that is, particular narrative, grammatical and rhetorical strategies – are more or less suited to particular subject matters, we might also begin to think of technique, subject matter and the relation between them in terms of selection. In fact, *selection* is not the right word, for the struggle of the author is not simply to choose, but to make, or at least to rework.

But what is it that engenders this struggle? Quite simply, the historical character of literary practice: it is because forms and contents are subject to ageing, because the meanings and values attached to them change over time, because techniques and themes once thought scandalous and avant-garde gradually become modish and then outmoded, that each new generation of authors is compelled to return to the question of style.[19] And if style is not simply form understood in relation to other forms, but also form understood in relation to content and to the history of this relation, then it is clearly a mistake to speak – as past stylisticians have been wont to do – as if the prose of the world could be divided between two or twenty basic styles.[20] For the passage of time and the pressures of place themselves ensure that the plain style of Philip Larkin is different from the plain style of Ben Jonson, just as the spare prose of J. M. Coetzee is different from the spare prose of Samuel Beckett, though the meanings attached to the former inevitably depend on those associated with the latter.

Field and Material

It follows that stylistic analysis entails comparison as well as description. In explaining their 'restricted concept of style', Geoffrey Leech and Michael Short therefore observe: 'A style is defined in terms of a *domain* of language use (e.g. What choices are made by a particular author, in a particular genre, or in a particular text).'[21] Although helpful as a starting point, the meaning of 'domain of language use' certainly requires further elucidation.

The question of context, norm and deviation is one that Coetzee himself addresses in the conclusion to his dissertation, where he first acknowledges the need to 'replace deviation from the norms of the whole language with deviation from some more limited norm', and then asks: 'What should this be?' The solution Coetzee adopts – considering Beckett's English fictions in relation to the 'external' norm of twentieth-century fiction as well as the 'internal' norm established by the works themselves – largely corresponds with the focus on genre, oeuvre and text Leech and Short recommend. If this is not entirely without relevance to the present study, Coetzee himself views his solution as provisional and wonders whether 'approaches which we today regard as divergent will always remain so.'[22]

In fact, the more pressing question is whether the kinds of contexts proposed by Coetzee as well as by Leech and Short give due emphasis to the historicity of style, and to the fact that authors at different times and in different places face horizons of possibility that are changed not simply by those elements of life with which historians, sociologists and philologists are directly concerned, but also by the pressures, tensions and dynamics peculiar to literary practice. Certainly, it is possible to give a more thorough account of these horizons, aided in the present case by the distinct yet complementary visions of Pierre Bourdieu and Theodor Adorno.

The wide-ranging theory of literary production proposed by Bourdieu has offered several literary critics a means of overcoming the apparent antinomies between contextual and formal analyses.[23] This is because it insists that a work has its meaning and value not directly within the fields of power and social relations, but rather within what Bourdieu describes as a 'relatively autonomous literary field', a competitive space in which successful position-taking depends on the capacity of a given work to distinguish itself from other works. It is because the grounds for distinction are aesthetic that the field's relative autonomy is ensured, since at least one principle of evaluation is therefore internal. The field may thus continue to be subject to external evaluative measures, such as volume of sales, and yet remain partially self-regulating, its participants struggling amongst one another for what Bourdieu calls 'degree specific consecration', the form of recognition bestowed by those within the field itself.

The peculiar logic according to which the literary field operates is of course nothing other than the logic of style, and this has several important consequences. To begin with, the temporality of the field comes to be determined internally, so that it is not the passage of years that marks time but rather the passage of literary generations, each of which endeavours to dismiss the achievements of its immediate predecessors as déclassé. The history of the literary field thus becomes the history of evolving forms and contents, articulated more in individual works than in the polemical manifestos of authors and movements.

In a similar fashion, the shape and structure of the literary field comes to be determined less by geography or social class than by shared traditions, institutions, networks and languages, as well as shared challenges, problems, themes and subject matters. Proximity becomes in this way a function not of common citizenship and domicile but of intensity of relation, and because a practice must distinguish itself to achieve recognition, it may in the end be closest of all to precisely those practices to which it is most vehemently opposed.

For this reason alone, an account of literary relations must always go beyond questions of influence and elective affinity. Indeed, to describe the domain within which an author's stylistic decisions are made and given meaning, it will be necessary to reconstruct the state of the field at the moment of the work's production, to recover those practices, debates, movements and institutions which have ensured, for the moment in question, that only certain combinations of forms and contents will give the impression of necessity.

Although it tends to privilege an author's struggles with predecessors over those with peers and rivals, there are nevertheless important respects in which Adorno's aesthetic theory prefigures Bourdieu's, not least in its attempt 'to understand art as essentially historical, whilst retaining a strong interest in aesthetic valuation', and thus to avoid the bad choice between internal and external analysis.[24] However, whereas Bourdieu's notion of the field relies on a metaphorics of the visual, and therefore prompts us to think of successful position-takings as consequent on clear-sightedness and choice, Adorno's account, and especially his notion of aesthetic material, acknowledges the labour that is expended in writing, the concerted effort that is needed to acquire and configure what is given. It acknowledges, in other words, that the positions occupied by literary works are not simply chosen, but made.

Where literature is concerned, Adorno suggests, the material is of course language, but it is also that agglomeration of themes and subjects, genres and techniques that the history of literary production presents to an author; or, rather, in which the author finds himself or herself always already situated. Thus, in his *Aesthetic Theory*, Adorno writes: 'Material, by contrast, is what artists work with: It is the sum of all that is available to them, including words, colors, sounds, associations of every sort and every technique ever developed. To this extent, forms too can become material; it is everything that artists encounter about which they must make a decision.'[25]

However, if this seems to imply an 'infinite warehouse of past practice', the historical and contingent character of Adorno's material means that the notion of 'availability' must be qualified.[26] In this regard, Adorno comments: 'The idea, widespread among unreflective artists, of the open eligibility of any and all material is problematic in that it ignores the constraint inherent in technical procedures and the progress of the material'.[27] In other words, as the consequence of changing environmental conditions and ongoing use, literary materials are always subject to processes of banalization. In being used, they can be used up. As such, at any given time and in any given space, only particular subjects and techniques will remain available for a work that is meaningful, that is capable of knowing the truth of the world.

These observations on Adorno's aesthetic material and Bourdieu's literary field may not do justice to the complexity and subtlety of either thinker, but should be sufficient for present purposes. What is of greatest importance here is that these notions help us to understand literary works historically and relationally. In thinking about the horizon of possibilities which gives meaning to aesthetic decisions, they prompt us to focus on the restrictions and openings of particular moments and to emphasize negative as well as positive relations. They prompt us, moreover, to consider writing not as a process of neutral choice, but rather as labour and competition, a struggle by and between authors to shape that with which they are presented, to overcome and master a set of problems, difficulties and demands, not by wholly intentional effort, but by means of craft: a practical knowledge and acquired habit that gives one the feeling of operating by instinct or intuition. That this manner of clarifying the nature of literary practice and the context of intelligibility also corresponds in important ways with Coetzee's own developing conception of the domain of aesthetic decisions is something that will emerge over the course of this study.

South African Literature as Field and Material

Used heuristically, the terms *field* and *material* help to flesh out the domain
of stylistic endeavour, and do so in a manner that invigorates the procedures of contemporary stylistics, which at least acknowledges, in contrast
with some earlier formalisms, 'that utterances (literary and otherwise) are
produced in a time, a place, and in a cultural and cognitive context'.[28] This
nevertheless presents us with a further set of questions: what is the field to
which Coetzee belongs and what is the material with which he is faced?

In previous critical responses to Coetzee's fictions, the question of literary context has certainly been raised, but there has been a tendency to focus
solely on lines of descent that lead from writers such as Kafka, Beckett,
Borges and Nabokov. The preoccupation with influence and indebtedness
implicit in these genealogies has meanwhile ensured that works by South
African authors are very seldom deemed relevant, except as indistinguish-
able further instances of a realism to which Coetzee's novels are fundamentally opposed. Yet his critical writings and reviews make clear that
Coetzee remained interested in the careers of his local peers and rivals,
and that he engaged critically with their works and the peculiar challenges
they faced. It is therefore one of the central contentions of this study that,
if Coetzee's *material* necessarily incorporates the products of centuries of
literary labour in several European languages, his *field* is South African.

Is it legitimate to view Coetzee in this light, when he has for so long
been regarded as a man apart? This is a question with which this study
as a whole is concerned and the answer will depend on whether it is possible to demonstrate the significance of Coetzee's local literary field to the
emergence and meaning of his bare style. To do this, it will be necessary
to consider Coetzee's novels alongside and against works of fellow South
African writers, and to re-examine the nature of his relations with metropolitan predecessors, especially Beckett, but also Vladimir Nabokov and
those authors associated with the *nouveau roman*. This cannot be mean-
ingfully undertaken in this introduction, but we can at least prepare the
ground for subsequent chapters by addressing certain challenges that arise
when such an approach is made.

To begin with, the fragmentation of South African life wrought by apartheid begs the question whether it is even appropriate to speak of a South
African literature, rather than several literatures corresponding to the
ethno-linguistic spheres carved out by the state's policies of separation.
Without wishing to adopt the perspective or tone of one recent critic,

who claims that his 'book overflies the colonial past' in order to treat South African literature as 'a single subject', I believe there are nevertheless grounds for speaking of a unified space, even while preserving a sense of the different conditions under which its writers lived and worked.[29]

It is helpful to remember here that, as Bourdieu explains, the constitution of the literary field may be the function of internal relations rather than external limits, so that the conditions of social existence need not in themselves be decisive for determining its boundaries, particularly as these will always be a stake in the struggle for legitimacy, and thus open to redefinition by succeeding generations of authors. That there is disagreement about who belongs therefore matters less than that the question is posed. Of course, what matters most is that the position-takings are related to one another, whether by affirmation or negation, but if the dynamics of mutual recognition and conflict are essential to the shape of the field, the durability of its boundaries very much depends on those local institutions that grant its outlines a measure of tangible existence.

The roles of such institutions in South Africa have been recently described in Peter D. McDonald's *The Literature Police*, which gives an extremely thorough account not only of the apartheid state's censorship regime, but also of an impressive range of local publishers, periodicals, literary awards and writers' groups.[30] Although it is not his immediate aim, McDonald thus provides much of the evidence necessary for attributing a singular existence to South African literature during the 1960s, 1970s and 1980s, albeit one marked by attempts at partition and secession. He does this not only by cataloguing the existence of these institutions, but also by describing their frequent disregard for the logic of apartheid in their consideration and inclusion of works irrespective of authors' ethno-linguistic backgrounds.

The processes that McDonald observes can be illustrated by examining two kinds of text he addresses only in passing: introductions to and anthologies of South African writing, which continued to emerge throughout apartheid, bearing the imprimatur of recognized agents (editors, critics, writers) and institutions (publishers, universities, state education boards). Amongst the earliest introductions was the 1925 *South African Literature*. Its author, Manfred Nathan, cast the net more widely than many who would follow, insofar as he included histories, travellers' accounts, ethnologies and biographies, but he also took the view, adopted subsequently in many surveys, that a consideration of South African literature could not restrict itself to works in a single language. However, while he therefore examined writings in English, Afrikaans and Dutch, he failed to mention any writings in indigenous languages, or even those produced in English and Afrikaans by 'non-whites'.[31] Nathan thereby ignored a problem that would become increasingly difficult as apartheid brought questions of race and nation more sharply into focus, and as significant black and coloured writers rose to prominence.

For some editors, the path of least resistance was to cleave to the classificatory system provided by the state. Amongst the outcomes were works such as Alan Lennox-Short's encyclopaedic collection *English and South Africa*, which offered a fairly comprehensive survey of genres and prominent writers and featured two short entries by Coetzee himself.[32] However, while it made sure to include a section on 'non-white' authors, it also marked their difference, which led the poet, novelist and critic Stephen Gray to comment: 'So-called coloured and black writers in English are, in this volume, relegated to a buffer zone between English white writers and Afrikaners in English translation, as if the race classifications of apartheid were a sound methodology for literary criticism to adopt as well.'[33]

In his own *Southern African Literature*, Gray would suggest that, though apartheid had affected 'every facet' of the literature of 'the subcontinent at the tip of Africa', not least by erecting barriers 'between black and white, between English-speaker and Afrikaner', it was still possible – indeed desirable – to speak of a single literary space. All that was required, if its ethno-linguistic divisions were not simply ignored, was some imagination. Gray's own solution was to use the figure of the archipelago to describe the particular kind of unity of Southern African literature, a series of islands linked beneath the waves, such that 'one does not readily see the connections between them'.[34]

However great the challenge faced by those responsible for overviews and introductions, the difficulty of defining South African literature was still more pressing for makers of anthologies because their choices and exclusions required explicit justification, even where the selection was already delimited by genre or period. Often, editors shuffled uncomfortably between biographical, thematic and formal definitions, attempting to skirt the categories of apartheid and also its geography. So, for example, in *Close to the Sun*, first published in 1979, G. E. de Villiers noted: 'The short stories in this anthology were all written by Southern African (as distinct from South African) writers. Although not all of the authors were born in this part of the world, all either have lived here, or are still living here. Apart from one or two, the stories are set either in South Africa or in a few of its neighbouring countries.'[35]

In other cases, an argument was made for the thematic and even formal continuity of all South African writing. In his introduction to *South African Writing Today*, published in 1967, Anthony Sampson suggested that South African works could be identified by 'the powerful sense of place, the feel of a vast and varied canvas', a sense of place produced by a 'language which seems ... to have come out of the landscape'.[36] Indeed, according to Sampson, South African writing had a 'special quality' given to it by 'the pull between the natural privacy of the writer, and the tide of outside events', a quality that emerged in all its peculiarity when the works of South African authors were contrasted with those of their metropolitan peers: 'While English writers have become preoccupied with intimate relationships, sensitive childhoods, fantasy or nostalgia, the South Africans cannot retreat – however they may want to – into these luxuries: they are compelled to come out into the world and there is no difficulty in knowing what to write *about*.'[37]

As the decades wore on, this kind of assurance might have become increasingly rare, but anthologies continued to emerge even in the years of 'total onslaught' and 'total strategy'. In 1986, for example, Coetzee was chosen, alongside André P. Brink, as editor of *A Land Apart: A Contemporary South African Reader*. The blurb on the Penguin paperback edition notes that Brink and Coetzee, 'two of South Africa's most important authors', had 'compiled a collection of English and Afrikaans writings that give a unique and vivid picture of the reality of life in South Africa during the past decade'. In their introduction, the editors themselves were far more circumspect, aware of the extent to which all attempts to establish the bounds of particular fields are consequent on contestable authority and inevitable exclusion: 'If the outlines of a map of contemporary South African writing do seem to emerge, the map should be used cautiously and within the limits very cursorily sketched in this introduction.'[38]

We might then say that, by means of a number of institutional interventions, the shape of South African literature was traced and queried throughout the twentieth century, and if its borderlands remained shadowy, its central territories were being ever more thoroughly charted. Of course, the constitution of a literature is always subject to contestation, and the success of these ventures is measured not by their capacity to determine an external reality accurately, but by the extent to which they impose their conceptions of this reality on other agents within the field.

In spite of this provisionality, were one to compose a palimpsest of all the surveys, anthologies and introductions produced in South Africa in the

1970s and 1980s, it would reveal an obvious agreement about those writers who could not then be left out. By 1986, Coetzee had clearly become one of these, and the fact of his involvement in texts such as *A Land Apart* as well as *English and South Africa* suggests that, far from seeking to distance himself entirely from his local contexts, he had, at least in the early years of his career, actively participated in their delineation. But what are we then to do with Coetzee's obvious investment in writers such as Beckett and Kafka?

One way of answering this question is by having recourse to the notion of the material. For though techniques and tools and themes can be transplanted, their utility may be more quickly exhausted in a new environment. This is not to discount their importance, because the horizon of possibilities will have been permanently altered by their existence, and an author who finds the practices of even his most admired antecedents somehow unsuitable may therefore better clarify the demands of the present – always a here as well as a now – by seeking to understand the causes of this inadequacy. In other words, though Coetzee could not have written as he did without Beckett, Kafka, Pound and a host of others, the peculiar situation in which he found himself meant that he could never have written as they did.

This peculiarity is a function not only of geographical location and choice of subject but also of alternative traditions, which can again be thought in terms of the material. For, though a British novelist of the 1980s – say Peter Ackroyd, Graham Swift or Angela Carter – might have incorporated techniques and themes from beyond Britain, he or she would not have attended – at least not to the same extent and with the same necessity – to the technical challenges faced by authors such as Olive Schreiner, Pauline Smith, Sarah Gertrude Millin and Alex La Guma. Yet, for Coetzee, the achievements and above all failures of these novelists were of real significance, shutting off particular avenues and making others unavoidable.

Another way of approaching the problem of Coetzee's indebtedness to metropolitan authors is to return to the notion of the field and to think about the ways South African literature might itself be connected to other literatures. Here again, Gray's introduction is a useful starting point: 'Like most archipelagos', he observes, Southern African writing 'is related to adjacent landmasses: in this case there are three of them – most importantly, the mainland of English literature, by language and historical circumstance; diminishingly, the British Commonwealth of literature; and increasingly, the continent of Africa which gives it its actual nourishment.'[39]

It is worth noting that Gray's geographical analogy becomes somewhat vague at this point – it is not entirely clear how these three landmasses are related to one another – and that he seems to discount the local significance of non-anglophone works. Nevertheless, it helps to give both clarity and nuance to an important point: proximity is a function of intensity of relation both within *and between* literary fields, and thus between writers in those fields.

The shared preoccupations and challenges of South African authors did not then preclude them from looking beyond their immediate contexts, or from belonging also to trans-national and even global fields, the existence of which likewise depended on a range of trans-national institutions, whether Pan-African, such as the Heinemann African Writers Series and Mbari Press, or metropolitan, such as the Booker and Nobel Prizes. It is important to acknowledge this, but it is also important to keep in mind that, though imported works undoubtedly constitute position-takings in relation to which local authors produce their own works, it is seldom the case that they act within the local field without being acted upon; without, that is, being mediated and modified by the contexts into which they are brought. On the contrary, set in relation to a different set of works and traditions, any writer's oeuvre will be shifted and re-aligned, given new meanings.

Something of this can be illustrated if we consider a review of Samuel Beckett's *Waiting for Godot*, staged in 1965 at the Little Theatre in Cape Town. The reviewer, Philip Segal, was then a senior lecturer at the University of Cape Town, who in other contexts was as staunch a defender of the universal values of the canon as one might imagine. Yet, having first quoted the play's opening lines and stage directions, Segal wrote: 'So – in a Karroo landscape with night approaching ... starts this investigation of pain, confusion, chaos, bestial horror and permanent illusion of life.' This is his only reference to the actual production – Segal makes no mention of actors or set design or direction – yet this brief allusion to the semi-desert of the South African interior invokes not only a certain place, but also its people (masters and servants and wandering wage-labourers), and, most important, an entire literary tradition in which this Karoo landscape frames narratives of isolation, abandonment and stalled longing for transcendence, and offers the approach of night as the only certain prospect.[40]

The processes involved in the staging and performance of theatrical works are clearly apposite here, but they should not be understood as different in kind from those more general processes involved in the mediation and modification of a particular work by its incorporation in a new set of literary contexts, for which the model of translation may be even more revealing. To produce a translation is to insert a work not only into different linguistic environments but also into different networks of literary relations; it is to make that work available to new readers by re-making it; and the result may sometimes be that the work in translation has a relevance and vivacity it lacked in its former contexts, and thus becomes a position-taking more central to the struggles of the field in which it is newly arrived. This is what happens, for example, when Ovid's *Metamorphoses* is translated by Arthur Golding and when James Macpherson's *Works of Ossian* enters a novel of Goethe's. It is also what happens when an otherwise minor Scottish poet, Thomas Pringle, is made the founder of a new literature of South Africa; or, indeed, when an Irish playwright working in French becomes the author of a strange new story of the Karoo.

Further Considerations

Field, material and *style* do not so much constitute the basis for a methodology as respond to and clarify a conception of practice and production that one finds in Coetzee's own literary criticism. This will become clearer as we proceed, but it is worth reflecting here that this approach to Coetzee through his own works at least attempts what Adorno describes as 'immanent critique', that is, critique 'which "remains within" what it criticizes,' and which 'starts from the principles of the work under discussion'.[41]

Even in this introduction I have tried where possible to draw on Coetzee's early scholarship and on contemporaneous theoretical and critical texts, of which several will be found referenced in the footnotes and bibliography of Coetzee's PhD dissertation. In each of the chapters that follow, the detailed exploration of style depends on a still closer engagement with Coetzee's subsequent critical essays, reviews and translations. If it is clear that his work as a graduate student in Texas was intended as a contribution to the discipline of stylistics, the critical and scholarly publications which came after it provide evidence of an ongoing interest, both wide-ranging and thoroughgoing, in theories of language, style and rhetoric. They provide evidence also of Coetzee's sustained engagement with a host of predecessors, peers and rivals, and this is no less significant.

Relying on Coetzee's essays and reviews for insights into his conception of literary practice is by no means without precedent; on the contrary, the publication in 1992 of *Doubling the Point*, in which many of these texts were anthologized, has made it easier for scholars to use them, along with the accompanying interviews conducted by David Attwell, as a way into interpreting Coetzee's novels.[42] Yet, though the use of these texts is not itself problematic, it is a matter of concern if critics should disregard the chronology of Coetzee's publications in order to use *Doubling the Point* as a kind of sourcebook, mining it for themes that can retrospectively be read into each of Coetzee's fictions.

In trying to avoid this, I have made an effort to situate each of Coetzee's early novels in relation to the critical and journalistic texts alongside which it was originally composed and published.[43] I have thought it particularly important not to use later materials to interpret works that, in some cases, preceded them by several decades. So, for example, where the early novels are concerned, little reliance is placed on the interviews with Attwell, and there is no reference at all to Coetzee's memorial fictions, *Boyhood* (1997), *Youth* (2002) and *Summertime* (2009), which in any case lie beyond the scope of this study insofar as they constitute a project that seems discrete, though by no means divorced from the rest of Coetzee's oeuvre.[44]

For related reasons, I have also avoided relying on the ubiquitously cited but generally misleading 'The Novel Today', which is so often used as evidence that Coetzee's literary practice was from the outset defined against any kind of realist mode.[45] Initially an address at a cultural festival organized by the South African *Weekly Mail* in 1987, 'The Novel Today' was a polemical intervention at a very particular moment in South African literature. More significant, certain of its claims contradicted, or at least simplified, much of what Coetzee had carefully articulated over the course of the previous decade and a half in numerous essays and reviews. That it has been so widely quoted, in spite of its idiosyncrasy and exclusion from *Doubling the Point*, says more, I believe, about the desire amongst critics to construct a particular narrative of Coetzee's career than about the text's relation to any of his earlier critical and literary concerns.

This is not to suggest that Coetzee's subsequent attempts to shape his own reception should be treated reverentially. On the contrary, it has been one of the aims of this study to treat them critically, and to look behind and beyond *Doubling the Point* by reclaiming the outlying and often submerged portions of Coetzee's oeuvre. Quite often, it is these neglected texts that have allowed me to question previous critical assumptions and to reconstruct important details of Coetzee's local literary environment, and thus to proceed to an examination of the meaning and effect of his prose style.

In Chapter 1, for example, after re-evaluating Coetzee's relations with Samuel Beckett, I look more closely at several pieces in which Coetzee developed his critique of the South African novelist Alex La Guma before turning to an analysis of the pared-down syntax of *Dusklands*, while in Chapter 2 the clues provided by several little-known reviews allow me to trace Coetzee's relation to a group of Afrikaans authors and thereafter to re-assess *In the Heart of the Country*'s repetitive use of words, phrases and story elements. My concern in Chapter 3 with the lyrical and rhythmic intensity of *Waiting for the Barbarians* entails an account of the lyric I's abandonment both locally and abroad; and in Chapter 4 I draw on Coetzee's writings on the tradition of the South African novel in English to describe the metaphorics of *Life & Times of Michael K*. Only in Chapter 5 do I shift my approach. Focussing on the changes in literary practice that mark Coetzee's middle fictions – *Foe* (1986), *Age of Iron* (1990), *The Master of Petersburg* (1994) and *Disgrace* (1999) – I pay less attention in this chapter to the essays, reviews and interviews of this period, and the interests and engagements by which they were marked, and instead read these novels in relation to those by which they were preceded.

If there is something that remains to be explained, it is my decision to divide Coetzee's oeuvre into 'early', 'middle' and 'late' fictions. Divisions of this kind are inevitably somewhat arbitrary, but I have tried all the same to produce a classification that has more than convenience to recommend it. Several of its grounds have to do with the kinds of institutional forces outlined in this introduction, which together helped to change Coetzee's standing, so that, by the publication of *Foe*, his transformation was under way from a man within to a man apart.

Even before the appearance of *Foe*, Coetzee's reputation had altered considerably, both at home and abroad, since the publication of *Life & Times of Michael K* had earned him his first Booker Prize. Though the award of the James Tait Black Memorial Prize to *Waiting for the Barbarians* in 1980 no doubt signalled his growing prominence outside South Africa, it was the Booker victory that confirmed Coetzee's international importance, and garnered not only considerable symbolic capital, but also the financial reward of the prize itself and the sales it generated. The significance of the award was by no means lost on those within South Africa: both the short-listing and victory were remarked in the local press, and one of the articles summarized the reviews published in Britain and addressed its commercial value quite explicitly.[46]

Whether or not influenced by his growing reputation, literary critics themselves became interested in Coetzee's work only in the early 1980s. Although it is not easy to draw a clear line between lengthy reviews published in specialist periodicals and survey articles in peer-reviewed journals, only at this time did the first critical essays focussed solely on Coetzee's novels begin to appear. Coetzee may or may not have been aware of the arguments these critics put forth, but what is important is that, from this point onwards, his novels came to be regarded as worthy of the kind of attention usually reserved for the most consecrated South African writers, and for the canonical metropolitan poets and novelists who formed the mainstay of English Literature departments in the Republic at least until the 1970s. At much the same time, certain local authors, reviewers and critics began to question what had previously been taken for granted: Coetzee's political commitment.[47]

If these changes in reception explain some of the tone of 'The Novel Today', it is worth noting also that *Foe* was to be the last of Coetzee's novels published in a distinct South African edition by Ravan Press. *Dusklands* had initially been put out by Ravan alone, but the four fictions that followed were each published by Ravan in South Africa, by Secker & Warburg in the United Kingdom, and by Harper & Row and then Viking in the United States. Ravan may not have been the publisher Coetzee had initially sought, but he had 'personally ensured that Ravan retained the Southern African rights to all his works up to and including *Foe*', and so long as this association lasted South African readers continued to meet with the Ravan logo that marked Coetzee's novels as local and imbricated them with radical and avowedly political writings.[48]

If these are what might be called institutional reasons for regarding *Foe* as a kind of watershed or fulcrum in Coetzee's career, there are also grounds for this understanding in the work itself. Though many of Coetzee's critics take *Foe* as the starting point for analysis of his oeuvre, seeing the novel as the culmination of a progressive, unilinear development, the reviews cited at the outset make plain that *Foe* struck a number of its initial readers as strange and unexpected, somehow incongruous with the previous fictions. In retrospect, the novel seems stranger still, and, in the trajectory of Coetzee's career, somewhat anomalous, not least for its use of the purposefully antiquated prose examined in Chapter 5. In other words, the very style of *Foe* marked a point between the end of the first phase of Coetzee's literary career and the beginning of the next.

By 1986, Coetzee was no longer a marginal upstart, but an internationally recognized novelist and critic. His fictions had changed the very shape and structure of South African literature, thereby ensuring that it would be in relation to his own literary practices that the next generation of South African writers would need to situate its works. The fact that even he would now have to contend with his reputation suggests what may be the only useful definitional characteristic of any author's 'late style': there is an 'early style' against which it must be measured. This is reason enough to treat Coetzee's early novels as the proper contexts for his middle fictions.

As for the late novels, they are likewise marked by further shifts in mode, and in particular a concern with generic boundaries and the distinction between works of fiction and works of fact; a concern which resonates with the questions asked of the boundaries between memoir, autobiography and confession in the trilogy of works recently collected in the volume *Scenes from Provincial Life*. But if *Elizabeth Costello*, *Slow Man* and *Diary of a Bad Year* therefore seem contiguous on broadly formal grounds, one should by no means overlook their shared thematic preoccupations and their orientation towards a new literary environment, that of Australia.

What it would mean to read Coetzee's late fictions within their Australian literary contexts is a question I leave for the future. Likewise, it remains to be seen whether *The Childhood of Jesus* will initiate yet another phase in Coetzee's career. In what follows, my aim is rather to clarify the relation of Coetzee's earlier fictions to those of his local as well as metropolitan peers and rivals, and thus to analyse and explain the aesthetic decisions that produced and gave meaning to his bare prose – a way of writing, I hope in the end to show, by means of which Coetzee both revealed and confronted a reality stripped of human relation.

Whether I am successful in this will determine how far this book is able to achieve its broader aims, which are: to propose a mode of stylistic analysis that leads from and back into a preoccupation with literary, political and social contexts; and to contribute to a re-orientation of postcolonial criticism towards questions of literary technique.

CHAPTER I

Neither Progress, Nor Regress
Dusklands *and the Emergence of a Literary Style*

The Mythic Birth of South African Modernism

Early in 1974, Coetzee's literary career was launched with the publication of *Dusklands*, described on its own dust jacket as the 'first truly major modern South African novel', a work measurable only 'by the standards of the best modern fiction, with no qualifications whatever'.[1] These striking pronouncements originated in a pre-publication review by Jonathan Crewe, one of Coetzee's colleagues at the University of Cape Town, and were finally explained only when the full text appeared in August 1974, in the South African journal *Contrast*. According to Crewe, Coetzee's novel identified itself with 'modern fiction' in two ways: first, it demonstrated an interest in the Western philosophical tradition; second, it adopted metafictional techniques. 'Like so much else in modern fiction', Crewe suggested, the two narratives of *Dusklands* were 'reflexive as well as referential'; they were 'fictions about fictions; about the fundamentally problematic question of the "meaning" of fictions; about the writing of fictions'.[2]

Crewe might not have determined altogether the course of subsequent literary criticism, but he certainly anticipated many of its central claims. *Dusklands* continues to be viewed as a wholly exceptional novel, at least in relation to other South African works, and, where its form is considered, reflexivity continues to be privileged above all else, including those stylistic qualities with which we are here concerned. If there has been any significant change, it is only in the shift from Crewe's 'standards' of aesthetic judgement to the terms of literary history: from being a work of 'the best modern fiction', *Dusklands* has become a work of, or after, modernism. Critics have proceeded to note Coetzee's 'many affinities with modernism'[3] and to insist that his work is a kind of 'late modernism' or postmodernism;[4] that it 'extends and revitalizes modernist practices'.[5] In each case, Coetzee is cast as the local inheritor and true heir of a metropolitan literary tradition, exiled perhaps, but bearing about him unmistakable marks and signs.

In contrast, the fictions of Coetzee's local predecessors and peers have come to be identified strictly with literary realism. At work here is an understanding of aesthetic progress according to which the various literary movements proceed as a matter of course from generation to generation, with each of their forms granted an ordained position on the path from antiquity to modernity. Beyond romanticism there is always realism, and beyond realism there is always modernism. It is therefore unsurprising that critics have viewed *Dusklands* as not only modernist but anti-realist, a negation of the supposed literary past. This has been both consequence and cause of an intensified focus on those reflexive features privileged by Crewe and to which Derek Attridge draws attention when he associates Coetzee's writing with the tendency of modernist fiction to foreground 'its own linguistic, figurative, and generic operations'.[6]

Linked to this notion of aesthetic progress is a conception of writers' relations that is modelled on patrilineal descent. However unintentionally, it produces lineages of great authors, and casts the non-consecrated aside as so much dead wood. In Coetzee's case, it has undergirded attempts to align his literary practice with certain of modernism's chief figures. Of these, Samuel Beckett has been especially prominent, and for good reason: Coetzee's interest in Beckett is clearly attested in several early interviews, and, more importantly, in research undertaken at the outset of his academic career, from which emerged not only his PhD dissertation but several journal articles published between 1970 and 1973, in which Coetzee concerned himself specifically with Beckett's fictional, non-dramatic prose.

Several versions of the genealogical descent from Beckett have been proposed. According to one critic, Coetzee lacked South African literary models for 'truth-telling' and so was forced to embrace 'the metropolitan modernists as literary fathers', turning to Beckett in particular to address 'his concern with ethics'.[7] According to another, it is from Beckett 'that Coetzee derives these narrative techniques and strategies' with which he 'abjures the use of a master-narrative and instead accepts a pure play of fabulation'.[8] A third critic goes so far as to identify Beckett as Coetzee's 'tutelary spirit', a guide in his struggle to get beyond language. It is in Beckett, more than in Pound, Eliot, Ford, Conrad, Nabokov or Faulkner, that Coetzee finds 'an author for whom nature and the world are problematic, because language cannot be taken for granted'. Indeed, it is Beckett who teaches Coetzee how to 'contemplate life as a Gnostic mystery'.[9]

Whatever their differences, each of these critics articulates an elaborated version of the story first sketched by Crewe. They have in common the belief that Coetzee's primary literary affiliation is with modernism and that he is specifically indebted to Beckett. Each therefore considers the anti-realist strategies of Coetzee's novels to be of signal importance, whether their purpose is to do away with the literature of liberalism, reject all master narratives, or transcend the hegemony of language. Finally, each critic situates Coetzee's novels in opposition to South African literary production, which is conceived as straightforwardly realist – either because it is convinced of its own capacity for truth-telling or because of its overt political commitment – and each assumes that realism is inherently opposed to modernism.

If we wish to tell the story of Coetzee's bare prose, it is important to recognize why previous critics have neglected it, and to acknowledge Coetzee's intense interest in Beckett's fictions and the use he makes of certain of their techniques. Yet, if the narrative of Coetzee's modernism and anti-realism is therefore not without some basis in fact, certain of its elements are troubled by closer scrutiny.

There is, to begin with, the problem of making any author the sign of a unified literary practice. Beckett, at least, belongs to that category of author whose adjustments in approach are so substantial that, even without considering his works for theatre and radio, it is necessary to differentiate between early, middle and late phases. This need has to do not only with the shift from English to French but also with real changes in form, which distinguish *The Trilogy* from *Murphy* and *Watt*, and works such as 'Ping' and *Lessness* from *The Trilogy*, and which include modifications to Beckett's 'anti-realism' (if that is what we wish to call it), since *Murphy*'s reflexivity is of a different order from the narrative disintegration of *The Unnamable*.

Coetzee was clearly alert to this: across several articles he argues for a gradual though determined movement in Beckett's career towards an 'art of zero'.[10] In the earliest of these essays, Coetzee observes that the 'play on the conventions of point of view' in both *Murphy* and *Watt* 'is the residue of an attitude of reserve toward The Novel, a reluctance to take its prescriptions seriously'. Because Beckett believes that 'Fiction is the only subject of fiction', that 'fictions are closed systems, prisons', he sets about disrupting 'the internal rules by which the game of the novel is played'.[11] His aim is to show up the 'illusionism of the realistic novel'.[12] For this reason, Coetzee says, *Murphy* and *Watt* are not wholly preoccupied with the discontinuity between word and world, but rather poke fun at the novel's conventions, in particular those conventions by means of which readers distinguish between levels of reality, separating out that of author from that of narrator, and that of narrator from that of narrative. Thus, certain codes are violated or subjected to irony, inconsistencies are introduced, and the authorial or editorial presence is occasionally signalled.

This 'attitude of reserve', however, whilst to begin with 'tentative and of questionable consistency', ultimately takes on greater significance, and proves in the end to be 'neither peripheral or [sic] transitory: it grows, and by the time of L'Innomable (1953) has become, in a fundamental sense, the subject of Beckett's work'.[13] In fact, according to Coetzee, each work of The Trilogy demonstrates an increasing radicalization of approach. Beckett's aim is no longer simply to expose the conventions of fiction, but rather to produce an aesthetic practice that is self-cancelling, in which the impulses towards fiction and silence negate one another and the narrative disappears. Initially, this aim is pursued largely at the semantic level, though not without effects on the syntax: each proposition, each statement of fact, engenders its own series of negations, and what emerges in The Unnamable is a decreative creation.

In the two essays of 1973, Coetzee largely maintains this position, which is modified only by the claim that it is with 'Ping' (1966) and Lessness (1969) – two short fictions – that Beckett properly arrives at his 'art of zero'. Indeed, it is suggested that even a work as late as Imagination Dead Imagine (1965) risks allowing words 'to assert themselves as illusion, as The Word in all its magical autonomy'. Therefore, however radical The Unnamable might seem, not until the publication of 'Ping' and Lessness does Beckett achieve a mode of writing that is 'nothing but a destructive commentary upon itself'.[14] In these later works, in which the principle of composition is the random combination of phrasal items, the decreative drive has been lodged within the syntax, which is now thoroughly irregular and fragmentary.

Whether or not convincing, this narrative of Beckett's changing art does trouble the claim that Coetzee's own practice was simply adopted from his predecessor; at the very least, we would have to decide which stages of Beckett's career to identify with Coetzee's work. Yet, in the scholarly literature, Beckett's fictions are often understood as uniformly anti-realist and entirely concerned with the chasm between word and world, and because Coetzee is assumed to follow Beckett, any sign of the latter's influence on the former is taken as evidence of a unity of practice and purpose.[15]

Now, if *Dusklands* is indeed an anti-realist work, and Coetzee an author who succeeds Beckett by extending the practices of modernism, one would expect Coetzee's oeuvre to begin where his predecessor's left off. To see whether this is the case, we might consider a passage from *Lessness*, quoted by Coetzee in one of his essays:

> Ruins true refuge long last towards which so many false time out of mind. All sides endlessness earth sky as one no sound no stir. Grey face two pale blue little body heart beating only upright. Blacked out fallen open four walls over backwards true refuge issueless.

> Slow black with ruin true refuge four walls over backwards no sound. Earth sky as one all sides endlessness little body only upright. One step more one alone in the sand no hold he will make it. Ash grey little body only upright heart beating face to endlessness. Light refuge sheer white blank planes all gone from mind. All sides endlessness earth sky as one no sound no stir.[16]

For Coetzee, these paragraphs, offering a 'taste of *Lessness*', demonstrate the work's 'basic principle of construction', which is 'repetition'.[17] Its units of construction are the sentence and the phrase, the clause having largely disappeared, since there is only a single unambiguous instance of a finite verb, *will make* in the simple clause, 'he will make it': nothing more than a promise of future action, relegated to the end of the sentence in which it appears, the identities of its pronominal subject and direct object left indistinct. Words that might otherwise have operated as verbs – *last, sound, stir, hold, light* – are restricted to nominal structures, and the occasional use of participles (*beating, fallen* and *gone*) simply emphasizes the stasis which pervades the work, and the sense of its marmorealized landscape.

Consisting of a set of fixed phrases, the syntax of *Lessness* is described by Coetzee as a 'rudimentary, nominalized syntax', one in which the possibility of action, movement and temporal flow is restricted.[18] If there is any motion at all, it occurs at the level of narration and belongs to the narrating subject, shifting perspective, moving through or around this impossible scene. Deprived of verbs, the text is also devoid of any sense of agency, of things acting upon other things or being acted upon, and the narrative drive is located only in the rhythm of the recombined phrases, which may or may not echo the repetitive rhythm of a heart beating in a state of repose. For Coetzee, *Lessness* is constituted by a literary practice which seeks, at the last, to cancel itself out; it belongs to a group of works that 'offer no day-dreams because their subject is strictly the annihilation of illusion by consciousness. They are miniature mechanisms for switching themselves off: illusion therefore silence, silence therefore illusion'.[19]

While it is a commonplace critical assumption that Coetzee cleaved to Beckett as master and mentor, it is hardly necessary to quote from *Dusklands* at any length to demonstrate the distance that separates it from *Lessness*. In contrast with the opaque and static planes, shapes and colours of the latter work, Coetzee's prose purposefully describes actions and their consequences in a syntax that respects the grammar of Standard English. To make this clear, it is convenient to quote precisely that passage in 'The Narrative of Jacobus Coetzee' so often seized upon as a marker of Coetzee's allegiance to late modernism, the passage in which Klawer dies and then reappears:

> The violence of the current at once snapped the knots that bound us and swept Klawer over the shallows into deep water. With horror I watched my faithful servant and companion drawn struggling downstream, shouting pleas for help which I was powerless to render him, him whose voice I had never in all my days heard raised, until he disappeared from sight around a bend and went to his death bearing the blanket roll and all the food.
>
>   The crossing took all of an hour, for we had to probe the bottom before each step for fear of slipping into a hippopotamus hole and being swept off our feet. But sodden and shivering we finally reached the south bank and lit a discreet fire to dry our clothes and blankets. It was late afternoon, there was a treacherous breeze, and, fearing illness above all else, I took care to skip about and keep my joints warm. Klawer on the other hand, having spread our clothing, squatted dismally before the flames clutching his nakedness and toasting his skin. To this mistake, and the mistake of donning wet clothes, I attribute his sickness. (100)

Of course, there is a surprise when we discover that Klawer is not dead, or not dead yet, but this surprise is of the kind found in *Murphy* or *Watt*, and belongs to that category of metafictional asides which are not properly anti-illusionist but rather jokes at the expense of convention. Keeping in mind the 'varieties of play' identified by Coetzee in his essay on *Murphy*, we might say that the passage marks an unexpected intrusion (or rather absence) of the author-as-editor, or at most a duplicity on the part of the narrator, which the author leaves extant.[20] At the level of plot, however, the economy of the narrative remains undisturbed: Klawer's death, occasioned by the river crossing, is inescapable.

In any case, given that the presentation of 'The Narrative of Jacobus Coetzee' is mediated by a translator ("J. M. Coetzee") and an editor ('S. J. Coetzee') as well as an author (J. M. Coetzee), it is always possible to attribute the transgression to one of these authorities. Indeed, unlike the excision and re-insertion of disjunctive 'compositional blocks' that Coetzee identifies in *Watt*, the second narration of Klawer's death appears motivated: it is offered as a revision, which, at the level of narrator and editor, creates a better impression on the reader; and, at the level of the author, is an ironic comment on the scope for mystification in narratives of exploration.[21] What is called into question, in other words, is not the reality of the fictive construct per se, but rather the degree to which the narrative's account of this construct is truthful.

It is not difficult to see straightaway that the 'anti-realism' of *Lessness* is of a different and more radical order, achieved by syntax as much as semantics. The prose of *Dusklands*, in contrast, is not only regular, but *simple, sharp, graphic* and above all *clear*. This clarity is achieved through: (a) use of clauses that are short, and more often simple or co-ordinated than embedded or subordinated; (b) careful handling of adverbials of place, time and manner; (c) preference for straightforward diction; and (d) avoidance of obscure constructions and analogies. That we are to understand these features in this way – that is, as productive of clarity – is suggested by Coetzee's 1969 essay on stylostatistics, where he identifies features typically associated with writing that is 'difficult', or semantically opaque. These include such quantifiable 'features of syntax as depth of embedding and phrase length, such features of diction as distribution of word lengths and rarity of vocabulary items' and such unquantifiable 'features as the remoteness of analogical components of metaphors'.[22]

However cursory, the comparison of passages from *Lessness* and *Dusklands* suggests the importance of reassessing Coetzee's relation to Beckett. Certainly, one must question any emphasis on formal similarities when the differences are at least as interesting, and perhaps more significant. Considered alongside *Lessness* and other instances of Beckett's later non-dramatic prose, there can be little about *Dusklands* that seems radically anti-realist. In fact, it is doubtful whether *Dusklands* approaches even *The Trilogy* in this regard. *The Unnamable* may proceed in a more regular syntax than *Lessness*, but its opacity goes beyond anything written by Coetzee, and it is preoccupied with the problem of reality and its representation in a way that Coetzee's early novels are not.

On the contrary, the moments of *Dusklands* usually identified with anti-realism in every case belong to those categories of authorial aside or narrative contradiction that poke fun at or unsettle novelistic conventions without wholly disrupting the representational power of the prose. As evidence, one might consider such instances as the following, from 'The Vietnam Project': 'My name is Eugene Dawn. I cannot help that' (1);

'I will not pretend that I cannot construe his speech word for word' (2); 'I am sorry there is no more of him in my story' (6); 'I write from (let us see if I can get this extravagance right) the Loco Motel' (36); 'One, two cars are pulling up, in the present indefinite this time' (40); 'A convention allows me to record these details' (44). None of these moments is much more than a sideways acknowledgement of the operational codes that govern fictional narrative, to which *Dusklands* largely submits.

This remains true of the novel's second part, even though the different versions of Jacobus Coetzee's adventures establish an ironic distance between reader and text. If S. J. Coetzee suspects the distortions engendered by the motives of the 'Castle hack who heard out Coetzee's story with the impatience of a bureaucrat', he raises the question of whether his own 'work of piety', and indeed the original account, are likewise distorted by ulterior motives (115). However, while there is clearly scope for mystification in every re-telling, the several versions do concur in certain basic data, and because each of the narrators is associated with particular ideological position-takings, the reader may feel rightly confident in the possibility of getting behind the obfuscation to the story's truth, encouraged in this by the implied authorial or narrative consciousness that occupies a position above or behind its various surrogates, subtly betraying them and exposing them to irony, if not always parody.[23]

I believe Coetzee's reflexive techniques are therefore best understood as gestures of acknowledgement, signalling fiction's permanent alteration through its encounter with the sceptical aesthetics of late modernism. This interpretation is lent support by Coetzee's observation (in an interview that is more recent and therefore less reliable as an index of his concerns during the composition of *Dusklands*), that there is 'only so much mileage to get out of the ploy' of anti-illusionism, that 'Anti-illusionism is ... only a marking of time, a phase of recuperation, in the history of the novel.'[24] The metafictional moments in *Dusklands* may thus be interpreted as signs of Coetzee's belatedness rather than his modernity, concessions to the fact that, in 1974, it was no longer possible or desirable to claim an unmediated relation between word and world.

Taking up this position does not mean dismissing the reflexive techniques of the novel as irrelevant, or refusing to see their role in demystifying discourses of colonialism, imperialism, liberalism and apartheid. It requires only that we recognize that there is, in *Dusklands*, little evidence of a desire to subvert the significatory and referential functions of language. The novel might then be seen to mark a movement away from the precipice of late modernism, or at least the radical aesthetics of Beckett's later works; to signal an acceptance, perhaps reluctant, of the process of naming; and to concede to demands for creative as opposed to decreative work. While it may mock conventions associated with certain kinds of realist novel, this is neither indicative of a thoroughgoing anti-realism nor in any sense profoundly innovative, a point to which we return in later chapters.

The purpose of revisiting the relation between Coetzee and Beckett is to enable a shift of focus and emphasis, from anti-realism to those features of language and narrative that contribute to the properly distinctive qualities of Coetzee's early novels, especially their spare intensity. First, however, we should attend to an important set of questions prompted by this realignment: Why was it that Coetzee distanced himself from the decreative mode of *The Unnamable*, not to mention 'Ping' and *Lessness*? What was it about the 'fiction of net zero' that caused him to turn aside?

It may be impossible to answer these questions conclusively, but Coetzee's critical writings offer intriguing clues. Of these, the most relevant is the essay on Vladimir Nabokov's *Pale Fire*, where Coetzee addresses the ambiguous effects of irony and reflexivity, arguing that the potentially decreative narrative strategies of the novel amount to little more than a ruse. Charles Kinbote's hallucinatory exegesis admittedly signals the dangers of reducing the novel to that level of reality in which its author exists, but the incommensurability of word and world, instead of a curse denying meaning to existence, becomes a guarantee that the work of art, whose only value is beauty, remains unalterable. The novel has, in other words, 'like a closed system of mirrors, shut itself off forever from interpretation and become a monument of unageing intellect'; it has become 'the frozen music of high art. The narrator spinning himself out of his own entrails behind Charles the Beloved turns out after all to be the imagination personified and triumphant.'[25]

Insofar as Nabokov remains committed to art and beauty, he falls short of Beckett's achievements, at least according to Coetzee, who says that radical art is that 'which, facing the abyss between language and the world, turns toward silence and the end of art'. In this sense, Coetzee adds, 'the most radical artist of Nabokov's generation is Samuel Beckett', whose 'most radically decreative work is *The Unnamable*'. In comparison, 'the radicalism of *Pale Fire* is half-hearted. *Pale Fire* interrogates its own fictional premises, but does so with an irony ... which nudges us toward consenting in the reality of its major construct in the Imaginary'.[26]

Coetzee's critique of *Pale Fire* suggests the impossibility of assigning univocal meaning to a particular set of techniques; it suggests, moreover, how little one is able to say of a work's properly distinctive and effectual features when one relies on such terms as 'realist', 'anti-realist', and 'modernist'. In the case of Nabokov, one would have, at the very least, to account also for those aspects of his prose that signal a commitment to the aesthetic: the profusion of sensual description, the prevalence of sound repetition, the proliferation of complex and elegant tropes. Together, these contribute to a style of writing that is purposefully lush and evocative.

It is precisely from this kind of literary art that Beckett had attempted to escape, at least according to Coetzee, who cites a letter in which Beckett explicitly repudiates 'Style'; by which he meant, Coetzee explains, 'style as consolation, style as redemption, the grace of language ... the religion of style that we find in the Flaubert of *Madame Bovary*', the beautifying of words which not only makes language an end in itself, but gives it primacy over all else.[27] Nabokov, on the other hand, had gladly embraced the 'religion of style': like Flaubert, he had repudiated a bad reality and turned to art as a means of transfiguring or at least transcending a world lapsed into alienation.

This, in any case, is Coetzee's opinion, though it is hardly controversial. Far more surprising, and far more significant too, is his belief that even Beckett had ultimately fallen into the trap of style: 'there is a second and a deeper impulse toward stylization that is common to all of Beckett's later work', Coetzee suggests, which is 'the stylization of the impasse of reflexive consciousness'.[28] Indeed, at a certain point in Beckett's career, this stylization is all that is left: works such as 'Ping' and *Lessness* may achieve a mode in which 'the promise of the charm' is finally and absolutely refused, but this mode is nothing other than hollow form.[29] Writing of the late fictions collected in Beckett's *Residua*, Coetzee therefore notes: 'Like a switch they have no content, only shape. They are in fact only a shape, a style of mind. It is utterly appropriate for an artist to whom defeat constitutes a universe that he should march with eyes open into the prison of empty style.'[30]

Thus, however stoic Beckett's resignation, Coetzee becomes sceptical of its value, something which he signals most clearly in the essay on Nabokov, where he claims *The Unnamable* as Beckett's most radical work, and insists Beckett's 'later fiction is merely the execution of a programme'.[31] Coetzee had come to believe, in other words, that Beckett's decreative project had arrived at a point at which what mattered was only the how, and not the what. The very great irony of this is that Beckett had ultimately produced an art as self-enclosing as Nabokov's. He may not have celebrated this accomplishment, but Beckett too turned from the world and was left only with the word.

If there was something that saved Beckett for Coetzee, it was the torment he felt in the need to speak and the belief that it was impossible to say anything: 'To Beckett this fictive covering is the shirt of Nessus. To Nabokov it is the emperor's new clothes, and imperial art consists in making the crowd really believe that the emperor is not naked.'[32] Nevertheless, what should now be clear is that, for Coetzee, the same gesture, the same self-enclosure and the same turning away from the world could be identified in both *Pale Fire* and Beckett's later works. It is with this in mind that we might begin to understand the mild reflexivity of *Dusklands*.

Orientations, Realisms, Realities

If *Dusklands* can be distinguished from Beckett's later works because its prose is clear and descriptive, this is hardly the only important difference. Assuming that Coetzee is correct when he says the subject of *The Unnamable* and later fictions is primarily the impossibility of escaping the prison-house of fiction, it should be clear that *Dusklands*, on the contrary, is concerned with the difficulty of being in the world, the difficulty of being in relation to others when such relations are poisoned by violent conflict. Thus, where Beckett's writings might speak of a turning from the world, Coetzee's novel suggests an orientation towards it.

As explained in the introduction, the kinds of stories an author tells, the subject matter that she or he chooses, may be as much an aspect of style as any linguistic or rhetorical feature. Furthermore, the different elements of a text are never wholly independent, because a kind of story will always be associated with a way of telling, a particular genre, a manner of expression and so forth, such that none of these elements can be changed without affecting the others. Yet a number of Coetzee's critics have committed the error of making an absolute distinction between subject matter and form. Though they recognize that he differs from Beckett in evoking 'a South African setting', they continue to insist that Coetzee adopts the 'postmodern techniques' of 'much European and American fiction'.[33] This approach, which treats the subject matter of Coetzee's novels as largely incidental, further encourages a response that stakes everything on the reflexive features of *Dusklands*. The outcome is that slew of readings which leap to defend the novel on the grounds of form, only to betray those grounds immediately. If, on the contrary, the question of form is taken seriously, one ought to consider *Dusklands* in relation to other South

African novels that are, in a very broad sense, about the same thing: the violence engendered by manichean struggle.

These include the novels of Alex La Guma, who belonged to the generation of local writers preceding Coetzee. Without being universally acclaimed, La Guma's first four fictions, published between 1962 and 1972, were widely accepted, at least in South Africa, as paradigmatic of a literature oriented towards the world. More significant, Coetzee had himself become interested in them. In September 1971, he produced the essay 'Alex La Guma and the Responsibilities of the South African Writer', which was followed in 1973 by his short entry on La Guma for the encyclopaedic *English and South Africa*, and, in early 1974, by the essay 'Man's Fate in the Novels of Alex La Guma'.

In the first of these pieces, Coetzee explicitly rejects that conception of linear aesthetic progress outlined previously in this chapter. Commenting on the manner in which the South African critic Lewis Nkosi pays homage to 'Western experimentalism', Coetzee notes that this attitude seems to involve 'a rather simple-minded view of absolute "technique" which, as in the myth of our science, can only progress, never regress'. What Nkosi fails to see is 'a whole spectrum of valid literatures open to Africa'. Concluding his essay, Coetzee is characteristically precise: 'The history of literature is not a history of discovery and progress, but rather a history of changing epistemologies and modes of expression that change with them.'[34]

These insights are clearly relevant to how we conceive Coetzee's relation to metropolitan modernism, yet they have seldom been remarked, in spite of the fact that Coetzee was writing about La Guma while he reworked his analysis of Beckett and drafted and re-drafted his first novel. Certainly, these pieces on La Guma have never been treated as a means of clarifying what is properly distinctive about the form of *Dusklands*. Yet it is here that Coetzee explains how a work can be about the world without necessarily being oriented towards it.

The way that critics have treated Coetzee's work on La Guma is not unrelated to the manner of its presentation in *Doubling the Point*, where there is no reference to the *English and South Africa* entry, and the significance of the essay of 1971 is obscured by the intimation, in a very brief note, that it was an earlier version of the article of 1974.[35] In fact, though portions of Coetzee's analysis remain consistent, his conclusions to the two longer pieces are markedly different. It is these differences that indicate Coetzee's changed understanding of the particular shortcomings of La Guma's novels.

The first essay focuses entirely on La Guma's *A Walk in the Night*. Coetzee is appreciative, and uses the framework proposed by Georg Lukács to read the novel as a work of critical realism able to depict a country in which consciousness of oppression has not yet produced conscious resistance to oppression. Coetzee praises La Guma's ability to envisage potential sources of resistance, even though these insights are denied to the characters. Deflecting the Lukácsian critique of naturalism, Coetzee asserts: 'La Guma is not a naturalist but a critical realist.'[36]

This assessment is then dramatically reversed, first in *English and South Africa*, where La Guma is associated with 'low naturalism' and the works of 'such naturalistic, proletarian writers of the 1930s as James Farrell, Richard Wright and John Steinbeck', and then in 'Man's Fate in the Novels of Alex La Guma', which insists that *A Walk in the Night* is *not* a work of critical realism. In both pieces, Coetzee emphasizes La Guma's attempt 'to overwhelm the real with an inventory of the names of things: torn newspapers, rotten oranges, tin cans, offal, mud, sweat, vomit, and so on', but where this inventorizing is initially read as the outcome of desire, it is soon viewed instead as a compulsion, which is traced in turn to a more fundamental flaw.[37]

Finally, the origin of La Guma's failure is identified as style – 'style is the great betrayer' – for in his style, La Guma reveals himself 'the inheritor of the worst excesses of realism'. Indeed, his novels, Coetzee claims, are replete with examples of the author 'straining after an effect no other than literariness itself'.[38] As evidence, Coetzee cites the following passage from *A Walk in the Night*:

> The room was hot and airless as a newly opened tomb, and there was an old iron bed against one wall, covered with unwashed bedding, and next to it a backless chair that served as a table on which stood a chipped ashtray full of cigarette butts and burnt matches, and a thick tumbler, sticky with the dregs of heavy red wine. A battered cupboard stood in a corner with a cracked, flyspotted mirror over it, and a small stack of dog-eared books gathering dust. In another corner an accumulation of empty wine bottles stood like packed skittles.[39]

Though he does not provide detailed analysis, Coetzee argues that we notice in the style of this passage, and others like it, La Guma's 'horror of a degraded world'.[40] He focuses in particular on the pattern of La Guma's noun phrases: 'an *old* iron bed ... *unwashed* bedding ... a *backless* chair ... a *chipped* ashtray ... cigarette *butts* ... *burnt* matches', arguing that 'everything named is named with its own gesture of repudiation. The signification of the passage is not a room and its details, but rather (a) a room, plus (b) horror of the room'. What the reader is presented with, Coetzee insists, is 'not only the interior of a certain room but an interior with the fingerprints of Literature all over it, an interior heavy with affect'.[41]

Coetzee's central argument, as I understand it, may be restated as follows: La Guma's literariness, signalled in his laboured conjuring of detail and his overblown characterization through connotative adjectival modification, makes an excuse of reality, insofar as the real is treated as a background against which to stage an attitude towards it, a particular configuration of sentiment that arises from the artist's subjectivity. Coetzee's focus here is on both the compulsion to inventorize and the manner in which La Guma un-names in the moment of naming. This mode of description is read as the product of a desire to transcend the 'things' themselves, to 'overwhelm the real'.[42] In this respect, Coetzee observes that 'La Guma's world, so overflowing with things, is nonetheless not an objective world, for the things themselves are overflowing with the writer's subjectivity'.[43] It is in this sense that La Guma is found guilty of the crimes Lukács detected in both naturalism and expressionism.

It must be emphasized here that, far from criticizing La Guma's work for attempting to describe reality, Coetzee suggests that its shortcomings lie in a hidden desire to get away from the badness of 'ordinary life', a desire perceptible in the compulsion to inventorize, and in the tendency to infuse the objective world with the colour of private emotion. In both respects, there is a principle of expansion or elaboration at work, in which Coetzee perceives a paradoxical wish to enrich reality, to aestheticize it and thereby to transmute or redeem it through the force of a narrating personality, turning the 'material world' – deemed insufficient, wanting, too poor – into something greater and more meaningful.[44] The thrust of Coetzee's final essay on La Guma, in other words, is that one can write explicitly about the world, and nevertheless turn away from it.

Rather strikingly, Coetzee's critique of La Guma thus recalls his criticisms of Nabokov, and indeed Beckett, both of whom were likewise said to have produced literary practices that turned from the world. In fact, there is much else that the late essays on La Guma, Nabokov and Beckett share, including the focus on syntactic features of style, and the use of Flaubert as representative of certain ideas about literature and its relation to the real. For in his discussion of *A Walk in the Night*, Coetzee notes: 'toward his world La Guma feels much like the Flaubert who wrote, "I execrate ordinary life. I have always withdrawn from it as much as I could. But aesthetically I wanted ... to get hold of it to the very bottom."' Coetzee invokes Flaubert again in the final paragraphs of the later essay, noting that each of La Guma's 'novels exposes us to a long-sustained shudder of revulsion – a revulsion that must confess in places to being merely fastidious' and 'that brings La Guma closest to the Flaubert who confessed his execration of "ordinary life"'.[45] These thoughts are then echoed in 'Samuel Beckett and the Temptations of Style', where Flaubert is once more understood as the artist who emblematically repudiates the world and turns to Style, a gesture subsequently repeated – in very different ways – by La Guma, Nabokov and even Beckett.

Since we are primarily concerned with the development of Coetzee's literary practice, it is irrelevant whether his analysis of these authors is convincing. The question of real importance is how far their own practices, as perceived by Coetzee, constituted specific position-takings in relation to which his was conceived, refined and given meaning. Coetzee's essays make clear that he was concerned above all with the manner in which very different modes of writing could result in a similar turning from the world, a similar literary introversion.

If Coetzee's critical practice is positioned against this introversion, there is every reason to suspect this attitude will inflect his literary practice also. We cannot, however, say whether this is the case without looking more carefully at *Dusklands* itself. For only by analysing those stylistic elements attributed significance by Coetzee – elements of syntax in particular – might we explain how he crafted a mode that could both achieve an orientation towards the world and avoid a repudiation of reality.

In the fourth section of the 'The Vietnam Project', Eugene Dawn sits in his motel room and struggles to write. To be more precise, he struggles to write in a manner suited to the 'complex natural reality' that surrounds him (38). Though he feels 'more or less adequate' to the 'dwindling subject' that appears in his mirror, he is stymied by the attempt to portray anything beyond himself, to 'spin … long, dense paragraphs' into descriptions of his setting, to provide his prose with 'the air of a real world through the looking-glass' (38). Instead, what is staged for the reader is an extraordinary moment of aesthetic failure, all the more pronounced for being written in what the narrator refers to as the 'present definite' (36). The time of narration and time of narrative are now almost identical, and every word that does not elaborate Dawn's vision of the 'snowcapped ranges' is a further marker of his artistic collapse. He is left to wonder whether he was perhaps not 'born to be a writer' (38).

This passage, properly reflexive, invites us to think about the ways in which the mode of the novel is and is not a kind of realism. It should be noted, in this regard, that Dawn understands the literary writer's task to be the encapsulation of 'complex natural reality', and believes this feat can be accomplished only in 'long, dense paragraphs', a phrase used twice (38). Dawn therefore tries repeatedly to describe his immediate environment, turning his attention finally to his room, before concluding weakly: 'I have already mentioned the oval mirror on the wall' (39). As the reason for his failure, Dawn suggests 'the problem of names': he lacks 'a lexicon of common nouns', and so feels unable to catalogue the plenitude of the world he sees and experiences (37–8).

While it is tempting to regard such a moment of reflexivity as a key to the mode and interpretation of the novel itself, there is reason for caution. Certainly it is a mistake to confuse the cerebral but paranoid narrator Dawn with the author Coetzee, not least because, when one considers the text of *Dusklands* carefully, Dawn's failure is not the novel's. Whilst the narrative may not contain any of those long, dense paragraphs describing natural reality for which Dawn yearns, passages of descriptive prose do occur, and these seldom give the impression of a problem with names. On the contrary, external reality is described in *Dusklands* with remarkable precision.

As an example, we might consider the following passage from 'The Narrative of Jacobus Coetzee':

> [1] On the morning of August 24 we arrived before a new range which we painfully ascended. [2] Toward evening the cattle scented water. [3] Flowing swiftly between steep banks we came upon the Great River. [4] The cattle had to be restrained from hurling themselves down the banks while we searched out a path.
>
> [5] The Great River forms the northern boundary of the land of the Little Namaquas. [6] It is about three hundred feet wide, in the rainy season wider. [7] In places the banks slope to small beaches where hippopotami graze and where we found traces of Bushman encampments. [8] In most places the current is swift; but Klawer, sent upstream to find a ford, came back to report a sand-shoal where we might safely cross. [9] It took two days to reach, for we had to retrace our way through the mountains and travel behind them parallel to the river.
>
> [10] North of the Great River we found ourselves among stony mountains, and for four days were compelled to follow the course of the Leeuwen River before we emerged upon the level grassy plain which constitutes the beginning of the land of the Great Namaquas. (68)

The description here may be touched by irony, but is nevertheless matter-of-fact and clear. As in the narration of Klawer's death, the syntax is regular and simple – clauses are relatively short, subordination and embedding are restricted – and diction is straightforward. Keeping in mind the critique of La Guma, one might further note that, while the narrator does not lack a lexicon of common nouns, these are kept from centre stage insofar as the passage avoids the subject-copula-complement structure, which is characteristic of descriptive prose because it is a means of fronting and therefore topicalizing noun phrases that name particular features of, say, a landscape or the interior of a room. In the first paragraph, the mountain range, river and banks belong to the rhematic parts of the relevant sentences (1, 2 and 3), as is the case in the third paragraph. Only in the second paragraph does the narrative pause to focus on particular features of the terrain, and only very briefly.

There is thus neither an attempt to inventorize, nor any sign of the expansion or embellishment one might have expected upon the first sighting of this Great River, hitherto undiscovered. Instead of being depicted lavishly, the river is viewed as a danger and obstacle, its salient features picked out and noted with terse economy. Furthermore, where adjectives are used – and they are used sparingly – they are simple and relatively objective, insofar as they tend to have nominal roots (*rainy, grassy, stony*) or to be drawn from a discourse amenable to mathematical rigour (*steep, level*). Thus, while the prose undeniably conjures a particular reality, there is no evidence here of any of the 'worst excesses of realism' that Coetzee discerns in La Guma.

Nor is this mode restricted to 'The Narrative of Jacobus Coetzee', for such passages are found also in 'The Vietnam Project'. Consider, for example, the description of the Harry S. Truman library:

> The basement (in fact the sub-basement, a stage in the downward expansion of the library) is reached via a spiral stairway and an echoing tunnel plated in battleship-gray. It holds Dewey classes 100–133, unpopular among Truman's clientele. The racks run on rails for compactness. The four security cameras that oversee the basement can be evaded in blind spots in the shifting aisles....
>
> My carrel in the library is gray, with a gray bookrack and a little gray drawer for stationery. My office at the Kennedy Institute is also gray. Gray desks and fluorescent lighting: 1950's functionalism. I have toyed with the idea of complaining but cannot think of a way of doing so without opening myself to counterattack. Hardwoods are for the managers. So I grind my teeth and suffer. (6–7)

Separated by half a page or so, neither paragraph suggests a difficulty with naming objects or things. In the first seven sentences, which largely relate the narrator's visual experience, one finds the following: *basement, sub-basement, library, stairway, tunnel, racks, rails, cameras, aisles, carrel, bookrack, drawer, stationery, office, desks, lighting.* If there is a contrast with the previous passage, it is the tendency to topicalize the relevant noun phrases. Nevertheless, what is offered is hardly a catalogue; only basic and indeed generic features are picked out, again in a syntax and diction that are regular and simple. Adjectival modification is likewise restricted – something foregrounded in the repetition of *gray* – and the few pre-modifiers used (*spiral, echoing, blind, shifting, little, fluorescent* and of course *gray*) are again denotative rather than connotative.

This analysis admittedly focuses on only a few grammatical features, but because these are precisely the features Coetzee picks out, they should be sufficient to illustrate the differences between the descriptive passages of *Dusklands* and those of La Guma's novels. Read against a mode identified by its excessive enumeration and characterization of material things, which it endeavours to bring to life by appealing to the plenum, the fullness of facticity, Coetzee's own writing might indeed be understood as *lean, taut, spare, stark, economical* and *austere.* If La Guma's prose tends to expansion, Coetzee's tends to contraction and reduction, and is therefore not simply a plain style, but one that is pared down, and which has its effect and meaning precisely in relation to what has gone before.

Moreover, in light of Coetzee's critique of La Guma, this pared-down description seems, perhaps counter-intuitively, to constitute a literary practice oriented, in its very grammar, towards the world. Its clarity and economy suggest, in other words, that the prose of *Dusklands* be understood as a purposeful overcoming of two forms of literary introversion, two forms of negating reality. One is then bound to ask: should the novel's mode not in fact be classified as some kind of realism? Of course, such an identification runs counter to the critical consensus that Coetzee's novels are primarily anti-realist, an opinion not only ubiquitous, but that originates, as we have seen, in the earliest responses to *Dusklands.* On the other hand, an identification with realism is not entirely without precedent.

In the August 1974 volume of *Snarl,* the literary critic Lionel Abrahams observed that, in *Dusklands* 'precise details' are presented and 'made dense with significant associations', and though he acknowledged that *Dusklands* 'boldly diversifies our fiction and relates it to modernistic modes', Abrahams therefore maintained that Coetzee's 'mode is realism'. Indeed, though he, like Crewe, believed the double narration of Klawer's death was reminiscent of Borges, unlike Crewe, and those who have followed him, Abrahams insisted that the novel's reflexive devices operated 'without dispelling the illusion'.[46]

To be clear, what is remarkable about Abrahams is not that he noticed the novel's descriptive qualities, but that he believed these to be significant. Crewe, after all, had also commented on the 'dense texture of "authentic", even documentary, detail' in *Dusklands*, and Attridge would later observe that its two parts 'make a claim to be documentaries of sorts'.[47] Both Crewe and Attridge, however, insist that the most important formal feature of Coetzee's novel is its reflexivity, which is effective 'in spite' of the writing's descriptive force.[48] Indeed, Attridge claims that, though 'Coetzee's intense prose can produce a readerly involvement that overrides all markers of fictionality', the power of the novels resides precisely in their metafictional moments, all other formal features, no matter how distinctive – or, to use Attridge's terms, inventive and creative – being merely temptations for those seeking solace in fiction.[49]

Why was it that Abrahams read the novel differently? Perhaps because his familiarity with the local literary context prompted him to the recognition that *Dusklands* was experimental only in relation to English-language authors in South Africa. Compared with the Afrikaans novels of André P. Brink and Etienne Leroux, on the other hand, *Dusklands* seemed to Abrahams less bewildering, for it lacked their 'surrealistic elements' and 'symbolic method'.[50] This suggests something of the relational significance of these authors, which will be further addressed in the following chapter. For now, we might focus instead on the fact that Abrahams's review offers a very different starting point from Crewe's.

But what then would it mean to think of *Dusklands* as a realist work? Certainly not that its mode be identified with the literary practices of La Guma or Flaubert. Rather, it would mean recognizing the emergence of a qualified or provisional kind of realism, one in which it was possible to accommodate the milder varieties of reflexive technique found in Beckett's early fiction, and acknowledge the linguistic mediation of reality; one in which fictionality could be foregrounded, rather than concealed. A realism, then, understood outside of any misleading opposition to modernism, and against the many ways the term has been used and indeed distorted in critical responses to Coetzee's writing.[51] For here, it has all too often been taken to indicate a single set of coherent practices, as if, between Daniel Defoe and Arnold Bennett, there was no change greater than the modernization of diction and idiom; as if the technological advances, cultural shifts, social and psychological theories and consequent alterations in schemas of perception of the intervening years had in no way affected attitudes towards reality and its representation.

Even were we to limit ourselves unnecessarily by conceiving realism as a mode or set of practices characterized by the desire to produce a reality effect, we would have to acknowledge that there have been innumerable modifications to this project, engendered not only by different ways of understanding the real, but also by the gradual hollowing out of convention, which causes once vital and vivid manners of description to age and become brittle. At the very least, we would have to acknowledge that the effect of the real is in fact several different effects, which Geoffrey Leech and Michael Short identify as *credibility* ('the likelihood, and hence believability, of the fiction as a "potential reality"'), *verisimilitude* (having to do with the 'thisness' of things), *authenticity* (what is described very closely resembles external reality), *objectivity* (description seems factual and based on observation) and *vividness* (what is described seems more real because more charged with affect and individual sensation).[52]

Dusklands may forego authenticity, but the world it creates is certainly vivid and credible, and, as we have seen, its descriptions often objective. Nor, finally, is it the case that all literary realisms necessarily imply philosophical realism, or, perhaps more important, that a philosophical realist will necessarily produce novels like Balzac's. At the very least, there is a confusion here between literary modes and philosophical positions, which are undoubtedly related, but not in the manner many literary critics think.

Given the connotations of *realism*, and the obvious misunderstandings surrounding it, why not jettison the term altogether? For two reasons: first, because it signals the moment of polemic in this study, directed against assertions of Coetzee's anti-realism; second, and more important, because Coetzee criticized La Guma precisely for trying to do away with the real, and thereafter shaped a literary practice intended to avoid the pitfalls associated with La Guma's writing.

Again, what is at stake here is not the capacity of a work to reproduce an unmediated reality, but rather its orientation towards the world – for it is this that makes it realist, in the sense I am using the term. Bertolt Brecht used it similarly: 'Realism is not a mere question of form. Were we to copy the style of these realists [Balzac and Tolstoy], we would no longer be realists. For time flows on.... Methods become exhausted; stimuli no longer work. New problems appear and demand new methods. Reality changes; in order to represent it, modes of representation must also change.'[53] To Brecht we might add Alain Robbe-Grillet, an author with very different allegiances, and whom Coetzee had been reading alongside Beckett: 'All writers believe they are realists. None ever calls himself abstract, illusionistic, chimerical, fantastic, fallistical.' Indeed, for Robbe-Grillet, 'Realism is not a theory ... which would permit us to counter certain writers by certain others; it is, on the contrary, a flag under which the enormous majority – if not all – of today's novelists enlist.... It is the real world which interests them; each one attempts as best he can to create "the real."'[54]

In this light, it is important to stress again that the orientation towards the world that affects the very syntax of *Dusklands* is sought in full awareness of the extent to which language mediates reality. To speak of the clarity and economy of Coetzee's prose is neither to suggest that Coetzee aimed at a transparent writing through which the truth of the world might be seen, nor is it to imply that plainer speech is more honest speech. One might accept as chimerical the notion of an absolute truth, waiting to be revealed by the right combination of magical words, and yet continue to insist that there is a great deal at stake in the kinds of truths that authors create for their readers.

Where works of fiction are concerned, an orientation towards the world is realized only insofar as a particular world is brought into being. In the case of *Dusklands* this is not only a world of violence and life-and-death struggle, a world in which full and fulfilling relations between self and other are rendered impossible by domination and oppression; it is also a world that is stark, stripped down, laid bare, reduced to its brute constituent parts. It is, in other words, a world brought into being by a particular style and, moreover, a particular syntax. The bareness of this world is something that we come to experience in reading the novel, due in part to the commonplace notion that a way of speaking is suited to a particular situation, or that a way of seeing the world produces a way of describing it.[55] Whatever its mechanism, *Dusklands* has left many of its readers affected by an encounter with something desolate and laid to waste.

Here it is worth emphasizing the properly dialectical meeting between the two aspects of style with which we are concerned: subject matter and syntax. The argument being made is not that, in looking at the world, Coetzee saw brutishness and then attempted to find a language adequate to it. Rather, an orientation towards the world produced a novel in which everything all at once speaks of a reality that is bad not because it is ugly or because it lies beyond discourse but because it is brute and also brutal.

Unity and Purpose of a Bare Prose

The account of *Dusklands* given thus far has largely ignored the novel's division into two parts, which are in turn composed of several sections. Yet one might ask whether *Dusklands* should not be thought of as two novellas, or an anthology of fragments, rather than a single novel, particularly given the degree of formal variation across the sections. Further work is clearly required to demonstrate the novel's stylistic coherence, keeping in mind that every prose work of reasonable length will be subject to a degree of variation (syntactical, lexical and rhetorical), and that this will be problematic only where the variation is substantial and cannot be explained in terms of the work's own aesthetic logic.

We might begin by considering the 'Afterword' of 'The Narrative of Jacobus Coetzee', attributed to S. J. Coetzee, panegyrist masquerading as pedant. The style of this section deviates noticeably from those passages analysed above, for its language is altogether more florid, as is clear from the manner in which the sighting of the Great River is recounted:

> [1] And so on 24 August Coetzee arrived at the Great River (Gariep, Orange). [2] The sight which greeted him was majestic, the waters flowing broad and strong, the cliffs resounding with their roar. [3] Here he might have rested all day, here have fixed his abode, enjoying the shade of the willows (*Salix gariepina*, not the weeping willow) and inhaling the cool breezes. [4] His Hottentots, glad of shelter from the scorching sun, had thrown aside their garments and lay naked in the shade or swam fearlessly in the stream. [5] The cooing of doves soothed his ear. [6] The cattle, unyoked, drank at the water's edge. [7] He saw that the banks, clothed in trees (*zwartebast, karreehout*), might furnish timber for all the wants of colonization. [8] He could not see that the course of the river was plagued with falls and rapids, or that it debouched on a particularly desolate strip of coast. [9] He dreamed a father-dream of rafts laden with produce sailing down to the sea and the waiting schooners. (128)

The prose of this passage is distinguished by the introduction of a more learned lexicon and an antiquated idiom (*to fix abode; to be laden with produce; to be glad of shelter; to furnish timber; to throw aside garments*). It is marked also by phrasal parallelism, which produces the anaphoric symmetry of sentence 3, and the rising triadic structure of sentence 2, with its noticeably strong rhythms ('the wāters flŏwing brŏad and strŏng, the clĭffs resŏunding with their rŏar'). One should note also the sound repetition (the alliteration of sentence 4 and the assonance of sentence 5), and the clichés of the pastoral idyll (sun, shade, breeze, birdsong, naked bodies frolicking in cool waters). Here, the fullness of the description, which does not lack in adjectives (*majestic, broad, strong, cool, scorching, naked, glad, plagued, desolate*), conjures the plenitude offered by the land to its conqueror, the richness of a complex natural reality that wants only for a purpose.

Now, from the point of view of S. J. Coetzee, the aim of this 'Afterword' is to idealize and justify the journey of exploration. However, from the point of view of the implied external narrator, its purpose is to expose the mystifications of a certain kind of scholarship. This is achieved through the pastiche of a learned style, which becomes increasingly parodic as the account's tendentiousness reveals itself. The question is whether there is any further purpose to this stylistic deviation; to which we might answer by noting, in the first place, that S. J. Coetzee's manner of speaking is one that has the fingerprints of rhetoric – if not literature – all over it. Indeed, the prose of the 'Afterword' displays certain of the 'excesses of realism' associated with La Guma. This need not be surprising, because the kind of scholarship S. J. Coetzee represents is thoroughly implicated in the desire to make the reader feel the truth of a particular reality and to endow that reality with a meaning beyond itself – its essential relation to a greater destiny. The consequence of this stylistic marking, however, is that the 'Afterword' comes to constitute a point of contrast internal to the novel, by means of which the predominant style is itself characterized and attributed some value or significance.

This is not to say that the prose of the 'Afterword' should be conflated entirely with that of La Guma's novels. Rather, a similar set of preconceptions about the nature of reality produces similar literary effects. Another of these effects occurs earlier in the 'Afterword', where we encounter an extraordinary series of catalogues, which function not only as inventories of reality, but also as a means of giving the weight of material fact to the journey described, and thereby substantiating its historical truth. To begin with, S. J. Coetzee itemizes the contents of his forebear's wagon: 'black, white and blue porcelain beads, tobacco, knives, looking-glasses, brass wire' and so on, culminating in 'three water-casks, a medicine chest, and many other things – civilization, in fact, *in ovo*' (125–6).

The catalogues do not end here, for S. J. Coetzee begins almost immediately to list the remnants of one of the expedition's halts (on August 18), including 'the ashes of the night fire, combustion complete, a feature of dry climates; faeces dotted in mounds over a broad area, herbivore in the open, carnivore behind rocks; urine stains with minute traces of copper salts; tea leaves; the leg-bones of a springbok; five inches of braided oxhide rope; tobacco ash; and a musket ball' (126). If one recalls the passage quoted from *A Walk in the Night*, of which Coetzee says that everything mentioned is 'named with its own gesture of repudiation', it is significant that everything named here is likewise already consumed, used up.[56]

Nor will any of it remain for long: 'The faeces dried in the course of the day. Rope and bones were eaten by a hyena on August 22. A storm on November 2 scattered all else. The musket ball was not there on August 18, 1933' (126).

There is a joke here at the expense of the compulsion to inventorize, but also at the expense of the notion that material things constitute a world of solidity, density and permanence, a world on which to stake claims for belonging. It is a joke which reads as the proclamation: no transcendence shall be discovered in the immediate materiality of the everyday. It is a joke carried to a rather macabre conclusion as the listing continues, revealing its mania and hidden desire in the inventory of bodily fragments: 'From scalp and beard, dead hair and scales. From the ears, crumbs of wax. From the nose, mucus and blood.... These relicts, deposited over Southern Africa in two swathes, soon disappeared under sun, wind, rain, and the attentions of the insect kingdom, though their atomic constituents are still of course among us. *Scripta manent*' (126–7). In fact, the real punchline is the section's final sentence: 'I hope I have succeeded in evoking something of the reality of this extraordinary man' (129).

In the case of 'The Narrative of Jacobus Coetzee', it is clear that the stylistic deviation of the 'Afterword' serves a particular purpose in the economy of the novel. What might then be said of 'The Vietnam Project', in which there are likewise moments in which the prose becomes more fulsome and indeed excessive?

It should here straightaway be noted that, as regards style, the 'Introduction' to Dawn's report causes few difficulties because its syntax remains simple, clear and pared down. More problematic are such passages as the one that immediately follows the description of Dawn's office:

> Gray planes, the shadowless green light under which like a pale stunned deep-sea fish I float, seep into the grayest centres of memory and drown me in reveries of love and hatred for that self of mine who exhausted the fire of his twenty-third, twenty-fourth, and twenty-fifth years beneath the fluorescent glare of Datamatic longing in dying periods for 5 PM with its ambiguous hesperian promise. (7)

The syntax of this sentence is noticeably more complex than that of the six sentences by which it is preceded, with a number of embedded and subordinate clauses, finite and non-finite. We encounter also a series of metaphors (including the extended metaphor by means of which the office light is figured as water, and the office as a seascape) as well as a more pronounced use of adjectival modification. With regard to the latter, whereas the previous six sentences make use only of *gray*, *little* and *fluorescent*, the final sentence, in its four clauses, introduces *shadowless*, *green*, *pale*, *stunned*, *deep-sea*, *dying*, *ambiguous* and the specifically poetic adjective *hesperian*, another sideways allusion to lands of dusk, of the setting sun.

If there is thus a shift from the barer prose that prevails elsewhere in the novel, the question is whether this deviation (like that of the 'Afterword') can also be explained in terms of the work's stylistic logic. Here we might recall the passage cited previously, where Dawn describes the writing he wishes to emulate and that which he actually produces, for though neither accords with that of *Dusklands* itself, Dawn's proposed model does bring him into relation with S. J. Coetzee, and, indeed, Alex La Guma, as well as the two authors to whom he more explicitly alludes, Saul Bellow and Patrick White, whose Herzog and Voss are both heroes of a certain kind of descriptive prose (38).

It so happens, however, that this hyper-descriptive writing is only what Dawn believes he *ought* to copy. His 'true ideal' is instead 'an endless discourse of character, the self reading the self to the self in all infinity', which relates Dawn rather to Beckett, insofar as it implies something like the mode of *The Unnamable* (40). While these two ideals might otherwise have seemed irreconcilable, the earlier discussion of varieties of literary introversion makes it clear that, from Coetzee's perspective, the aesthetic practices of Beckett's later fictions and La Guma's novels are not incommensurable, for both enact a turning away from the world. Nor is it accidental that such practices constitute Dawn's models, for he is a character not only on the verge of breakdown, but thoroughly introverted.

There are a number of ways to read Dawn's condition. The terms of his own narrative, however, suggest the relevance of existential phenomenology, particularly as articulated in R. D. Laing's *The Divided Self*.[57] From this point of view, Dawn's condition seems the product of what Laing calls ontological insecurity, one feature of which is a split between a secreted inner self and a loathed external self. That this is Dawn's predicament is suggested in those passages which reveal his mechanical sexual relations with Marilyn (8, 11), and those which treat his body as something not only separate but alien and threatening, the 'parasite starfish' (7), 'revolting body' (7), 'enemy body' (8), 'tyrant body (33), the 'hideous mongol boy who stretches his limbs inside my hollow bones' (40).

The concluding section of 'The Vietnam Project' offers little prospect of full recovery, for it reveals that Dawn has yet to grasp the distinction between things and their names:

> It has all come down to this (I ease myself in and tell over the clear, functional words): my bed, my window, my door, my walls, my room. These words I love. I sit them on my lap to burnish and fondle. They are beloved to me, each one, and having arrived at them I vow not to lose them. They lie quiet under my hand: they wink back at me, they glow for me, they are placid now that I am here. They are my fruit, my grapes growing for me. They are the stars in my tree. Around them I dance my slow, fat, happy dance of union, around them and around. I live in them and they in me. (45)

Advised by his doctors to 'form stable relationships' with things in the world, Dawn believes he does so 'by cathecting my love on to my room' (45). However, the contents of this cell escape him as much as did the contents of his motel room and everything that lay beyond it.

Throughout his narrative, Dawn's psychic decay is characterized by a damaged sense of the real and an inability to be in the world. According to Laing, this condition may eventuate as easily in a repudiation of a reality (which might come to be experienced as so many threatening and fragmented objects, of which the external self is the closest and therefore most dangerous), as in an understanding of the external world as a potential source of regeneration for a deadened inner world ('There is no doubt that contact with reality can be invigorating' (38)). However, while Dawn's ontological insecurity may be explicable in thematic terms, it causes certain technical difficulties for a work committed to an orientation towards the world. For how does the novelist both characterize the introverted first person narrator and achieve such an orientation?

One solution is to establish a distance between the character narrator Dawn and the work's implied external narrator. This, I have suggested, is accomplished in the motel room passage and in other such reflexive instances, and it is further achieved whenever the reader feels able to discern a truth lying beyond Dawn's paranoia, that is, in moments of dramatic irony, such as when Dawn insists on the reality of Marilyn's affair. But there is another important means of effecting this distance, and here we return to the passage describing Dawn's grey office.

Across the seven sentences that constitute this passage, there is, as indicated, a stylistic shift, but there is also a parallel movement from immediate sensory perception to memory of sense perception to Dawn's affective response to his environment. We might then say that the passage stages a subjectivization of reality, or that the world of the narrative, which is mediated by the focalizer Dawn, becomes obscured by his pathology. In such a moment, what is described is no longer the reality of the novel, but rather Dawn's particular reality, which has its own style, characterized by heightened metaphoricity and by certain of the 'excesses of realism'. This is a matter taken up in greater detail in the third chapter, but we might observe here that the function of such moments is clearly related to that of the 'Afterword', insofar as they too constitute points of stylistic contrast, and might therefore be understood in terms of the work's own logic.

Insofar as its stylistic variation appears motivated, *Dusklands* should indeed be treated as a single coherent work, a view in any case supported by the manuscripts.[58] The various drafts of the novel are contained in a number of notebooks, collected in six folders. Though their contents are somewhat chaotic, it is immediately apparent (the notebooks are carefully dated) that the earliest drafts are versions of 'The Narrative of Jacobus Coetzee'. Indeed, it seems likely that 'The Vietnam Project' was not begun before the novel's second part had been largely completed.

In reading successive drafts of 'The Narrative of Jacobus Coetzee' one discovers a decided shift from a properly mimetic narrative voice towards a more neutral voice, less identifiable with any particular historical or sociocultural idiom. So, whereas earlier drafts characterize the narrator, through his language, as a crude frontiersman, revisions entail a smoothing out of the prose: the abandonment of particular syntactic patterns, such as parataxis, and of clumsy and colloquial expression, as well as the eradication of noticeably rudimentary lexical items.

To be properly substantiated, these rather vague impressions would require a more rigorous analysis, which cannot be undertaken at present. Nevertheless, the drafting of the novel indicates a gradual stylistic unification of its different parts, and thus provides further evidence that, at least in terms of its compositional principles, the work coheres.

This brings us closer to the present chapter's conclusion, and one of its most important claims. For if *Dusklands* is animated throughout by a single set of stylistic principles, and thereby produces a prose and a world that is bare and stark, it has yet to be explained what this means. Here, we might return briefly to the final part of 'The Vietnam Project' and to one of those reflexive gestures by which a distinction is effected between the novel's implied narrator and the character narrator Dawn:

> besides going numb I am also sweating a lot and turning white, in a fishy way. Also, something which I usually think of as my consciousness is shooting backwards, at a geometrically accelerating pace, according to a certain formula, out of the back of my head, and I am not sure I will be able to stay with it. The people in front of me are growing smaller and therefore less and less dangerous. They are also tilting. A convention allows me to record these details. (43–4)

There are a number of things to say about this passage, by no means the least significant of which is that the convention mentioned in the final sentence is one that allows a character narrator to be both agent and teller of an event. In the normal course of things, this does not seem a problem, but what is described here is an impairment of consciousness, which yet proceeds in a measured, collected fashion. What is thus foregrounded, at this crucial moment, is the presence of the implied narrator, the proper origin of the novel's spare prose.

Admittedly, in the second sentence, with its subordinate clause embedded in the first noun phrase, and its twin adverbials inserted between 'backwards' and 'out the back', there is a minor stylistic departure, as Dawn's derangement impinges on the syntax. The writing, however, will very shortly regain its simplicity, and indeed its clarity:

> Holding it like a pencil, I push the knife in. The child kicks and flails. A long, flat ice-sheet of sound takes place.
>   That is what he was talking about, the thing he wants me to put down. It is the fruit-knife from the bedside table. The ball of my thumb still carries the memory of the skin popping. At first it resists the orthogonal pressure, even this child-skin. Then: pop. Perhaps I even heard the pop through my hand, as in quiet country one hears a faroff locomotive through the soles of one's feet. Someone else is screaming. That is my wife Marilyn, who is also here (my mind is quite clear now). (44)

Here, the sentences are again short, and their structure relatively simple. Whether Dawn's mind is in fact clear, and in spite of the ways reality remains somehow distant and fragmented, the description of the stabbing is notable for its precision, its restricted use of the straightforward and largely denotative adjectives *long, flat, quiet, faroff, clear*, and *orthogonal*.

What is portrayed here is the culmination of Dawn's psychotic breakdown, a scene that, in both structural and semantic terms, is the climactic moment of 'The Vietnam Project'. It is also a moment of intensely vivid and graphic description, the lucidity of which seems all the greater because of its horror. What is more, because the times of narration and narrative are out of kilter, everything appears to happen in slow motion, which only heightens the intensity of the passage. Together, these features create an impression of the prose being stripped down as the narrative's focus is restricted and sharpened, and what we find at the centre of its field of vision is an act of deadly violence that the writing itself suggests is its cause and consequence. It is in this moment of violence, in other words, that both the reality and the prose of the novel seem their starkest.

At this point, another general observation about the manuscripts of *Dusklands* may be helpful: the drafting process itself suggests some kind of relation between Coetzee's bare style and descriptions of violence because amongst the earliest drafts we find versions of the opening passages of 'The Narrative of Jacobus Coetzee', giving advice on the manner in which Bushmen are to be hunted and killed. A considerable portion of a short passage is taken up with horrific detail, a disquisition on murder, rape and atrocity delivered throughout in a measured prose.

Such scenes, of course, are found throughout the novel. There may be relatively few passages in which physical surroundings are described in any detail, but depictions of violence are both frequent and so positioned as to become focal points. In 'The Vietnam Project', we are led inexorably to the revelation of the photographs hidden in Dawn's briefcase, images of the brutal reality that pushes him to breakdown. As each photograph is displayed, the reader encounters a further instance of Coetzee's descriptive prowess. Of course, these are not representations of violent acts per se. The reality of war is mediated by the photographic and cinematic forms and separated in time and space from the moment of narration. This distance might be said to explain the relative composure of the writing in these cases.

No such explanation exists for the climactic scene of 'The Narrative of Jacobus Coetzee', however, in which one reads of the massacre of the Hottentot village. It is clear from this passage that the most straightforward prose is reserved for the most explicitly brutal scenes. The murder of Adonis is exemplary:

> He would not take it. I stamped. His lips seeped blood, his jaw relaxed. I pushed the muzzle in till he began to gag. I held his head steady between my ankles. Behind me his sphincter gave way and a rich stench filled the air. 'Watch your manners, hotnot', I said. I regretted this vulgarity. The shot sounded as minor as a shot fired into the sand. Whatever happened in the pap inside his head left his eyes crossed. (111)

There is little need here to repeat the syntactical analysis offered previously. The qualities are the same, and the stark force of the description is in any case best left unparsed.

For the sake of clarity, it is worth summarizing the argument I have been making: because of the ways moments of violence are positioned in the narrative, they are prioritized structurally and thematically. The fact that the writing is noticeably bare in such moments is a means both of ensuring the descriptions are vivid and intense, and of suggesting a particular relationship between violence and bare prose, such that each invokes the other. Thus, the bareness of reality itself comes to be related to violence.

It is not difficult to think why this might be the case, at least if one keeps in mind, in broad outline, the manner in which human relations have been understood by, amongst others, Jean-Paul Sartre, Martin Buber, Frantz Fanon and R. D. Laing, all of whom Coetzee appears to have been reading during the period in which his early novels were conceived and composed. Each of these writers, whom we might very roughly identify as existentialists of one kind or another, drew in important respects on Hegel, whom Coetzee had likewise been reading, and in particular on Hegel's understanding of the necessity to the self of the other's recognition. In this case, however, it is Fanon who seems of greatest relevance, given his immediate concern with the nature of colonial societies, which he characterizes as thoroughly 'manichean' and saturated with violence, a state of existence that blocks recognition and the kind of being-in-the-world that Laing identifies with ontological security, and which Fanon describes in *Black Skin, White Masks* as a person's 'human reality, different from his natural reality'.[59]

In Fanon's terms, violence comes to be understood as the essential mode of relating in colonial societies. It is, in the fullest sense of the term, brutalizing. By this one does not mean simply that it hardens attitudes or corrupts morals, but that it ensures people come to be treated as things, as brute insensate matter. It ensures that reality is stripped of all human relation, deprived of what Buber calls the I-Thou. The fact that such a state of affairs is often conceived not only as basic, simple or foundational, but as debased, denuded, stripped away, pared down, reduced, laid bare, is given testament in the terms used by philosophers as divergent as John Searle ('brute reality') and Giorgio Agamben ('bare life') to describe a non-social world.[60] Whatever the intentions of these philosophers, reality without human relation is characterized not simply as that which subsists, but as reality-minus, which at least suggests hope of or aspiration towards a being-in-the-world.

This allows us to return to La Guma, and the particular manner in which Coetzee understands his failure. In view of what has been said previously, La Guma's mistake was to focus his attention on the epiphenomena of a bad reality. He was concerned by and fascinated with the materiality of the world, in which he perceived reality's badness, and he responded by attempting to reproduce this reality as a plenum: he piles up, in a kind of pyramid of death-in-life, objects and details and the features of faces and hands, but, finding that even this is not enough to account for the real, he infuses these many things, this It-world, with his own subjectivity, hoping both for redemption and transcendence, but effecting only repudiation. In this, he is echoed by Jacobus Coetzee, who describes the 'mountain of skin, bones, inedible gristle, and excrement' he leaves in his wake as his 'dispersed pyramid to life' (84).

What La Guma does not see is that reality only appears as an agglomeration of things because it has been stripped bare, and no excess of detail can alter this fact. The right response, Coetzee's work intimates – the valid, appropriate and responsible response – is a literary practice in which the truth of this reality is recognized as one of brute facts, a practice capable of laying bare, in a series of shattering moments, the cause of all this bareness, which is a violence conceived not simply in terms of individual acts of aggression, but as the basic structure of relations in certain societies and at certain times.

Based on his critical essays and first novel, it seems Coetzee believed he was faced with a reality in which life had indeed been reduced to brute relations. This posed a challenge, requiring at the very least an orientation towards the world. Other orientations, whatever their merits, were inadequate: an art that attempted to redeem reality by aestheticizing it would only restate the transcendence of beauty and spirit; an art, such as Beckett's, that rejected the very possibility of meaning and resigned itself to existence in the buzzing, booming confusion, whilst railing against this imprisonment, likewise led to introversion and empty form; a feasible response, therefore, was to refuse both bad choices, neither to progress nor regress, but, instead, to produce a way of speaking and seeing, which was not only turned towards the world, but able to assert something about its particular reality. The consequence of this double negation is the distinctive prose style we encounter for the first time in *Dusklands*.

CHAPTER 2

New Dimensions
In the Heart of the Country's *Repetitions*

Reading Coetzee's second novel, *In the Heart of the Country*, one encounters again the prose of a world laid bare. Its syntax is pared down, the sentences relatively short and simple, the use of adjectival modification and adverbials limited by requirements of clarity and precision. In scenes of brutal violence, its writing too becomes markedly spare. If anything, it is a starker work than *Dusklands*. Yet, if critics have considered the question of formal development at all, they have tended to view the novel as more purposefully anti-realist, finding evidence for this in the numbering of its passages and its more frequent narration of contradictory events.

In the previous chapter, I argued that a misconceived relation between Coetzee and Beckett had encouraged readings of the former's fictions in which undue emphasis was given to their disjunctive moments. In the present chapter, I follow a different route, tracing in greater detail Coetzee's position in the South African literary field. Here also, a partial view has prompted a focus on his writings' metafictional gestures, largely by engendering a belief in his status as modernizer of local literature. This status, which is hardly touched by the question of whether his works were as radical as Beckett's, depends instead on the assumption that South African fiction, prior to Coetzee's emergence, was bogged down in genres and techniques long abandoned by metropolitan authors. Only through clarifying what is mistaken in this assumption might we articulate the true basis for Coetzee's break with his local predecessors and peers, even the most avant-garde.

Men of the Sixties, Men of the Seventies:
Coetzee and the Sestigers

Published in 1977, *In the Heart of the Country* was immediately celebrated by the South African press as a major achievement. Afrikaans critics were especially appreciative, none more so than André P. Brink, who chose the novel as one of his books of the year.[1] It built on the achievement of *Dusklands*, Brink said, which had itself changed the 'image of South African history' and 'added a new dimension to our local prose – both Afrikaans and English'.[2]

Yet, when earlier reviewing *Dusklands*, Brink had been notably less enthusiastic, believing that many of 'the possibilities' inherent in the work's 'manifold perspective' had not been realized. In fact, he said *Dusklands* lacked not only 'the subtle complexity' of Doris Lessing's *The Golden Notebook* or 'Nabokov's archetypal *Pale Fire*', but also the 'momentum of a simpler framework', and that, in thus falling 'between two stools', it was less impressive than it might otherwise have been.[3]

Brink was especially irked by assertions of the novel's originality. *Dusklands* was not, he commented acerbically, '"the first truly modern South African novel" as the publishers proclaim'; he could easily 'think of a dozen titles, Afrikaans and English, ... as truly modern and South African', some of which were 'in fact better'. Indeed, the novel's 'hyper-conscious exploitation of the site of narration' only prompted Brink to link Coetzee with the Sestigers, a group of Afrikaans writers of the 1960s to which he had himself belonged. Identifying Coetzee as an 'Engelse Sestiger', Brink observed that if *Dusklands* had been 'written in Afrikaans, and ... published a decade earlier', its author might even have become one of the group's central figures.[4]

Brink was by no means the only local reviewer who baulked at Ravan's claims or was reminded of the Sestigers. We have seen already that Lionel Abrahams found echoes in *Dusklands* of Brink's own fictions, as well as Etienne Leroux's, and Ursula Barnett explained that, though Afrikaans speakers were often 'equated with conservatism', it was the Sestigers who had been the local 'pioneers in the field of the avant-garde novel'.[5] Even Jonathan Crewe was careful to observe, in the version of his review that eventually appeared in *Contrast*, that: 'In *Dusklands*, the modern novel *in English* arrives in South Africa for the first time.'[6]

Who, then, were these Sestigers? What, if anything, had Coetzee to do with them? And why, only a few years after Brink's disappointment with *Dusklands*, did his review of *In the Heart of the Country* speak of the 'new dimension' Coetzee had added to South African fiction?

As early as 1961, N. P. van Wyk Louw, the pre-eminent Afrikaans poet and critic of the mid-twentieth century, was complaining of 'gemoedelike lokale realisme', a 'genial' variety of South African literary realism char-acterized by its thematic preoccupations with either life on the farm or urban alienation. Concerned with its stultifying effects, Van Wyk Louw was nevertheless hopeful, for in several recent fictions he found it abandoned in favour of '"surrealist narrative", "magical prose", the fantastic narrative setting', modes of writing he associated with Lautréamont, Kafka and Henry Miller.[7]

To begin with, the canon of emergent Afrikaans writing included only a few works. However, given considerable impetus by Van Wyk Louw's intervention, the movement was greatly energized by the publication of *Sestiger* in 1963. Although the journal was short-lived, its eight issues provided a platform for several of the twentieth century's most prominent Afrikaans authors, including Brink, Breyten Breytenbach, Bartho Smit and Chris Barnard. The actual fictions produced by these Sestigers may not in the end have been as surrealist as Van Wyk Louw wished, but each certainly arose from the conviction that the Afrikaans writer could no longer 'pour his new themes or thoughts' into what Bartho Smit called the 'ossified forms' of the past.[8] Instead, new modes were required, and these were sought in the novels of Joyce, Faulkner, Beckett, Kafka, Miller, Sartre and Camus, as well as in Nederlands authors such as Cees Nooteboom, L. P. Boon, W. F. Hermans and Simon Vestdijk, whom Van Wyk Louw insisted were of special relevance to the regeneration of Afrikaans literature.[9]

Some indication of how the Sestigers viewed themselves is found in Brink's *Aspekte van die nuwe prosa*, which aimed to situate the Afrikaans renewal in relation to broader metropolitan trends: towards a thoroughgoing relativism, an 'exploitation of all aspects of the novel's structure', and a particular interest in 'time as an active structuring factor'. Brink believed the Sestigers' own efforts were best understood under two headings: 'Eksperimente met styl' and 'Eksperimente met struktuur'. With regard to the former, he claimed the Sestigers were reshaping syntax in order to create new meanings, whilst exploring the 'texture of language itself', the possibilities inherent in its existence both as sound and as 'the *word on paper*'. As for structure, Brink argued that 'in place of the traditional chronological model with its sporadic shifts in perspective – though always within the framework of "reality" – a variety of new forms had appeared that incorporated manifold realities or layers of meaning' and that depended, in particular, on mythic palimpsests.[10]

Thus, according to Brink, the Sestigers had rejected cultural nationalism in favour of cosmopolitan aestheticism. Yet they continued to write in Afrikaans – at least for the time being – and remained committed to rejuvenating South African literary practice.[11] To this end, several amongst them had reworked local genres, particularly those associated with the myths of Afrikaner nationhood and history. In his *Die groot anders-maak*, for example, Jan Rabie had tackled the narrative of exploration by writing of the early *trek* into the interior of the Cape from the perspective of a group of Khoekhoe. Etienne Leroux, on the other hand, had offered estranging visions of the farm and *plaasroman*, or farm novel, in his surreal and unsettling *Silberstein* trilogy.

Brink therefore had good reason to believe Coetzee's originality had been overstated. Much about *Dusklands* and its author undoubtedly seemed familiar to him, and this impression would have grown only stronger in subsequent years. With regard to Coetzee's affiliations, for example, his special relationship with Nederlands writing would become increasingly apparent, first in his translation of *Een nagelaten bekentenis*, a novel by Marcellus Emants, and then in his translation of and commentary on Gerrit Achterberg's sonnet sequence, 'Ballade van de gasfitter'.[12]

This relationship itself depended on some knowledge of Afrikaans, which Brink took for granted, and which would become evident in several early reviews and articles written by Coetzee in that language. A facility with Afrikaans should not, of course, be taken as evidence of any ethno-linguistic identity, particularly given Coetzee's sense that Afrikaners would be unlikely to accept him as one of their own, though he would neither wish nor be able to withdraw unilaterally from their community.[13] His linguistic ability does, however, point towards a matter of far greater relevance: Coetzee's concerted engagement with Afrikaans literary culture.

His studies of the *plaasroman*, collected in *White Writing*, are now well known, but as early as 1977 Coetzee had published a revealing critique of Ross Devenish and Athol Fugard's film *The Guest*, about an episode in the life of Afrikaans poet Eugene Marais, whose work Coetzee knew well enough to question the filmmakers' departure from Leon Rousseau's biography, *Die groot verlange*. Coetzee was critical also of their representation of the Meyer family, which perpetuated, he believed, the stereotype of the 'Boer', not least in making Afrikaans characters 'speak a variety of English no human has ever spoken'.[14]

Although it was not unusual for English-speaking South Africans to take an interest in Afrikaans writing and history – the very existence of *The Guest* makes this clear – what Coetzee demonstrated in this review was not simply a knowledge of, but also a certain protectiveness towards Afrikaans and its literature, an attitude as proprietary as it was critical. Something of this attitude is present also in Coetzee's early fictions, which presented characters and locales clearly recognizable to an Afrikaans readership, and parodied moribund local genres in a manner reminiscent of the Sestigers: whilst 'The Narrative of Jacobus Coetzee' poked fun at journals of exploration and nationalist scholarship, *In the Heart of the Country*, in spite of its status as the first of Coetzee's novels published abroad, aimed directly at the conventions of the *plaasroman*.

Nor was there any attempt to conceal these resemblances: when the South African edition of *In the Heart of the Country* was eventually published by Ravan in 1978, much of its dialogue was in Afrikaans. Early reviewers, it is true, were likely to have read the British edition, but Brink would certainly have known that portions of the novel had appeared already in the journal *Standpunte*.[15] This choice of venue was itself significant. Founded in 1945 by Van Wyk Louw, *Standpunte* had thereafter aligned itself with what Peter McDonald has called the *volk* avant-garde.[16] Though some of its glamour had faded by 1976, the journal was still prestigious, and by choosing it to publish sections of *In the Heart of the Country* Coetzee made only more explicit the novel's entanglement with the themes and history of Afrikaans literature. He might also have done a great deal to guarantee its favourable reception in the Afrikaans press.

In a number of ways, then, Coetzee's designation as an 'English Sestiger' might be justified, for he resembled the *volk* avant-garde in its distinctive pattern of literary affiliations and its approach to the materials of South African literature. Indeed, he sometimes behaved *as if he were* an Afrikaans novelist.[17] Complications arise, however, when it comes to the question of Coetzee's engagement with the Sestigers themselves.

There are, to begin with, few direct references to the movement in Coetzee's non-fiction, and certainly none of those essay-length critiques that helped, in the previous chapter, to clarify his relation to Beckett, Nabokov and La Guma. Moreover, when Jean Sévry raised the question, in an interview conducted in 1985, Coetzee conceded that the Sestigers had been 'one of the most interesting movements to emerge in South African writing', but rejected altogether the possibility of his indebtedness to them, insisting that any similarities were at most the consequence of convergent evolution or shared tradition. When Sévry went so far as to suggest Coetzee's novels 'had something in common with' the writings of the Sestigers, that his works were in fact 'a prolongation' of a trend initiated by them, Coetzee's response was hardly encouraging: 'It is quite right that the mode that I have chosen is very similar to what Leroux has been doing, but at the same time I don't find any affiliation between Leroux and myself. I didn't get there by reading Leroux.'[18]

The stridency of this denial might be considered reason enough to abandon the question of Coetzee's relations with the Sestigers, though it might just as well be taken to indicate, if not an 'anxiety of influence', then something like it, a desire on Coetzee's part to distance himself from those South African authors closest to him in generational and aesthetic terms. We should certainly keep in mind that, as his international reputation grew, Coetzee tended ever more emphatically to situate himself as a man apart from local writing, whilst affirming his connection to major metropolitan figures. Again, Sévry's interview is revealing, for, having elicited Coetzee's somewhat bad-tempered assertion of autonomy, he asked about a more canonical forebear: 'Now quite a few critics keep pressing comparisons between yourself and Kafka. I suppose you feel rather irritated with it?' Far from being irritated, Coetzee readily acceded to this comparison, explaining that 'one's responses are very different, to being compared to Leroux on the one hand and with Kafka on the other. Kafka is such an enormous presence in modern literature that for one to deny totally that he has been affected by Kafka would be extremely foolish'.[19]

There may be something disingenuous in this double movement of affirmation and denial, but this is beside the point. Instead, we ought to observe that Sévry, in pressing Coetzee to consider his literary relations, framed his inquiries throughout in the familiar terms of influence and indebtedness. As such, he could not but fail to ask the more pertinent question, about the significant differences between Coetzee and his local predecessors. Coetzee himself seems to have raised this very question, at least in one early text, 'Lughartig, met erns'. For in this 1975 review of Stephen Gray's *Local Colour*, Coetzee linked Gray's novel to *Dusklands*, and then situated both works in relation to those of the Sestigers.

However vaguely, the link is suggested even in the features of *Local Colour* that Coetzee selected for praise, since in speaking of its descriptive force, as well as its 'formal aspect', 'language use', 'composition' and 'sense of structure', he echoed those terms in which his own novel had been received. The association is then made a good deal firmer in the review's closing sentences. For here, Coetzee described Gray's novel as ''n aantreklike bydrae tot die vernuwing wat die Engelse prosa in Suid-Afrika deesdae belewe, 'n vernuwing waarin ons jonger skrywers en kleiner uitgewers die voortou neem', that is, 'a sensitive contribution to the renewal that English prose in South Africa is currently experiencing, a renewal in which our younger writers and smaller publishers are leading the way'.[20]

That Coetzee included himself in 'our younger writers' follows not only from the recent success of his own novel, but also from his and

Gray's shared involvement with Ravan Press, the 'smaller publisher' likewise responsible for *Local Colour*. Indeed, it is difficult to imagine anyone familiar with *Dusklands* and its reception mistaking Coetzee's meaning. What would really have caught the attention of *Beeld*'s Afrikaans readers, however, was Coetzee's repeated use of the word *vernuwing*, renewal, because in speaking of 'die vernuwing wat die Engelse prosa in Suid-Afrika deesdae belewe' Coetzee was implying a connection between his and Gray's emergence and that, a decade previously, of authors such as Brink and Leroux. For the arrival and project of the Sestigers had from the very beginning been conceived as a 'vernuwing in die prosa'.

Of course, notions of renewal and revival have been central to many artistic movements, but this should not distract us from the particular resonance the phrase 'vernuwing in die prosa' had acquired since N. P. van Wyk Louw first used it as the title for his study of the failures and prospects of Afrikaans literature. This resonance had not a little to do with Van Wyk Louw's specific argument, his belief that 'The general level of culture attained by a modern people is measured above all by the *prose* that is written, enjoyed, valued, endured or even permitted by its members.' For, if a people's prose could be treated as an index of its existential condition, the stagnation that Van Wyk Louw discerned in Afrikaans writing became a cause for real concern, and the 'vernuwing in die prosa' that he sought a matter of cultural survival.[21]

Whether or not their understanding of the need for change was identical with Van Wyk Louw's, those authors whose arrival he heralded in *Vernuwing in die prosa* gladly accepted his terms, and the notion of a 'renewal in prose' spread rapidly through Afrikaans critical discourse. The phrase itself recurred frequently in the pages of *Sestiger*, in the first number of which Jan Rabie noted that, while no 'renewers of the poetic arts' had emerged in the early 1960s, 'prose' could already 'boast of such works as *Sewe dae by die Silbersteins* and *Lobola vir die lewe*'.[22]

'Vernuwing in die prosa' was indeed so often repeated that it became something like the Sestigers' motto, its association with the movement continuing well into the 1970s. The clearest evidence for this is found in the proceedings of a symposium dedicated to an appraisal of Sestig, hosted by the University of Cape Town (UCT) between 12 and 16 February 1973.[23] More than a decade after Van Wyk Louw's study, J. D. Miles observed: 'It is today widely known that the *vernuwing* of Afrikaans prose brought about various shifts of accent and even radical changes to the so-called older prose.'[24] Likewise, J. C. Kannemeyer, critic, literary historian and

Coetzee's eventual biographer, insisted: 'With Sestig, Afrikaans literature brought about a *vernuwing* that was not limited to poetry alone.... For the first time in our literature, poetry, prose and to a lesser extent drama developed at the same time and in the same measure.'[25]

The notion of renewal – and especially a renewal in prose – was thus prominent enough to head the list of the movement's chief features, and was regarded as such even by its critics, such as Jack Cope, who remained sceptical of the Sestigers, no matter how much they had 'talked about renewal' or desired 'to bring into Afrikaans writing what they found freely treated in other literatures'. Indeed, Cope's article is proof not only of *vernuwing*'s resonance, but of the permeability of boundaries between literatures in English and Afrikaans, a matter he addressed directly in suggesting that all 'creative writing produced by the people of this country', regardless of the languages used, should be seen as 'aspects of a national literature', particularly in view of the 'innumerable threads of interchange and cross influence between the various writers'.[26]

Recently appointed as a lecturer to UCT's Department of English, J. M. Coetzee may well have attended the Sestigers symposium, joining several hundreds of Afrikaans speakers, English speakers, and those, like him, whose allegiances were more ambiguous. Kannemeyer's biography suggests Coetzee was indeed present, but the matter is not crucial. In his review of *Local Colour*, Coetzee's awareness of the Sestigers' project was implied in a concatenation of terms and ideas entirely familiar to the readers of *Beeld*: the present as moment of literary crisis, a new movement led by younger authors and smaller publishers, and, above all, a renewal in South African prose. With Coetzee's knowing use of *vernuwing*, repeated for rhetorical effect, the recent history of Afrikaans literature was thus summoned, made suddenly pertinent to an assessment of Gray's novel, and, by implication, his own.

What would yet have remained ambiguous was the precise nature of the relationship between the two moments of prose renewal to which Coetzee gestured. Did his *vernuwing* suggest only that his generation was belatedly extending the Sestigers' challenge by repeating their iconoclasm in a different linguistic domain? Or was this new *vernuwing* to be interpreted in a more profound sense, as a reinvigoration of *all* South African prose, and therefore an overturning of the Sestigers themselves?[27] Perhaps Coetzee's review traded intentionally on this ambiguity, but it certainly seems from Brink's very different responses to *Dusklands* and *In the Heart of the Country* that one could answer either way.

If we still cannot say what prompted Brink's change of heart, it is now at least clearer that Coetzee was not only aware of the Sestigers, but also in certain respects similar to them, albeit determined to keep his distance. It seems, moreover, that Coetzee was himself prepared to pose the question, however implicitly, which we will need to consider further: of whether and in what ways his early novels – *Dusklands* and *In the Heart of the Country* in particular – marked a departure for and from South African literature.

Renewal and Repetition: André P. Brink

The critical writings and reviews on which we have focussed thus far are helpful guides to authors' engagements, but insufficient if we wish to understand their actual practices. To explain what Brink meant, for example, when he spoke in *Aspekte van die nuwe prosa* of the Sestigers' experiments with narrative structure and the textuality and texturality of language, we will need to address the works themselves.

For this purpose, Brink's own novels are most apposite, and not only on the grounds of common authorship: from the very outset, he had been identified with the 'vernuwing in die prosa'. Indeed, though Etienne Leroux was often regarded as the greater literary talent, it was Brink who gave the movement much of its direction, producing early in his career an extraordinary range of writings, including his celebrated novels, *Lobola vir die lewe* (1962), *Die Ambassadeur* (1963) and *Orgie* (1965), as well as the prize-winning play *Caesar* (1961), the travel journal *Olé* (1965) and a startling number of translations.[28]

Nor was he unaware of his contribution: in *Aspekte van die nuwe prosa*, Brink happily discussed his novels' achievements alongside those of his peers. Thus, when describing experiments with narrative structure, he cited *Die Ambassadeur*, a novel set largely in near-contemporary Paris, which jettisoned the conventions of 'genial local realism' by giving several overlapping and competing accounts of an extra-marital affair between the South African Ambassador and the bohemian Nicolette Alford.[29]

The narrative's structural complexity arises in the first place from its multiple perspectives. These are thematically motivated by the unattainability of perfect understanding, which is staged already in the novel's opening chapter, narrated by Stephen Keyter, a young diplomat. Keyter's desire to 'discover the whole truth' and his belief in his capacity for disinterested judgement are undercut by his misinterpretation of events and by the revelation that his detachment is the consequence of a profound mistrust of others, which soon compels him to stalk the Ambassador and Nicolette in order to repeat the primal scene that haunts him (45).

There are thus limits to vision and understanding, confirmed by shifts in perspective; but there are also limits to thought and feeling, and these are expressed by the use of different narrative modes: 'first person' or character narration in chapters 1, 3 and 4 ('Third Secretary', 'Ambassador', 'Nicolette'); 'third person' or external narration in chapter 2 ('Chronicle'); and mixed character and external narration in the final chapter ('Coda'). Ways of speaking, we come to understand, produce and are produced by ways of being in the world.

Keyter's cool discourse, for example, cannot accommodate the intensity of immediate experience: 'It is difficult to describe this impression … because I am steeped in constipated officialese. Words are too formal, and certainly too smug, too polished for recording primary impressions' (9). Similarly, the novel must change from the external narration of the second chapter, where the Ambassador is focalizer, to the character narration of the third chapter, because, in meeting Nicolette, he discovers a new way of living: 'How can I speak of her chronologically if she has no chronology? For she is simply a sort of continuous present tense, a book one starts reading in the middle and which has no cover, title page, beginning or end' (127). Here the peculiarities of Nicolette's being are explicitly figured in terms of narrative structure (the temporal ordering of events), syntax (a particular tense and aspect) and even a certain textural configuration (a book without covers and paratexts).

Through the novel's structures and themes, the impossibility of understanding others comes to constitute its central drama. Indeed, each moment of crisis is consequent on mistaken or partial sight. In this regard, Brink's use of the technique of repeated narration is of signal importance. This becomes clear if we consider the sequence of events that begins with Nicolette's flight from Stephen's apartment, leads to her first visit that same evening to the Ambassador, and concludes with her second visit the following morning. Elements of this sequence are narrated first by Stephen (43–5), then in 'Chronicle' (65–82, 112), again, briefly, in the Ambassador's narrative (190), and finally by Nicolette (217–18). It is this sequence of events, moreover, that comprises the focus of the report Stephen sends to the Republic, and of the investigation it initiates. And yet, though each iteration reveals something new, uncertainty remains, and the final impression is of facts whose interpretation is constantly subject to change, an impression guaranteed by the ordering of the narrative, which allows the final word on these events to Nicolette, who believes that uttering thoughts in 'plain words' makes them 'vulgar and no longer true' (225).

Hardly a comprehensive analysis of *Die Ambassadeur*, this should nevertheless clarify how far the form of Brink's novel is aligned with a commitment to hermeneutic openness. Moreover, in being thematically foregrounded, its multiple perspectives and modes point towards the 'site of narration' itself, the site at which these perspectives and modes are chosen and arranged. In this way, narrative structure comes to be identified as a source of meaning in its own right.

In *Orgie*, Brink's experiments with structure continue, though he cites the novel instead as an example of experimentation with style, with language's textuality and texture.[30] In this respect, *Orgie* – a bewildering account of a couple's relationship dissolving in the midst of an orgiastic masked ball – is one of the most extraordinarily avant-garde works of South African literature. To begin with, its reader encounters a text printed the wrong way, parallel rather than perpendicular to the book's spine, and further distinguished by a variation in the font, size and colour of its type. Thus, with its first words, the novel demands a reorientation of reading practices, emphasizing the materiality of the book in hand: its dimensions, weight, the look and feel of its paper and print.

The most disorienting aspect of *Orgie* is not, however, its axial shift, to which one is soon enough accommodated. Rather, it is the use of an idiosyncratic interpretive schema, set out at the book's beginning in a manner reminiscent of initial stage directions:

OPSET

PERSONE

hy   sy

TYD

'n hede

'n verlede

'n duur

PLEK

saal van 'n kunsbal, Kaapstad: 20ste eeu n.C

feesgebou en tempeltoring, Babilon: 18de eeu v.C.

What follows this scene setting is a narrative in which the events thus occur simultaneously in two places, one contemporary (an artists' gathering in Cape Town), and one ancient (a festive hall in a Babylonian temple-complex); a text moreover, in which there is a constant movement of the narrative between a past (*'n verlede*), a present ('n hede) and a time of duration (**'n duur**), indicated by the change from italicized to roman to bold font; and which, finally, is narrated by two personages (they can hardly be called characters), he ('hy') and she ('sy'), whose utterances are separated, for the most part, into two columns.

However unusual a reading experience this implies, one is constantly surprised by a novel that breaks its own rules. There are moments, for example, in which the narrative voices compete side by side; moments when the boundary between the two seems to dissolve and words flow towards one another across the page; moments in which a third central column appears (implying the existence of at least one additional personage); moments, finally, in which the text collapses into a pile of jutting and truncated phrases crossing one another at different angles (79) and even moments in which words disappear altogether, vanishing into an empty blankness or the darkness of an ink-washed page (93).

Nor is Brink's experimentation with texture and text in *Orgie* limited to typography, the '*word on paper*'; language as 'sound structure' also plays its part. Examples are too numerous to describe in any detail, but the following instance is illustrative:

> Teen die muur met die skrikwekende skilderwerk
> naby die donker venster sit ek, en die groot saal druis
> en draai, iewers 'n trom, iewers 'n trompet, en die
> groteske gemaskerde wesens woel verby, rook kolk
> om my tafeltie, die aarde kantel voort, die laaste
> sterre tol: kabaal kabbala kabbel krabbel brabbel
> babbel babel –

> (Against the wall with the appalling painting
> nearby the dark window I sit, and the great hall sways
> and spins, somewhere a drum, somewhere a trumpet, and the
> grotesque masked beings toss and turn past, smoke swirls
> on my little table, the earth tilts forward, the last
> stars reel: cabal cabala babel scribble scrabble
> babble Babel –)

Of particular interest here is the list of alliterative words that form a series at once phonological and semantic, and which, along with the beating drum and screeching trumpet, recurs throughout, constituting a phonic background texture. It is also worth noting, however, the passage's parataxis and its somewhat irregular ordering, which offers an exemplary demonstration of Brink's claim that in the works of the Sestigers 'crumbling worlds' are described in a 'crumbling syntax'.[31]

Repetition and Renewal: J. M. Coetzee

The typographical experiments in *Orgie* may be unusual in fictional prose, but Brink's manipulation of narrative perspective would have been wholly familiar to any reader of Faulkner's *As I Lay Dying* or Joyce's *Ulysses*. Nevertheless, in the South African literary context, the use of these techniques ensured a break with the past, and certainly with 'gemoedelike lokale realisme'.

Viewed alongside such purposefully avant-garde works as *Die Ambassadeur* and *Orgie*, it should be reasonably clear why the claims made for *Dusklands* were questioned by local reviewers. Nor could *In the Heart of the Country* have fared much better on these grounds, in spite of its numbered passages and more pervasive use of repeated and contradictory narration of event. For even these adaptations hardly constituted a renewal of South African prose. Although the numbering of passages is certainly unusual, this is less for the numbers themselves than for their location (we frequently encounter numbers as chapter and section headings), and though striking at first, this typographical modification soon becomes familiar.

As for the contradictory narration of event, Coetzee had used this technique in 'The Narrative of Jacobus Coetzee', both in the passage recounting the deaths of Klawer, and in S. J. Coetzee's reconstruction of his ancestor's expedition. With *In the Heart of the Country*, it is simply more widely deployed: things are said to have occurred, events to have taken place, which seem in the end not to have happened at all. The murder of Magda's father, for example, related on page eleven, belongs to a portion of the novel that is in a sense revoked, but later echoed when she kills him a second time. This death too is then set aside, as the novel concludes with her caring for a man in old age.[32]

Here, the use of a single narrator ensures that the contradiction cannot be explained by a difference in perspective, as is largely the case in *Die Ambassadeur*, and, for the most part, *Dusklands*. On the other hand, as in *Dusklands*, the disjuncture remains semantic (rather than lexical or grammatical) and the repetition is explicable in terms of the logic of the narrative itself (Magda is mad and hallucinating or bored and fantasizing). As such, when considered as an experiment with narrative structure, *In the Heart of the Country*'s more obvious use of contradictory narration is best understood as a change in degree, rather than in kind.

If we remain committed to the idea that Coetzee's early novels added a new dimension to South African prose, it therefore becomes necessary to look elsewhere than these aspects of the novels. Or, rather, it becomes necessary to look at them otherwise than in the context of a break from 'gemoedelike lokale realisme' and the invention of local modernism. Instead, we might consider how some of those features that seem to offer the clearest indication of Coetzee's anti-realism might just as well be understood to contribute to that terse economy remarked in *Dusklands* from the outset, and which had become, in Coetzee's second novel, nothing if not more intense.

For, if one concludes a reading of *In the Heart of the Country* feeling that it offers stark descriptions of a stark place, this is not only because Coetzee's syntax remains taut and spare, and his use of adjectival modification curtailed. If a sense of claustrophobia pervades the novel, this is not only because its central character is trapped on a farm and in language. It is also because there is no escaping the enclosure of the first person narration and its almost monotonous repetition of words, phrases, figures and, indeed, events, a claustrophobia and monotony only heightened by the use of passages whose brevity is signalled in their numbering. As such, it becomes possible to see in Coetzee's second novel an intensification of strategies of repetition and enclosure, and thus of bareness itself.

Beginning with narrative repetition, we can understand how ubiquitous a phenomenon it had become by focussing on the novel's semantic level and on textual units larger than the clause and sentence. What we then see, over the course of the narrative, is that a great many things happen several times over: a new bride arrives on the farm; the father tempts the bride; Magda enters the kitchen seeking an explanation for Ou-Anna's absence; the father is killed; Magda requests Hendrik's assistance; the aftermath of death is expunged; Magda tries to bury her father; Magda is raped; Hendrik is captured; airmen fly over the farm; Magda tries to communicate with the airmen.

These repetitions are not all of the same kind, but comparison is possible if we divide them into several classes of repeated narration and repeated event. For this, it is helpful to have some notion of frequency, a term from narrative theory. In the definition offered by Shlomith Rimmon-Kenan (drawn in turn from Gérard Genette), frequency refers to 'the relation between the number of times an event appears in the story and the number of times it is narrated (or mentioned) in the text'.[33] With this in mind, it is possible to identify several different frequency structures.

Rimmon-Kenan uses the term 'iterative' to describe the single telling of a repeated event, an example of which is encountered on the novel's first page: 'I am the one who stays in her room reading or writing or fighting migraines' (1). The iterative, in other words, may be used to describe actions that are habitual. A particularly striking example occurs at the end of the novel, where there is a return to the routine of life on the farm: 'I feed my father his broth and weak tea. Then I press my lips to his forehead and fold him away for the night' (137).

If the iterative refers to a single telling of an habitual occurrence, Rimmon-Kenan uses the term 'singulative' for 'telling once what "happened" once'.[34] Since actions and events can recur without being habitual, there is no reason to exclude the singulative from the present discussion, particularly as we encounter instances of its use in the narration of Magda's repeated struggle to rouse Hendrik from his drunken stupor (passages 128, 133) and to squeeze her father's body into a porcupine hole (passages 180–3, 185).

In each case, the effect is largely comic, for the events in question belong to the category of thwarted attempt, the staple of farce. Neither death nor burial can be achieved with ease or grace; both, in the end, are bungled. Needing Hendrik's help, Magda crosses the riverbed with purpose: 'I am running now as I have not run since childhood.... I am wholly involved in my mission, action without reflection' (65). This heroic posturing is dissipated in failure, as the narrative resorts to the slapstick of hurled kitchen implements, quixotic broom charges, drunken stumbling, playground cursing, and, in the end, Magda's retreat, 'panting and toiling through the riverbed again', and her subdued return, 'trudging now, tired, fed up' (67, 68).

We come finally to the repeated narration of a single event, for which Rimmon-Kenan reserves the term 'repetitive', and which we have touched upon in Brink's *Die Ambassadeur*. Magda's discovery of Ou-Anna's absence is a straightforward example: in each of the passages 78, 79, 80 and 81, a version of this event is recounted. In the first, we have only a brief description of an empty kitchen; in the second, Magda, finding her father, initiates a dialogue of some length; in the third, Magda's father addresses her immediately and no conversation ensues; in the fourth, Magda again enters an empty kitchen, but the emptiness provides an opportunity for metaphysical speculation. The details of these accounts vary, but, lest there be any doubt that they refer to the same basic event, the passages make careful use of certain words and phrases to ensure both cohesion and coherence. So, for example, both 78 and 79 begin 'I stand', while 80 and 81 begin 'Or perhaps', a connective phrase that also establishes the link between 79 and 80. This parallelism, by means of which the passages are constituted as a larger textual unit, is complemented and reinforced by the echoing of lexical items in the outermost passages. In both 78 and 81 we find 'empty kitchen', whilst in the former we also find 'The stove is cold' and 'rows of copperware', and in the latter, 'the cold stove' and 'rows of gleaming copperware' (36–7).

If this is a relatively straightforward example of the repetitive, *In the Heart of the Country* contains instances that are less transparent. Twice in the narrative a new bride arrives on the farm, and twice there follows, seemingly ineluctably, the death of Magda's father. However, in the first telling, the new bride is Magda's stepmother and the killing a murder, whereas, in the second, the bride is Hendrik's, and the death largely accidental. Nevertheless, between these two sequences of events there is clearly a correspondence, one that is emphasized, as in the previous example, by phrasal and lexical repetition. The novel begins: 'Today my father brought home his new bride. They came clip-clop across the flats in a dog-cart drawn by a horse with an ostrich-plume waving on its forehead, dusty after the long haul' (1). This first section, which concludes with the news that the father 'does not die so easily after all', that there is a 'second chance', is followed by one in which a new bride arrives on the farm once again: 'They came clip-clop across the flats in the donkey-cart, dusty after the long haul from Armoede' (16, 17).

In this case, it is more difficult to argue that the same occurrence is narrated twice, for what we encounter here is not the kind of adjustment consequent on faulty memory or shifts in perspective, which are the basis for the repetitive's use in *Die Ambassadeur*, for example, or in Faulkner's *As I Lay Dying*. Nevertheless, the two versions may be paraphrased in the same way, the same sequence of basic events reduced to the same story. They are, in other words, variations on a theme. The real difference between this instance of the repetitive and the one previously discussed therefore lies in the degree of abstraction required to reveal the similarities that bind together what will always be distinct passages of the text.

There is more to say about Coetzee's use of the repetitive, but we might note in the meantime that it is only one of several categories of narrative repetition, and that, when these categories are viewed in relation to one another, they can be seen in terms of the work's more fundamental repetitiveness. What remains to be shown is precisely how this narrative strategy contributes to Coetzee's bare prose style when it seems, on the contrary, to violate the principles both of economy and precision, saying too much and at too great a length.

Here it is the prominence of the iterative – the single telling of a repeated event – that provides an insight into the function and effect of narrative repetition in general. After all, this prominence is related directly to the fact that, in the world of the novel, very little happens, the days passing by in a ceaseless round of routine actions and encounters. The tedium of this existence – the 'savage torpor' of rural life – is one of the narrator's central preoccupations (138). Magda longs for adventure, but this is hard to come by. Indeed, from a certain point of view, some of the narrative repetitions may be explained by the fact that, if she is not mad, Magda is at least bored, and prone to enlivening fantasies.

From a very different perspective, the repetition of events may be seen as a stylistic choice that signifies a limitation on resources. Coetzee is forced, in other words, to make do with what little is available to him, which is barely sufficient, and which requires that the same compositional blocks, the same basic narrative units, be arranged and rearranged. The paring down of narrative elements is something which is only emphasized by the brevity of the work and, indeed, the numbered passages into which the spasms of prose are so tightly packed.

If repetition might therefore be said to foreground the limitations of both story and text – both the restrictive existence of life on the farm, and the restricted resources of the novel – it is more easily understood as a fundamental component in the production of Coetzee's bare prose. A narrative self-consciously in search of incident, staving off the boredom of the desert, is forced, it would seem, to eke all it can from its reduced repertoire. In certain moments, the novel reads even as if blood were being drawn from stone. It is precisely in such moments that one comes to exist – and to feel one's existence – in the brute reality produced by Coetzee's novels.

However striking, narrative repetition is itself only one aspect of a more basic repetitiveness characteristic of Coetzee's writing in general and of *In the Heart of the Country* in particular, and that is no less operative at the levels of word and phrase. Though a number of open category lexical items are repeated in almost exorbitant fashion, the effect is anything but lavish. It likewise tends to produce a sense of spareness. This undoubtedly has something to do with the particular words and phrases that are repeated, amongst which we find: *desert, stony, stone, stone desert, flats, dry, dust, dusty, dull, dark, black, bush, pebble, green, grey, insect, tedium, monotony, loneliness, solitude, vacuum*. But it is also a consequence of what this repetition again suggests: a limited repertoire of words and phrases.

Perhaps the most prominent instance of lexical repetition involves the morpheme *dust*, which appears at least thirty-five times in a narrative that is all of 137 pages long, and with sufficient insistence to have been chosen as the title of the novel's film version.[35] In view of its definition in the OED, 'earth or other solid matter in a minute and fine state of subdivision, so that the particles are small and light enough to be easily raised and carried in a cloud by the wind; any substance comminuted or pulverized; powder', there is something rather neat about *dust* being at once an irreducible fact of the material reality described by the novel, and an elemental lexical particle that constitutes the narrative. Of course, for any biblically minded reader, *dust* has from the very outset connotations of the elemental, the origin and destination of existence: for dust thou art, and unto dust shalt thou return.[36]

We encounter *dust* in the very first of the novel's numbered passages, in the phrase 'dusty after the long haul' (1). *Dusty*: this is how one enters the realm of the narrative, which is, as we so often read, the middle of nowhere. And so it is that the daily, habitual return to the homestead of Magda's father is described in the following terms: 'When he came in hot and dusty after a day's work' (9). Here, it is not only the word that is repeated, but its narrative and syntactic contexts: arrival and adverbial phrase. These are precisely the contexts in which we encounter it again in the twenty-seventh passage, 'dusty after the long haul', the thirty-eighth passage, 'dusty after the long haul from Armoede', and in the forty-first, 'Hendrik arrived one afternoon, a boy of sixteen, I am guessing, dusty of course' (12, 17, 20). Nor does the break in the narrative, after the first set of murders, interrupt this repetition. In the forty-ninth passage, we read that 'Hendrik brought back his girl from Armoede, the dust rising lazily behind the cart, the donkeys toiling up the path to the cottage, weary after the long haul' (25).

If arrival on the farm is one of the semantic contexts in which dustiness is encountered (so often preceded by a long haul), in later portions *dusty* appears in the text rather as a descriptor of Magda, sign of her status as an old maid. We find for example: 'All my life I have been left lying about, forgotten, dusty, like an old shoe' (41); 'an unused body now dusty, dry, unsavoury' (44); 'that dusty hole' (86). Otherwise, *dust* spreads through the novel – it is that which sifts and falls to the ground, that which coats rooms and floors and unused schoolhouses, that in which one lies and to which one will ultimately return.

For the reader too, dust gets everywhere, though its ubiquity and abundance signal only bareness, both of the prose and of the reality to which it corresponds and which it produces; on the one hand, it is the elemental particle of loneliness and lack of use, and on the other, its recurrence warns that the lexical cupboard is bare. As much as every empty room gathers dust, so *dust* reveals a compositional necessity that has nothing to do with elaboration or an art of *copia verborum*.

The fact that repeated morphemes are so often clustered, such that particular words co-occur with particular phrases and events, is itself significant, since it indicates a relationship between different levels of repetition in the novel. Certain situations attract to themselves certain words and configurations of words, establishing within the narrative a set of conventional associations that come to have their own logic.

This is something the narrator acknowledges in such a moment as 'Hendrik arrived one afternoon, a boy of sixteen, I am guessing, dusty of course' (20). It is the phrase 'of course' that gives the game away: dusty, *of course*, for how else could one arrive at the farm and in what other terms could such an arrival be narrated? In this way, the work calls attention to the fact that lexical and phrasal repetition cannot be dissociated from narrative repetition, and that the basic units of composition are neither words nor events, but rather textual blocks in which internal relations are a matter of convention and coherence. It therefore becomes apparent that restriction operates not at the level of particular linguistic or narrative items, but at the more fundamental level of literary practice.

This matter can be elucidated if we recognize that repetition at one level does not necessitate repetition at another. So, for example, in the works of certain authors, narrative repetition might become an occasion for 'elegant variation'; but in the case of *In the Heart of the Country* we are made only too aware that there is nothing extra with which to add flavour to the 'thin porridge of event' (23). In this novel, the different levels of repetition co-occur as distinct blocks, something that is explicitly registered in moments of reflexivity such as the one cited earlier ('of course' is a minor violation of the separation between author and narrator, or between narrator and character). This ensures that what might otherwise have seemed the product of the author's linguistic deficiency or the narrator's psychological compulsion is understood instead as consequent upon the paring down of compositional elements. What is intimated, in other words, is that lexical and phrasal repetition is a function of choice, a matter of style.

This might help us understand one of the general functions of reflexivity in Coetzee's novels. It is certainly one of the effects of reflexive uses of the iterative, such as: 'I am the one who stays in her room reading or writing or fighting migraines' (1). This may be a description of a particular character's habits, but it is also the marking of a type, the performance of a pre-determined role, for the sentence might have been written *I stay in my room reading or writing or fighting migraines* without losing the form of the iterative.³⁷ When 'the one' is inserted into the subject complement position, however, the privations of rural life can be seen also as the limitation on narrative elements: Magda is not simply an old maid starved of adventure on a South African farm, but a character in a novel the constituents of which are determined by generic conventions, and, moreover, by compositional principles of economy and precision.

It is precisely because Magda herself is revealed at every turn to be as much a compositional unit as the events in which she participates that the repetitiveness of the novel comes to be understood as an element of literary practice, rather than a consequence of her insanity or boredom, or life in the Karoo. And though it is possible that the limitations are those of a particular genre, rather than the author's style, the novel's final page suggests it would yet have been in keeping with the *plaasroman* to have filled out the narrative with descriptions of 'the melancholy of the sunset over the koppies, the sheep beginning to huddle against the first evening chill, the faraway boom of the windmill, the first chirrup of the first cricket, the last twitterings of the birds in the thorntrees, the stones of the farmhouse wall still holding the sun's warmth, the kitchen lamp glowing steady' (138).

In illustrating the effects of lexical and phrasal repetition, a number of instances might be discussed, but an analysis of the most prominent should suffice. Almost twice as prevalent as *dust*, the morpheme *ston(e)* appears at least sixty-three times and for the first time in the novel's eighth passage, in which the farm and homestead are encountered: 'In a house shaped by destiny like an H I have lived all my life, in a theatre of stone and sun fenced in with miles of wire' (3).

Over the course of the novel, *stone* becomes an inescapable feature both of the farm and its narrative, introduced into various phrases that are themselves repeated. *Stone desert* is one of these, but we find stone everywhere, as plaything and building material, as home to insects and marker for the dead. Indeed, we find sticks and stones, goats and stones, bushes and stones, dreams of stones; we encounter stone and scrub, the cool stone house, stone chips, the stone floor.

As with *dust*, *stone* is characterized as something fundamental. In one set of linked passages and phrases, stone belongs to a category of objects associated with the 'mere phenomenon', 'elementary life', all 'that does not signify but merely is', an 'insentient universe where everything but me is merely itself' (131, 12, 9, 67). So it is that Magda speaks of her 'iron intractable risible determination to burst through the screen of names into the goatseye view of Armoede and the stone desert', to experience a vision of 'each bush and tree, each stone and grain of sand, in its own halo of clarity, as if every atom of the universe were staring back at me' (18, 127).

If the stoniness of this fictional reality is therefore a sign of a world laid bare, the repetition of *stone* again ensures the starkness of the prose itself. In a certain respect, however, the meaning of *stone* differs from that of *dust*, for the former is used also to figure the language of the narrative, which is described early on as a 'stony monologue', a set of 'lapidary paradoxes', 'the rocks of words that I have never heard on another tongue' (12, 8). The association appears again fleetingly when Magda attempts communication with the postal boy, 'the words dropping heavily from my lips, like stones', before being made emphatic towards the novel's end, when Magda begins to compose her stone messages to the airmen (124).

In the 248th passage, Magda reveals: 'I have tried forming messages with stones, but stones are too unwieldy for the distinctions I need to make' (128). The process of gathering, painting and arranging these stones, first into words of 'letters twelve feet high', expressing quite plainly her predicament and desires, next into the 'POEMAS CREPUSCLRS', and finally into 'ideographs', is described between the 255th and 257th passages (132–3). Here we read that 'there has never been any shortage of stones in this part of the world', though of course, we know this already, having encountered on what amounts to every second page some reference or other to the stony landscape of the stone desert and the stone house (132).

Now, if stones can be used to make words, certain words or ways of speaking might be said to have something in common with stones. This notion is prepared from the outset, though only in the final passages do we come fully to understand the meaning and proleptic force of the phrases 'lapidary paradoxes' and 'stony monologue'. For it is here that it becomes apparent that the narrative itself has been composed of elemental units that are arranged and rearranged, shifted about, and made into patterns both satisfying and alarming. It is here, in other words, that the novel seems to acknowledge that its language is stony, which is to say – in a context in which stone is associated with minimal existence – that it is reduced, pared down, a language from which everything extraneous has been stripped away and which produces a reality of 'elementary life' and 'elementary states' (12).

From Enrichment to Economy

It is telling that in naming her compositions 'POEMAS CREPUSCULARIAS', poems of twilight, of dawn and dusk, Magda initially runs 'short of stones' (132). The restrictions on her literary resources are thus made explicit, and we find evidence of Coetzee's increasing awareness of his own writing's distinctive qualities. As to whether this intensification of bareness played any part in Brink's change of heart, this we cannot know, though we might at least try to explain how it further set Coetzee's novels apart from those of the *volk* avant-garde.

What is so far lacking is a broader sense of the literary practices that characterized the Sestigers' works, and the manner in which Coetzee construed them; how he related them, in other words, to those he had critiqued in his essays on La Guma, Beckett and Nabokov. This lack can be remedied by considering the scholarly writings that Coetzee produced alongside *In the Heart of the Country*, in which he reiterated the dangers attendant both upon an outmoded realism and a too radical or celebratory anti-realism.

In 'The First Sentence of Yvonne Burgess's *The Strike*', Coetzee again took aim at one of his local peers for writing in a manner too conventional and literary. He suggested that *The Strike*, a novel published in Johannesburg in 1975, was composed throughout in a language so 'automatized' that the work might as well have been produced by the codes of fiction and 'without an author'. Here too, the problem with a certain kind of realism was not its concern with reality, so much as its failure to get outside of literature. Coetzee described several alternatives to this automatized writing: one might, he said, 'write a work of criticism in the form of fiction in which the codes of the Novel ... will be exhibited and decoded', an enterprise that he associated with the *nouveau roman*; or, if one accepted the impossibility of transcending the 'illusionism of Realism' one might, 'like John Barth', resort to 'a Nietzschean gaiety'; finally, one might do as Borges's Pierre Menard, and simply re-compose a masterpiece of the literary past, trusting that, 'In language', as Coetzee put it, 'there are no stable and positive elements. Elements achieve definition only through their reciprocal differences, and all shift their boundaries continually with the passing of time'.[38]

These assertions – clearly resonant with the arguments of Coetzee's earlier articles – were repeated more extensively in 'Achterberg's "Ballade van de gasfitter"'. Here Coetzee reproduced his critique of late modernist and postmodernist literary introversion by associating Achterberg's verse with what he called the 'poetics of failure', a mode again identified with Nabokov's *Pale Fire*, John Barth's *Lost in the Funhouse* and Beckett's *The Unnamable*. Coetzee described this poetics as a 'program for construct- ing artifacts out of an endlessly regressive, etiolated self-consciousness lost in the labyrinth of language', one which was 'ambivalent through and through'. It was the proper mode of a poetry in which 'the formula no longer refers to something … but to nothing', a kind of literature in which 'the formula formulates itself, turning in upon itself'.³⁹

Coetzee's critical positions thus remained largely consistent during the period in which *Dusklands* was completed and *In the Heart of the Country* composed. The question is how to situate the Sestigers' fictions in relation to the automatized writing of La Guma and Yvonne Burgess, as well as the poetics of failure, the self-enclosing self-referentiality of Barth, Nabokov and the criticism-as-fiction associated with the *nouveau roman*. The matter is by no means straightforward, for the Sestigers' novels could not be said either to have been produced by the codes of fiction, or to have exhibited these codes in any thoroughgoing way. Their anti-realism, such as it was, tended to be less that of regressive, labyrinthine reflexivity than of fantas- tic phantasmagoria.

This in itself may be important, however, if it prompts our recogni- tion that the Sestigers were concerned less with the absence of meaning than with its abundance, and that complexity arose in their works not from a frustration with illusionism, but as a consequence of proliferat- ing characters, points of view, modes of narration and layers of reality. It was thus a complexity of expansion, of greater depths and heights, of richness and, above all, enrichment, a complexity very different from that in Beckett, Borges or Robbe-Grillet, and some way distant even from that in Nabokov and Barth. In a sense then, the Sestigers were not unlike Coetzee, for though they drew explicitly on metropolitan traditions, the significance of their works depended on a set of local practices and posi- tion-takings, and could only be misrecognized were they now forced into the straitjacket of 'local modernism'.

Indeed, it is precisely because they were responding in the first place to what Brink had identified as 'a drought-and-poor-white-prose' that the works of the Sestigers are best understood in terms of an aesthetics of enrichment.⁴⁰ Nor is it difficult to see how this aesthetics accorded with their broader project, their determination to use literature to transmute a stagnant world, to transcend a reality of strict social, communal and religious mores. For the need to bring an Afrikaans readership into contact with the enlivening currents from abroad required, in Brink's own terminology, the rushed 'exploitation' of all those resources the novel had accrued over its several centuries of existence, which could be made immediately available either through translation or through adoption, adaptation and incorporation.

What followed was a sometimes feverish experimentation with as many techniques as possible, both across and within the works in question. In the case of Brink, this helps explain the mania with which he undertook translations, the incredible generic range of his own oeuvre and the very striking formal differences between works of the same genre, such as *Die Ambassadeur* and *Orgie*. Indeed, it suggests why, in *Orgie*, it was not sufficient that the novel institute a new set of rules for reading, but had also to break those rules, and in as exorbitant a manner as possible; and why, in *Die Ambassadeur*, there needed to be not only a play of perspectives, but also a play in modes, the purpose of which had to be explicitly signalled lest the reader mistook it or missed any moment in what became, in effect, a display of literary riches.

If it is much clearer already how their very bareness set Coetzee's works apart, it is important to note that the Sestigers' aesthetics of enrichment is only partially explained by technical proliferation and variation. As much as Coetzee's style entailed a certain subject matter, the Sestigers' practices too were constituted by a particular sense of the world, which gave rise to a distinctive thematics of solitude and the terrible struggles of consciousness and desire.

To explore this aspect of the Sestigers' renewal, we might again consider Coetzee's understanding, which we can infer from *In the Heart of the Country* itself, since the novel might be read from a certain perspective as a satire upon attitudes and orientations with which the Sestigers were identified. To see this, however, it is necessary to return briefly to the argument made in the previous chapter, that the effect of Coetzee's prose style, and the sense of its unity, depends to some extent on the establishment of a distance, often ironic, between the novels' various character narrators and the implied narrators standing above or behind them.

The way that *In the Heart of the Country* engenders this distance is by a parody of Magda's longing for both immanence and transcendence, which is not wholly unlike the parody of Eugene Dawn's desire to describe the plenum of existence. In certain respects, it is true, Magda's self-descriptions are more convergent with Coetzee's literary practice than Dawn's. She longs neither for an absent lexicon of common names nor for a discourse of pure reflexivity, understanding all too well that 'Words are coin', that 'Words alienate' (26), and being sufficiently wary of compulsive listing: 'The frenzy of desire in the medium of words yields the mania of the catalogue' (26). Yet she fears lest she be regarded as no more than a 'stone-moving, word-building intelligence' (133), recognizing a need (which sets her apart, for example, from Beckett's Molloy) for 'more than merely pebbles to permute, rooms to clean, furniture to push around: I need people to talk to', for 'how long can one go on building patterns before one longs for extinction?' (119).

Nevertheless, a vein of dramatic irony is yet deposited in the spaces between the narrative as it exists and as Magda wishes it to be. Her desire, to begin with, is to be or become 'a poetess of interiority, an explorer of the inwardness of stones', a desire she acknowledges as the 'vain urge of my consciousness to inhabit' everything it encounters, to penetrate the 'ecstasy of pure being' in which 'the stones and bushes of the veld hum with life' (35, 49, 48). A desire, then, which associates her with Sydney Clouts, whose verse, Coetzee had suggested, 'subjects the world of things out there ... to an imperial demand to open itself to the imagination; as soon as these things yield themselves, the poem enters them, takes them over, and inhabits them'. Indeed, Coetzee had noted of Clouts that his 'poetry records a struggle to inhabit a world penetrated ... by the intense presence of the pebble in his hand (stone is, throughout his work, the irreducible other)', a struggle, that is, for transcendence through access to the immediacy of being.[41]

Magda's articulated desire thus aligns her with a poetic tradition described by Coetzee as Romantic, and this is nowhere clearer than in her lament for the loss of a primal language, to which belong the words *ons* (we), *ek* (I) and *jy* (you): 'There are few enough words true, rock-hard enough to build a life on, and these he is destroying' (35).[42] Here, Magda not only invokes the terms of Martin Buber's *I and Thou*, which Coetzee likewise identified with the 'Romantic tradition'; she seems also to commit herself to what Coetzee described as Buber's 'myth of the fall into the quotidian from an original state of relation'.[43] In this way also, Magda is implicated in an idealism grounded on the possibility of transcendence, and which is at odds with a literary practice in which paring down is a means of responding to and creating a certain kind of reality, rather than finding a path to essence and a world of true being.

To see clearly the parody of Magda's Romanticism it is of course help-ful to know Coetzee's critical writings, but hardly essential, because the narrative itself exposes the naïveté of Magda's belief in a vanished primal tongue. On two distinct occasions, Magda explicitly blames the loss of her rock-solid language on her father's wooing of Klein-Anna. She wonders: 'How can I speak to Hendrik as before when they corrupt my speech?', and, at a later point, insists that 'The language that should pass between myself and these people was subverted by my father and cannot be recov-ered' (35, 97). On these occasions, what is excluded from Magda's under-standing is that, even in Buber's idealist terms, the truth of the I and the You (which is reciprocity) cannot exist in a world of unequal relations: if it is not possible to say You without meaning It, this is because the death struggle between lord and bondsman casts a pallor over all existence.

One might then say that the novel knows something that Magda does not, which is that the stoniness of its own language has nothing to do with a longing for transcendence. There is no essence broached with the right combination of terms, no Word that is the Rock. On the contrary, all that is inevitable is that stone will at some point become dust, which will sift and rise and be scattered to the winds. Nor does Magda know that the novel's bareness is not the unfortunate consequence of life on the farm, but rather a response to and creation of a certain kind of reality, governed by violence and domination.

The tension between the Romanticism of Magda's desires and *In the Heart of the Country*'s realism (understood, again, as an orientation towards the world, not a set of fixed codes) is thus one source of the dramatic irony necessary for the differentiation of implied narrator and character narra-tor. Another arises from Magda's preoccupation with the vacuum at the heart of being, her sense of abandonment by a non-existent God in a cold universe of dead matter. For this preoccupation with the thoughts and themes of existentialism is not only at odds with her Romantic longing for transcendence, but also, and again, with an understanding of solitude as a function less of man's essential being-in-the-world than of a structure of social relations from which reciprocity has leached out.

Coetzee's own interest in existentialism, remarked in the previous chapter, is further evidenced in his essay on Achterberg, which refers not only to Buber, but also to Sartre and Kierkegaard. However, though he deploys its terminology in his critical writings and each of his early nov-els, he does so always with that attitude of sceptical reserve encountered in the narrative of *In the Heart of the Country*; a scepticism that returns us, finally, to Coetzee's understanding of the Sestigers. For, if there was any particular philosophy underpinning the Sestigers movement, it was that of existentialism, whether this was gleaned directly from the works of Sartre and others, or whether, as Brink claimed, 'the bond between Sestig and existentialism' arose because 'the world itself, of which every writer is at least a seismograph or barometer, made an existential way of living and writing unavoidable'.[44]

Whatever its origin, this bond between Sestig and existentialism was more than apparent in fictions that revolved around experiences of alienation and encounters with the nothingness at the heart of being. If such experiences and encounters seem to fit awkwardly with an aesthetics of enrichment, we should remember that what they promised above all was a freedom from social constraints, and, more important, that the 'gemoedelike lokale realisme' of previous literary generations had often sacrificed the individual for the sake of the collective.

It was, in any event, precisely the bond conjoining the Sestigers and existentialism that added further resonance to Coetzee's decision to cast Magda as a kind of existentialist, as well as a kind of Romantic. For the dramatic irony born of parody that marks the boundaries between Magda and the novel's implied narrator thereby came also to signal the distance between the Sestigers and Coetzee, a distance measured precisely by the extent to which *In the Heart of the Country* exceeded the early works of Sartre and Buber by recognizing violence and domination as structuring factors in the production of colonial solitude and alienation. This recognition was lacking in the Sestigers' works, which, principally concerned with the liberation of consciousness from social constraints, ignored those material conditions that sustained a life too barren to be enriched by art alone.

Although they had sought to broaden the narrow horizons of local literature by turning towards metropolitan art and philosophy, what the Sestigers thereby produced was an art of flight, rather than confrontation. This was something to which *In the Heart of the Country* gestured in its parody of Magda's romantic-existentialist longings. What may yet be surprising, given Brink's response to *Dusklands*, is that, by 1974, several of the Sestigers had themselves come to accept this. Brink, for example, had stated at the Sestigers symposium that the movement's time had passed and that its achievements had been marred by a failure to face up to the reality of apartheid.

In fact, Brink had begun to address this failure in his own fiction, with the publication in 1973 of *Kennis van die aand*. The first Afrikaans novel banned by the apartheid state, it eschewed 'fantastic narrative' and took up political themes, and thereby marked a break in Brink's career as well as in Afrikaans literary culture. In an interview conducted soon after the publication of *In the Heart of the Country*, Brink reflected on this break, remarking that his 'previous writings' had been a 'very experimental sort of fiction', but that he now wished to 'explore the basic questions' of his origin, and of 'the forces and the places and the people' that had shaped him. It was for this reason, he said, and because he wanted 'to try and understand not only something more about myself, but about the whole world that I came from', that his writing had become 'so much more South African orientated'.[45]

If this explains something of his personal motivations, Brink's address at the UCT symposium had previously offered a broader account of the reasons for moving on from Sestig. Discussing the movement's origins and contexts, he attributed the Sestigers' general orientation to what he characterized as belatedness, or perhaps immaturity. For Brink observed that, though the Sestigers had followed Beckett, Kafka and Joyce, they had not yet met with Robbe-Grillet, Saul Bellow and Günter Grass; though they had been familiar with Freud and Jung, they had known nothing of Laing; though they had immersed themselves in existentialism, they had heard nothing of Fanon and *Wretched of the Earth*; though they had lived in the aftermath of the Second World War, they had not yet experienced Vietnam; and though they had spent time in Paris and Amsterdam, they had never yet engaged with the truth of South Africa.[46]

This is as clear an expression as any imaginable of the generational gap that divided Coetzee from the Sestigers, as much as the Sestigers from themselves, and explains Brink's desire to begin afresh. What it does not explain – indeed, what it makes more difficult to understand – is Brink's initial designation of Coetzee as an English Sestiger, which, given what he had recently said of the movement, could only be understood as a denigration, in spite of his assurances to the contrary. The oddness of Brink's response to *Dusklands* is only exaggerated when one considers that the novel was quite obviously more engaged with those very truths he believed the Sestigers had ignored.

Provided we attend more closely to certain assumptions informing Brink's work both as a critic and novelist – especially assumptions about the structure of the literary world and the nature of literary technique – we might identify one cause of Brink's sense that *Dusklands* offered only more of the same. For it is clear that Brink, like Van Wyk Louw, envisioned literary hemispheres marked by distinct fictional modes, a straightforward or realist mode on the one hand and a complex anti-realist mode on the other. Along with this sense of a bipolar literary world came the conviction that particular techniques were eternally wedded to particular effects and meanings.

Such an understanding is manifest as much in *Aspekte van die nuwe prosa*, where Brink suggested that the techniques of contemporary renewal had been derived from Cervantes and Laurence Sterne, as in his review of *Dusklands*, where he spoke of *Pale Fire* as an 'archetypal work'. From this vision of the literary world it followed, moreover, that in his own re-orientation Brink should have abandoned whatever technique he deemed experimental, and, finally, that he should have misrecognized the achievement of *Dusklands*, because he could not have understood the novel otherwise than as a work that fell between two positions, being neither sufficiently complex nor sufficiently direct.

Thus, in his idealism, Brink failed to appreciate the insight found by Coetzee in Borges's Pierre Menard, that literary practices acquire meaning relationally, in a field of shifting values, and that specific techniques have meaning only in particular works, that is, in particular combinations of forms and contents. Of course, this insight need not prevent us from adducing general effects of given techniques in a given moment and literary field. It requires only that we proceed with caution, in the knowledge that any analysis founded on an absolute division between content and form, and which fails to return to the work to test hypotheses, risks the kind of misunderstanding found in Brink's review of *Dusklands*.

The work itself, in other words, becomes the initial context in which a technique has value. This can be clarified if we turn one last time to a comparison of Coetzee and Brink and if we focus on those strategies with which we have previously been concerned: the repetition of words and phrases, and the contradictory repetition of events. If we consider *In the Heart of the Country*, it is obvious enough that only some of the novel's lexical items are repeated, and that they together belong to and produce a very particular world, one that is dry and hard, elemental and bare. In *Orgie*, on the other hand, where lexical and phrasal repetition is no less marked, the recurrence of such a sequence as 'kabaal kabbala kabbel krab-bel brabbel babble babel bybel' helps instead to augment the impression of confusion, of constant noise and constant motion.

A similar point can be made regarding narrative repetition. Whereas *Die Ambassadeur* repeatedly narrates events that are chosen precisely for their ambiguity, Coetzee's use of the repetitive makes especially resonant those events that manifest the violence inherent in and productive of the novel's brute reality. This is especially apparent in the repeated narration of Magda's rape, which is worth considering in greater detail precisely because of the difficulty it presents for identifying and distinguishing between accounts and occurrences.

It is all too clear that there are distinct reports of the rape itself in passages 206, 207 and 209, but passages 205 and 208 may well be further instances. Passage 205 culminates in the following: 'I roll over on my back and lift my knees. This is how a bitch must look; but as for what happens next, I do not even know how it is done. He goes on kicking at my thighs' (104). Here, the uncertainty about 'what happens next' suggests there is more than kicking, though if this is rape, it is elided by the narrative. Similarly, the logic of the passages' division indicates that 208 may also be an instance of elided narration.

As to the number of occurrences, there is uncertainty here because of the shift in scene from kitchen to bedroom, an uncertainty exacerbated by patterns of lower-level repetition. For, while it seems clear that 205, 206 and 207 recount more or less the same sequence of events and happenings and include many of the same lexical and phrasal units, 208 and 209 largely dispense with these. It is only Magda's assertion in 208, 'Jy raas net met my, jy praat nooit nie, jy haat my net', which resonates with her pleading in 207, 'Waarom haat jy my so?', and Hendrik's assurance in 209, 'Sal nie seer wees', that distantly echoes Magda's cries in 206 and 207, 'Jy maak my seer' (105–7). These phrases occur in the English-language edition as: 'You do nothing but shout at me, you never talk to me, you hate me' (116); 'Why do you hate me so?' (115); 'It won't hurt' (116); 'You are hurting me' (115).

Now, given these uncertainties, it may seem plausible to read this use of the repetitive as an indication of a radical discontinuity between word and world, exposed by the irreducible differences between each instance. In the first place, however, such a reading threatens to mystify the relationship between repetition and difference. Since every repetition involves at least two instances, some variation is required to distinguish them. On the other hand, to perceive repetition, two different events must be regarded as in some senses the same. In other words, as Rimmon-Kenan observes rather matter-of-factly: 'no event is repeatable in all respects, nor is a repeated segment of the text quite the same, since its new location puts it in a different context which necessarily changes its meaning.'[47]

More important, any reading that focuses only on the repetitive's disjunctive effect fails to confront the significance of *what* is repeated. For, in spite of the uncertainties, it remains possible to discuss each of these narrative instances as a version if not of the same event, then at least of the same act, the rape of Magda by Hendrik, a brute fact that remains inescapable, an act of violence that is foregrounded by this repetition, and that, whatever its status in the reality of the fiction, must be endured by the reader over and over again. It is an element of the narrative, more-over, assigned an origin beyond Magda's fantasy or desire precisely inso-far as the site of composition is revealed, not only by the inconsistencies themselves, but also by Magda's failure to grasp the reasons for Hendrik's hatred. Thus, for the implied narrator, the rape becomes an immovable stumbling block, a source of difficulty and irresolution.

Ignoring the nature of this event means, finally, being unable to rec-ognize the general character of events repeatedly narrated, and thus their relation, not only to one another, but also to lexical and phrasal repeti-tion, and, indeed, to those other elements of grammar and rhetoric that serve to produce the bareness of Coetzee's prose and thus the bareness of a reality stripped of human relation. For those moments on which the narrative catches, those events at the heart of its repetitives, have to do in every case with an encounter that is also a confrontation, moments in which relations of domination are witnessed and instantiated. Some are acts of violence as horrifying as Magda's rape; but even such moments as the discovery of Ou-Anna's absence (passages 78–81) or the wooing of Hendrik's bride (passages 67–8) speak of a manichean reality.

Here again, one therefore discovers a relationship between features that produce the writing's spareness and acts proceeding from and lead-ing towards a brutal world in which even the possibility of reciprocity has drained away.

CHAPTER 3

Poetry and Perspective
Lyrical and Rhythmic Intensity in Waiting for the Barbarians

In a 1978 interview with Stephen Watson, J. M. Coetzee acknowledged literary engagements that have since gone largely unremarked: 'if we are talking about influences ... film has had a lot of influence, and also a lot of 20th Century poetry.' Asked whether he had 'anybody in particular' in mind, he responded: 'Well, quite a lot of people. In the first place Pound, Rilke, Zbigniew, [*sic*] Herbert, Neruda – these are all people whom I've probably read with more intensity than I've read any novelist, and I can't believe that it hasn't left a mark.'[1] There is little reason for us to believe differently, but if we take Coetzee at his word, where might this mark be found?

In Coetzee's own poetry, which had appeared in publications of the University of Cape Town prior to his removal to Texas, the imprint of Pound is unmistakable. However, by 1978 this vein had largely expired and, in speaking with Watson, Coetzee was clearly thinking more of his recent creative output than his juvenilia, or his occasional labour as translator and critic of verse. The real question then is whether we might catch in Coetzee's mature works some trace of this intense encounter with poetry, if not with these particular poets. It is precisely this question I wish to pose here. Answering it, we might shed light on a further set of literary contexts, and on the nature and meaning of the *lyricism* and *rhythmicity* of Coetzee's writing; and, ultimately, its *force* and *intensity*.

Poetry, Lyricism and Bareness

Occasionally, the poetry of others enters Coetzee's prose directly, as in 'The Vietnam Project', where the narrative is suddenly interrupted, without warning, by the verse of John Berryman's *Dream Songs*: 'Books have begun to roll out, I know about the suburban sadists and cataleptic drop-outs with Vietnamese skeletons in their cupboards. But the truth is that like huffy Henry I never did hack anyone up: I often reckon, in the dawn, them up: nobody is ever missing' (10). No citation is given, but to those unfamiliar with it, the presence of Berryman's poetry is indicated by the disturbance to the prose of a slightly irregular syntax and a regulated pattern of stressed syllables, by the odd use of colons (which, in fact, mark line breaks), and, in the second sentence, by the alliterative runs on /h/ and /n/ and the light assonantal runs on /ɪ/ and /ɛ/.[2]

Quite often, however, Coetzee's prose falls into passages of regular rhythms and patterned sounds without the aid of borrowed lines. Indeed, for his introductory account of rhythmic prose, Simon Featherstone chooses the first paragraph of *In the Heart of the Country* as a paradigmatic example. He notes in the novel's opening sentences 'a careful deployment of rhythm. The first sentence is almost in verse metre, with four regular stresses, "Today my father brought home his new bride", a rhythmic pattern repeated at various points in the paragraph'.[3] To this pattern of stressed and unstressed syllables, one might add other kinds of sound repetition, including the alliterative run on /br/ in the first sentence, and on /k/ in the second sentence, 'They came clip-clop across the flats' (1).

But is it appropriate to take such features as evidence that Coetzee's writing is sometimes 'nearer to poetry than narrative', as Jane Gardam puts it in her review of *Foe*?[4] Do regular rhythm and sound repetition make prose poetic? Some encouragement for this view is found in 'Surreal Metaphors and Random Processes', an essay likewise published in 1978, where Coetzee notes that English sentences could be made to seem like 'sentences of English poetry' by encoding for three things: the regulation of rhythm ('that stress and unstress should alternate'); pronounced sound repetition (such as that involved in end-rhyme); and the originality and prominence of metaphor.[5]

With this in mind, it is not difficult to find in Coetzee's early novels other passages in a poetic strain, in which prosodic and phonemic patterning is combined with heightened metaphoricity. The opening section of *Waiting for the Barbarians* provides an example in its final paragraphs:

> I cārry my slēeping-mat ōut on to the rāmparts where the nīght brēeze gīves some relīef from the hēat. On the flat roofs of the town I can make out by moonlight the shapes of other sleepers. From under the walnut trees on the square I still hear the murmur of conversation. In the darkness a pipe glows like a firefly, wanes, glows again. Sūmmer is whēeling slōwly towārds its ēnd. The ōrchards grōan ūnder their būrden. I have not seen the capital since I was a young man.
>
> I awake before dawn and tiptoe past the sleeping soldiers, who are stirring and sighing, dreaming of mothers and sweethearts, down the steps. From the sky thousands of stars look down on us. Truly we are here on the roof of the world. Waking in the night, in the open, one is dazzled.[6]

The passage's noticeably poetic quality is doubtless due to its invocation of bucolic themes: the night breeze, the moonlight, murmured conversation, the end of summer and the bounty of nature, the watching stars. But it is no less the consequence of a marked use of metaphor – the pipe as fire-fly, the change in seasons as rotation of a wheel, the personification of the orchards as expectant mother, the stars as eyes, the earth as house – and a tendency towards sound-patterning, evident, for example, in the balanced repetition of /m/ and /t/ in 'I can make out by moonlight', where /m/ fronts the stressed syllable and /t/ closes the unstressed syllable. There is a similar patterning of /s/ and /w/ around stressed syllables in 'Summer is wheeling slowly towards', and pronounced alliterative runs on /s/, /p/, /t/ and /ŋ/ in 'tiptoe past the sleeping soldiers, who are stirring and sighing, dreaming of mothers and sweethearts, down the steps'. Moreover, as in the passage cited from *In the Heart of the Country*, one finds that the prose tends to fall into familiar rhythmic groups of four and five stresses, as in the first sentence with its almost anapaestic measure, or the slower, iambic movement of sentences five and six.

Later, when the Magistrate's failed morning of hunting is described, these features recur:

> Sometimes, on a good morning, I am enabled to live again all the strength and swiftness of my manhood. Like a wrāith I glīde from brāke to brāke. Shod in boots that have soaked in thirty years of grease, I wade through icy water. Over my coat I wear my huge old bearskin. Rime forms on my beard but my fingers are warm in their mittens. My ēyes are shārp, my hēaring is kēen, I snīff the āir like a hōund, I feel a pure exhilaration. (39)

Here again, the strong, regular rhythms verge on the metric. In the second sentence, for example, there is the suggestion of an iambic tetrameter. This is echoed in the first two clauses of the final sentence, which, together with the iambic trimeter of the third clause, hint at the beginnings of a poem in common measure. There are, in addition, several noticeable instances of sound repetition – the light runs on /s/ in the first sentence, on /reɪ/ in the second sentence, on /w/ in the third and on /m/ across the two clauses of the fifth – and the metaphorical component is likewise present, in those two similes by which the Magistrate lends himself attributes of a supernatural kind: ghostly silence and ease of movement, and the sensory acuity of an animal bred for the hunt.

In certain moments, then, in passages where sound and stress become noticeably prominent, Coetzee's prose does indeed bear the mark of a feeling for verse. Nor has this gone entirely unnoticed: readers have spoken from time to time of the strange lyricism of Coetzee's novels. Thus, Beryl Roberts, in her review of *Life & Times of Michael K*, remarks its 'lyrical but economic language', while Charles Larson describes *In the Heart of the Country* as a 'lyrical puzzle'.[7]

In both cases, *lyrical* suggests the musical or song-like qualities of language, which are inevitably related to those phonemic and prosodic features already detailed. Yet, if they are requisites of language that strikes us as sonorous, some semantic prompting may also be required, as Adam Piette explains in his study of sound repetition in narrative.[8] There is certainly evidence of this in the passages cited previously. In the first, the Magistrate can 'still hear' murmured conversation, and there are references to groaning, sighing and tip-toeing. In the second, the Magistrate's 'hearing is keen', and the simile that likens him to a wraith draws attention, if not to sound, then to its absence.

Sonority is not the only way, however, in which the lyric is invoked in Coetzee's novels, for when the poet Tom Paulin described *In the Heart of the Country* as an 'intellectual lyric', he recalled the term's association with affect and interiority rather than song, an association central to a tradition traceable to Hegel's *Aesthetics*.[9] There, *lyric* primarily designates a subjective mode, as it does in a number of subsequent theories. Georg Lukács, for example, distinguishes 'lyric', which fixes on the 'inner life of man' and 'his feelings and thoughts', from both 'tragedy and great epic', which 'present the objective, *outer* world'.[10] In this sense, Coetzee's lyricism would be a function less of poetic prose than of a narrative mode that forges connections with a genre of verse.

These connections have to do of course with Coetzee's use of first person character narrators (Dawn, Jacobus Coetzee, Magda, the Magistrate), whose monologues are frequently introspective, concerned with the nature of self and being. More important still is the manner in which these private thoughts, feelings and fantasies impinge upon the reader, as they do even in *Life & Times of Michael K*, in spite of its partial abandonment of homodiegetic character narration. For an association with the lyric depends above all on the capacity of narrative to produce an impression of interiority, and of intimacy with a singular subject. This, at least, is the understanding favoured by Magda, in the passage midway through *In the Heart of the Country* to which Paulin refers, where she declares her allegiance to a direct expression of the self and of things in themselves: 'My talent is all for immanence, for the fire or ice of identity at the heart of things. Lyric is my medium, not chronicle' (71).

Of course, Magda's misfortune is to be trapped, if not in chronicle, then certainly in narrative. Yet the poignance of her claim and the neatness of Paulin's phrase clearly resonated with Coetzee's publishers: 'intellectual lyric' found its way onto the dust jackets of the Ravan and Secker & Warburg editions of *Waiting for the Barbarians* and *Life & Times of Michael K*, and thereafter onto Vintage editions of *In the Heart of the Country* and *Dusklands*. If for no other reason than this, Coetzee's lyricism has acquired a certain currency, though the term's real value, it seems to me, is that it suggests the strange entanglement in his writing of economy and emotional intensity, as much as the character of his narrative mode.

If Coetzee's early novels are thus *lyrical* or *lyric* on at least two grounds, these are not, in the end, unrelated: sonority often coincides with certain semantic, thematic and narrative features. Thus, in the first of the passages cited previously, the shift into lyricism begins with the Magistrate's isolation on the rooftop and is further occasioned by a drift into reverie and delight in melancholic beauty familiar from Keats's 'To Autumn'. As the passage moves to its conclusion, memories of youth are exchanged for a brief vision of the sublime insignificance of man's existence in an infinite universe. Similarly, in the second passage, the hunt presents an opportunity for immersion in solitary being, even a kind of solipsism, and for the thrilling memory of a youth long past. Feeling at one with himself and the natural world, the Magistrate enjoys the exhilaration of a consciousness projected into all that surrounds it, in a passage that recalls the verse of Thomas Pringle, progenitor of South African poetry: 'Afar in the desert I love to ride,/ With the silent Bush-boy alone by my side: / When the sorrows of life the soul o'ercast, / And, sick of the Present, I cling to the Past.'[11]

Nor are these the only moments in which this association between lyricism and the lyric 'I' is established. Throughout the novel, one finds a more musical and figurative prose coupled with, or leading into, scenes of privacy, reverie, bucolic delight and movements of interiority. Thus, in the opening paragraphs of the third chapter, immediately prior to his attempts to explain himself in writing, the Magistrate describes 'Nature's cornucopia' and the signs of the returning spring in sentences such as the following, heavy with alliteration, assonance and stress: 'the ghost of a new warmth on the wind, the glassy translucence of the lake-ice' (57). Later, in the midst of his escape, and with the 'heat of midday' descending, there is again a lyrical pause as the Magistrate lays himself 'down on the bed in the sweet remembered scent of flowers' and thinks of 'These days, these hot spring days already becoming summer', and how easy he would 'find it to slip into their languorous mood' (93–4).

The motions of slipping, gliding and slowly subsiding themselves become markers of such moments, which are likewise occasioned by passage through the town gates. Thus, when the Magistrate takes 'the old road that curves behind the west wall' to walk amidst the excavations 'undone by driftsand', he imagines settling himself down to 'be blistered by the sun and dried by the wind and eventually frozen by the frost' (100). Later, the Magistrate again sets off, this time to 'wander down the wide road to the lakeside', fully alive to the beauty of his surroundings: 'Behind me the sun is setting in streaks of gold and crimson. From the ditches comes the first cricketsong. This is a world I know and love and do not wish to leave. I have walked this road by night since my youth and come to no harm' (132). Here, the various elements of the novel's lyricism are very much in the foreground; we find not only the familiar sound repetitions, but also a gradual subsidence ('The ground beneath my soles grows soft; soon I am walking on soggy marshgrass, pushing my way through reedbrakes, striding ankle-deep in water in the last violet light of dusk'), as well as a consciousness attuned to sound and sensation ('Frogs plop into the water before me; nearby I hear a faint rustle of feathers as a marshbird crouches ready to fly'), which ultimately turns in upon itself: 'Calf-deep in the soothing water I indulge myself in this wistful vision' (132–3).

This rhyming of musicality, subjectivity and pastoral pleasure is by no means restricted to *Waiting for the Barbarians*. Reading *In the Heart of the Country*, one likewise encounters passages of song-like and figurative introspection, and lyric is similarly related to a 'kind of story' to which Magda feels herself especially drawn, an 'art of memory', 'the weave of reminiscence in the dozing space of the mind' (43); related also to 'hymns' of solitude and the farm, of 'nostalgia for country ways' and 'the beauty of this forsaken world'(138).

But if one therefore encounters moments of lyricism elsewhere in Coetzee's early novels, it is important to remember that readers of *Waiting for the Barbarians*, and *Life & Times of Michael K* too, were no less struck by the economy and simplicity of the prose. Without being as starkly repetitive as *In the Heart of the Country*, both, indeed, are short novels that make use of a limited cast of named characters and a reduced repertoire of events; and both are concerned with a structure of relations that is or that becomes manichean, and is the background for a failure of reciprocity.

The question then is how the occasional lyricism of Coetzee's writing is related to its more pervasive and fundamental spareness. An answer suggests itself if we turn once more to the Magistrate's morning of hunting, which culminates in the following: 'The mōvement is smōoth and stĕady, but perhăps the sūn glīnts on the bărrel, for in his descĕnt he tūrns his hĕad and sĕes me. His hŏoves touch īce with a clĭck, his jăw stŏps in mid-mŏtion, we găze at each other' (39). To begin with, as in several of the paragraphs it follows, the passage progresses by alliterative and assonantal runs, for example on /s/, /m/ and /muː/, the stresses fall like beats, and our attention is focussed on these phonological elements by references to steady motion and certain sounds; abruptly, however, in the final sentence, sonority fades and the rhythm is halted, as the climax anticipated by the three-stress pattern and parallel construction of the first two clauses is arrested and disappointed in the third. Yet, to have fulfilled its promise, the final clause need only have been substituted with something like *his găze turns băck my ŏwn*. Then, the rhythm would have seemed emphatic.

Instead, there is a subtle shift, a sudden deflation of the narrator's lyricism. Disappointment finds expression in stylistic modulation, and the writing is robbed of its fluidity much as the hunt is 'robbed ... of its savour'. The thematic cause of this minor departure, suggested by the narrative itself, is truly revealing. For the Magistrate's impotence arrives with his recognition of only two possibilities: 'either the proud ram bleeds to death on the ice or the old hunter misses his aim' (39–40). Faced with these alternatives, the Magistrate's potency – his sensed self-fullness – drains away in another of those moments when death encroaches.

An encounter with annihilation is thus the proximate cause of this tonal shift. Lurking in the background, however, is a disturbing thought: that the Magistrate and Joll are not so different after all. For the latter has spoken, in the novel's opening section, of a hunt in which he participated, of 'a huge antelope he shot' and 'a mountain of carcases' left behind (1–2). Nearness to Joll, it would seem, has no less an impact on the poetry of the prose than disappointment, something confirmed when we recall that the Magistrate can enter his state of contemplative reverie – in the first of the passages cited – only upon parting from his unwelcome guest. Thus, lyricism comes either as relief or in a pre-lapsarian state of grace, and is threatened, before or after, by a reality the starkness of which it makes us feel more keenly. Indeed, lyricism is the context in which the world is laid bare.

We therefore begin to discern a complex modulation in or of the narrative, a movement between different modes, which occasions or is occasioned by changes in subject matter, and which is a means of producing significant contrasts. This is something touched upon already, in relation to *Dusklands*, but the distinction there was simply between a sparer prose and one marked by an expanded syntax and intensification of metaphor. In *Waiting for the Barbarians*, certain thematic and phonological elements become relevant, though this perhaps suggests only that lyrical prose is but one of several varieties reserved for moments of interiority, or simply respite from the world at hand.

Further evidence for this comes as soon as we consider passages which may not be song-like, but which are nevertheless characterized by an expanded syntax. In a good many instances, these too describe movements of interiority, as when the Magistrate thinks what it might take to cleanse oneself of the taint of torture (12); how he might have ignored Joll's activities (21); of the oddness of his relationship with the barbarian girl (43); of his 'yearning' for 'the familiar routine ... the approaching summer, the long dreamy siestas' (75); of his fear of death and his desire for comfort (95–6); of the negligible value of any protest against bloodlust (104); and of the meaning of the 'eventful year' that has passed (154–5). In each case, the average sentence length, which is 15 words for the novel as a whole, increases to at least 24.2, and to as many as 41.8 words.[12]

This may be a crude measure of expansiveness, but the pattern is striking: moments of reflection are clearly recounted in a prose that lacks the terseness found elsewhere in the novel. If we exclude passages of dialogue (which tend, for obvious reasons, to be the most compact), this terseness is nowhere more obvious than in scenes of violence and degradation. To make this clear we might consider such a scene:

> [1] The Colonel steps forward. [2] Stooping over each prisoner in turn he rubs a handful of dust into his naked back and writes a word with a stick of charcoal. [3] I read the words upside down: ENEMY... ENEMY... ENEMY... ENEMY. [4] He steps back and folds his hands. [5] At a distance of no more than twenty paces he and I contemplate each other.
>
> [6] Then the beating begins. [7] The soldiers use the stout green cane staves, bringing them down with the heavy slapping sounds of washing-paddles, raising red welts on the prisoners' backs and buttocks. [8] With slow care the prisoners extend their legs until they lie flat on their bellies, all except the one who had been moaning and who now gasps with each blow.
>
> [9] The black charcoal and ochre dust begin to run with sweat and blood. [10] The game, I see, is to beat them till their backs are washed clean. (105)

Here, the average sentence length is 14.9 words and there is no subordination of finite clauses, except in sentences 8 and 10. Indeed, half the sentences are of the simplest kinds. Of those adverbials present in the remaining clauses, the majority are of manner or place, and serve to specify action or clarify position. Of the eleven adjectives used as pre-modifiers, one is an enumerator and four are adjectives of colour, their use again determined by a principle of precision rather than elaboration. The remaining adjectives, *naked, stout, cane, heavy, slapping* and *slow* are all, except for *cane* (which is in any case a noun used as a modifier), of Germanic provenance, and characteristically straightforward. What is more, those features identified as markers of lyricism are now for the most part absent. There is occasional use of sound repetition – the /b/.../k/ of 'backs and buttocks' – and intensified rhythmic stress – 'begīn to rūn with swēat and blōod' – but this remains localized, and there is certainly no broader pattern established across the sentences. The passage is neither sonorous nor marked by an overt use of metaphor. All that is left of the deeply rhythmic is the dull and bloody repetition of the word ENEMY and the assiduous beating of the barbarians.

Since we have now repeatedly observed the relation between terseness and violence, the purpose of this analysis is to confirm and clarify the presence, in *Waiting for the Barbarians* as in Coetzee's other early novels, of a range of narrative modes or voices, each associated with a particular thematics. One of these is a barer mode, which comes into its own in those passages of necessity and violence that constitute climactic moments; another is a mode of interiority, characterized by a more expansive prose, and which is further modified to produce a properly lyrical voice, marked by sonority and metaphoricity, and concerned with the past, the natural world and the nature of being as much as with the self.

This is not, of course, to abandon the general characterization of Coetzee's prose as spare and economical. It is simply to observe that there are degrees of spareness, and that the narrative varies its tone and adopts different voices as it progresses. Nor do these shifts and inflections serve the purpose only of alleviating monotony: the association between bareness and failed reciprocity, and indeed the very sense of this bareness, depends on the existence of passages in which the prose is more expansive, sometimes even more rhythmic and indeed lyrical. For if I am startled by the beating of these barbarians, and if I feel this moment as a laying bare, this is at least partly because, in the passages preceding, I have accompanied the Magistrate in his reflections, and experienced intimations of a more fulsome world of thought, and sometimes even of song.

The Rhetoric of Rhythm

What is remarkable about this account of public violence is that, as spare as it may feel, the writing does not become elliptical, feverish or staccato. Instead, it creates an impression of measured coolness and steady progression. This has at least something to do with the ordered clarity of the passage, the fact that each sentence describes a distinct act or set of acts, and that there is a high level both of coherence and cohesion across the sentences. But it has to do also with a feeling that the narrative is slowing down, that 'slow care' is a quality as much of the description of the barbarians' beating as their reaction to it.

This feeling, alluded to previously in relation to *Dusklands*, is encountered elsewhere in the novel, most strikingly in the description of the Magistrate's hanging. It is to be contrasted with a sense of stasis, on the one hand, and rapid movement on the other; or, to put it in narratological terms, its scenic qualities are to be related to passages of pause and of summary and ellipsis.[13] The former, of course, include those moments of reflection described previously, but what is of interest here is that passages of summary, especially those marked by a shift into the durative, are likewise characterized by a somewhat expanded syntax. So, for example, across the five paragraphs leading into the hunt – which describe the arrival of winter, relations with the barbarians in years past and the Magistrate's preoccupation with 'old recreations' – the average sentence length is 20.4 words (38). Similarly, in the first section of chapter 4, the average sentence length of the final thirteen paragraphs (describing the routines of the Magistrate's imprisonment and the thoughts they prompt) is 21 words; and in the third section of the fifth chapter, which is durative almost throughout, it is 20.1 words.

It is when contrasted with these other varieties of movement – the rapidity of durative description and the stasis of introspection (both of which suggest a position outside narrative time) – that the progress of the narrative in the scenes of beating and hanging, for example, comes to seem measured, steady, methodical. Yet, if this is a further illustration of the significant qualitative contrasts created by internal shifts of syntax and narration, it directs attention also to certain quantitative or at least temporal dimensions of reading, to the ways in which the broader movements of Coetzee's novels are shaped and controlled; that is, to their peculiar rhythms, and indeed their rhythmicity.

Although stylisticians and narratologists alike have largely abandoned the study of prose rhythm, Coetzee's interest in the matter surfaces early on, his most explicit comments coming in his doctoral dissertation. There, he claimed that the 'generative principle behind the language of *Watt*' – a principle that determines the novel's structure and syntax – is rhythmical. As a consequence, Coetzee explained, one perceives in *Watt* a binary pattern, 'a rhythm of one *against* another: question against statement, answer against question, objection against answer, qualification against objection'. So pervasive and persistent is this rhythm, moreover, that the 'halting beat under the words becomes more audible than the words themselves', and though the 'rhythm could not exist without the words, ... finally it is the rhythm alone that we hear'.[14]

The focus here may be mostly on the rhythmic qualities of *Watt*'s sentences, but Coetzee is elsewhere concerned with the broader shape of narratives, the relationship between their various parts, and their effects on a reader's experience. It is these features of narrative that he addresses, for example, when he reflects on his own writing, in an interview with David Attwell:

> *In the Heart of the Country* is not a novel on the model of a screenplay, but it is constructed out of quite brief sequences, which are numbered as a way of pointing to what is not there between them.... (If you want to confirm that *In the Heart of the Country* is no screenplay, you have only to view Marion Hänsel's film version, *Dust*, which retains virtually none of the sequence divisions and indeed none of the quite swift *pacing* of the novel. It loses a lot of vitality thereby, in my opinion.)
>
> If I had to give examples of the kind of film whose style imprints *In the Heart of the Country*, I would cite a short film by Chris Marker called *La Jetée* and the film *The Passenger*, put together by colleagues of Andrzej Munk after Munk's death from sequences he had completed plus some stills. What impressed me most about films like these was, paradoxically, what they could achieve through stills with voice-over commentary: a remarkable intensity of vision ... together with great economy of narration. More than economy: a rapidity, even a forward-plunging quality.[15]

Once we have set aside those comments that relate specifically to the visual qualities of the films, what remains in evidence is Coetzee's interest in regulating the movement and '*pacing*' of narrative; an interest, that is, in the rhythmic properties of storytelling and their possible effects: in this case, a feeling of intensity, of being swept uncontrollably onwards.

It is precisely this interest, moreover, that animates the oddest of Coetzee's mature writings, and also the least written about: 'Hero and Bad Mother in Epic', his only original published poem of the 1970s and 1980s, which appeared in the year of his interview with Watson.[16] Although it has long been deemed of little relevance to an appreciation of Coetzee's oeuvre, this work, I think, offers some of the most intriguing insights into his

understanding of poetic effects – including those to do with rhythm – and
the uses to which these might be put in the composition of narratives.

Hero and Bad Mother in Epic, a poem

dusk seeps up the entrail of the seaborn nude
the vegetable sleeps in its circle
the bedroom drowses
the casino is swathed in tidal melancholia
the nude awaits the hero   5

mounting the entrail of the seaborn nude
toward the sleeping vegetable
toward the poisoned goose with its melancholy aftertaste
comes the naked philatelist of fiction

the philatelist climbs the entrail of the poisoned nude   10
who rules over the luck-swathed fiction
of castaway matriarch
punctual chimera
spider of solitude
the philatelist climbs the entrail of the nude   15
toward a bedroom where a sword drowses

the drowsy sword in the spare bedroom
of the casino in the tidal nude
awaits the philatelist of melancholia
through the symmetrical aftertaste of goose   20
the castaway philatelist gropes
he circles the poisoned casino
and enters the bedroom of the nude of solitude
where the sword of fiction drowses
the seaborn philatelist brandishes the sword of fiction   25

the nude feels the punctual sword in her entrail
is it the poisoned chimera she wonders
stirring in her entrail?
is it the symmetrical matriarch
the spare philatelist   30
the tidal goose from the castaway bedroom?
is it the bedpost of fiction
the aftertaste of solitude
the vegetable of melancholia?
is it the vegetable of melancholia mounting the entrail of the seaborn nude?
(what stirs in her entrail   36

is the punctual instrument of the drowsy philatelist)
in a drowsy circle near the punctual casino
in the tidal entrail of the lucky nude

waits the chimera of solitude   40
swathed in spare fiction
with castaway sword he beheads the chimera
the punctual philatelist vanquishes the chimera of solitude
and enters the symmetrical casino of fiction

the matriarch of melancholy sleeps in the tidal casino   45
the poisoned philatelist gropes through its symmetries
his search is perplexed
where is the seaborn matriarch?
without the seaborn matriarch where is the lucky fiction?

in the final symmetry of the casino of solitude   50
the poisoned vegetable mounts the sleeping matriarch
the philatelist arrives at the seaborn bedroom of the casino in the nude
as the spider mounts the symmetrical matriarch
the spare philatelist is filled with the melancholia of melancholia
upon the symmetrical matriarch he turns his castaway sword   55
and the tidal casino in the drowsing nude is filled with the fiction of solitude
the spare philatelist transfixes the punctual matriarch

the philatelist	the bedroom	the spider
the casino	MOONBURST	the goose
the matriarch	the sword	the fiction 60

past the sleeping vegetable and the poisoned goose
with its melancholy aftertaste
the castaway philatelist descends the entrail of the sleeping nude

but the nude of solitude is dreaming new dreams
the downfall of calligraphy she dreams   65
the documents of panic
the iron in the milk
the axes of sleep
the perfumes of the dead
the geography of caution   70
the crocodile of blood
the counterfeit footfall
the terrible tailor
the shadowy root
the feminine kingdom   75

It is first of all important to acknowledge that if 'Hero and Bad Mother in Epic' has hardly been mentioned in scholarly literature, and has otherwise been treated with suspicion, this is because it is a computer poem. Produced at a remove, written not by the poet but by the code he writes, it has about it a whiff of illegitimacy and parlour games. Reasons for taking the poem seriously are nevertheless suggested by the conditions of its composition, details of which can be gleaned from 'Surreal Metaphors and Random Processes', where Coetzee describes a program able to generate lines of precisely the kind found in his poem. Indeed, the examples given in the essay – 'philatelist of solitude' and 'The nude with the haggard fingernail disdains the schoolboy of splendour' – share with the lines of his verse not only a common lexicon (one provided, incidentally, by Neruda's poetry) but also a common syntax, as is clear from such examples as 'nude of solitude' and 'the spare philatelist transfixes the punctual matriarch' (ll. 23 and 57). While this confirms that 'Hero and Bad Mother in Epic' emerged from Coetzee's computer experiments, it also makes clear that the code he describes was designed to generate nothing more than lines with 'the unexpectedness and originality of "real" poetry'; lines which Coetzee in any case had to cull from 'the detritus' of 'thousands of other lines of less intrinsic interest' thrown up by random process.[17]

Sifting and selecting these outputs would have been, moreover, only a preliminary step, since Coetzee speaks of the need to produce not lines, but 'English sentences', to which 'additional "poetic" rules' would then be applied. And though he may otherwise have regulated rhythm or rhyme, the '"poetic" rules' he chose in this case aimed instead at 'semantic originality' and striking metaphorical phrases, because, Coetzee observed, a 'machine which produced original metaphors might have attention paid to it. A machine which produced imitations of traditional metrical patterns, however impeccable, would certainly be ignored'. All of which suggests that, in making 'Hero and Bad Mother in Epic', Coetzee not only selected and arranged the sentences generated by his 'algorithm for the production of original metaphors', but also, in certain cases, broke them up, and in others, ran them together.[18]

The grammatical variations of 'Hero and Bad Mother in Epic' support this view: following the first stanza – in which there is a single simple sentence in each of the five lines so that the line breaks coincide with syntactical breaks – the sentences begin to vary in length and complexity, stretching over lines or being sundered by them. Line division is in turn augmented by parallelism, rhythmic patterning and sound repetition, alliteration in particular. So, for example, in the second stanza, whose four lines make up a single simple sentence, the anaphora that links lines 7 and 8 is complemented by a fairly regular rhythmic pattern (four, three, five and four stresses, rising in lines 6, 7 and 8, falling in line 9), as well as alliterative runs on /n/ in line 6 and /k/ and /f/ in line 9. By these means, repeated throughout the poem, the line is given integrity as a unit.

It is therefore quite wrong to think of 'Hero and Bad Mother in Epic' as nothing more than a computer poem, for the computer has been used to generate only 'poetic' building blocks, which are subsequently arranged, altered, extended and even broken down, first in the climactic dissolution of the ninth stanza, and then in the epilogic eleventh stanza.

Even with regard to this 'poeticizing' function, the computer's contribution is gradually exposed and devalued by the poem itself, which, in one sense, comes to constitute a phenomenology of metaphor. The collocations I find so striking to begin with are slowly revealed as products of something closer to chance than poetic inspiration, and are thereby deprived of the implicit intentionality that I presume when identifying a phrase or clause as metaphorical. This becomes clearer when the unfolding of the poem is considered more carefully.

In the first stanza, in which the scene is set, I encounter semantically unusual lines, but, prompted by familiarity with the obscure verse of the modernists, I try to make sense of them. It may not be possible to give content to each term (to what can 'vegetable' refer?), but I proceed regardless, however hesitantly: dusk cannot seep, strictly speaking, for it is not a liquid, but a time of day; nevertheless, its progress may be experienced not only as gradual and chilling, but as something corporeally affective, so long as 'entrail' is read as referring to the gut, site of intuitive knowledge. As for the 'seaborn nude', her identity is unclear, though, if the psychoanalytic references of the title are any clue, she may be the bad mother, the villain of the piece. In any case, she is not unfamiliar: her image belongs not only to pictorial art (Botticelli's *The Birth of Venus*, Duchamp's *Venus Descending the Stairs*) but to poetry also, and in particular Wallace Stevens's 'The Paltry Nude Starts on a Spring Voyage'.[19] In solitude, then, sheltered within a complex pervaded by her state of depressed anxiety, the nude awaits her Nemesis.

The hero, for whom the reader is prepared by the poem's title, as well as by the final line of the first stanza, enters on the scene in the second stanza, the delayed main verb and subject of its single sentence further contributing to the sense of rising expectation. Here, I encounter more of those strange collocations – mounting the entrail? the poisoned goose? – and I continue trying to make sense of them, encouraged by the repetitions of earlier associations that help fix meaning: *seaborn* is still attached to *nude*, in the manner of heroic epithet, and the vegetable, whatever it is (a beanstalk perhaps?), continues to sleep. The phrasal echoes that link lines 1 and 2 with lines 6 and 7 emphasize these repetitions, ensuring also that the hero who is awaited in the final line of the first stanza is identified with the philatelist of fiction who arrives in the final line of the second.

Here, however, something begins to impede my progress: not the shift in descriptor, or even the strangeness of the hero's occupation; rather, a repetition that introduces troubling contradictions. For I read of the hero's nakedness. Is it not the villain who is unclothed, who has in fact been characterized chiefly by her nudity? Not that it is impossible, at this stage, to resolve the matter: nudity and nakedness may mean different things, as they do in the visual arts.[20] Yet suspicion lingers, for how is it possible to reconcile the 'poisoned goose' of line 8 with the 'poisoned nude' of line 10? Is the nude both vegetable and goose, sleeping beauty and progenitor of the golden egg? Perhaps. The poem continues and these concerns recede, as I am encouraged both by the introduction of new characters – the spider of solitude, castaway matriarch and punctual chimera are all compelling additions – and by the repetition of line 3's collocation of 'bedroom' and 'drowses' in lines 16 and 17, as well as the more obvious repeated description of the philatelist climbing the entrail of the nude towards the bedroom.

But doubt flows in again more powerfully at the fourth stanza, in which the severe constraints imposed on the poem's lexicon begin to emerge at the same time as the collocative consistency is forcibly abandoned. The phrasal units of the first three stanzas – such as 'the casino swathed in tidal melancholia', the 'seaborn nude', the 'philatelist of fiction', the 'castaway matriarch' and the 'poisoned goose with its melancholy aftertaste' – are dissolved and reassembled from the fourth stanza onwards.[21] I continue to come across arresting collocations, but these now consist of increasingly familiar words: 'tidal nude' (l. 18), 'philatelist of melancholia' (l. 19), 'castaway philatelist' (l. 21), 'poisoned casino' (l. 22). In the final line of the fourth stanza, even the epithet 'seaborn', its attachment to the nude seemingly guaranteed by the history of art itself, is forced to migrate, becoming affixed to the only other protagonist assured singularity by the poem's title, the heroic philatelist.

It therefore becomes impossible to stabilize the referents of the poem's various lexical units, and phrases which hitherto gestured so imaginatively to poetic truths are unmasked as the inevitable products of a rule-governed machine, intended perhaps (given the limited lexicon, their appearance is at least foreseeable), but not meant. Yet this development does not put a stop to the poem or its reading. It simply discourages over-involvement in the most obvious 'poetic' features, the 'surreal' metaphors, which function only on the condition that they are presumed to conceal inspired insights.

If we become convinced that any given collocation is a product of chance, we can no longer consider it meaningful, unless we construe chance itself as something closer to Fate, as Coetzee suggests in 'Surreal Metaphors and Random Processes'.

But if we gradually come to overlook the unusual collocations (it is no longer possible to think of them as metaphorical), there is nonetheless something that pulls us onwards; that produces a sense of relation between the parts and that gives the whole a particular shape. In fact, there are several things that do this, including features of syntax and phonology. Verbs are especially important, for the twenty-five that appear – simple, mostly monosyllabic, unencumbered by adverbs, and almost entirely of Old English or French provenance, attested no later than the fourteenth century, the exception being the climactic *transfix* – are used to structure the poem, to make it cohere, since the stanzas are constituted through the use of clusters of related verbs denoting specific actions.

In the first stanza, for example, a combination of intransitive verbs (*seeps, sleeps, drowses*), an agentless passive construction (*is swathed*) and a denotation of inactivity (*sleeps, drowses, is swathed, awaits*) contribute to a picturing of the scene that is very much staged. In the second, there is a similar arrangement around the single main verb *comes*, supplemented by the participle *mounting*, while in the third this 'motion towards' is specified in the verb *climbs*, which governs both of the main clauses. And so the story unfolds: a journey is made, confusion is overcome, initial tasks are accomplished and finally the villain, who all the while has awaited this end, is vanquished, the hero returning home. So it is that we move from opening, to the climactic tableau of stanza 9 (illuminated by *MOONBURST*), to dénouement, to the coda of stanza 11.

In this, we are guided not only by the coherent progression of verbal clusters, but also by those cohesive pressures earlier remarked, the rhythmic regulation ensured by the use of parallelism and sound repetition. This is nowhere more evident than in the fifth stanza. The interrogative sentence of lines 27 and 28, with its embedded declarative 'she wonders', is followed by three further interrogative sentences, which build together to the climax of line 35, and the parenthetical aside of lines 36 and 37. At the level of the sentence, the pattern, *Is it the X?* (VSsC), is established in the first, and repeated in each of the three sentences that follow. The elision, in the second and third sentences, of the relative sub-clause, with its progressive verb and prepositional phrase, contributes as much to pacing as to cohesion.

The same is true of the further use of parallelism at the level of the clause, for, echoing the triadic structure at sentence level (if the pattern is stated in the first sentence, the second, third and fourth sentences move steadily towards a restatement), the second and third sentences are composed of three interrogative clauses each. Here, it is operator and dummy subject that are elided in the second and third clause, so that the pattern VSsC/ sC/ sC is established. Further contributing to the progressively rising tempo of the stanza, a parallelism operates also at the level of stress, which is more regular than elsewhere in the poem.

It is structures such as these that become apparent once the seemingly metaphorical collocations are de-emphasized, structures for which the program described in 'Surreal Metaphors and Random Processes' does not code, and by means of which the work not only holds together, but continues to have meaning; continues, indeed, to feel dramatic. For, however much the poem teases its readers with fantastic phrases sliding abruptly into nonsense, its parts are so divided that they constitute a series of action-based episodes, and these are so related that, with an impressive economy, their progression is given a particular shape: stasis, mounting tension, moment of crisis, dissolution. What the poem is therefore about is not so much, or not only, the story it recounts; instead, it is about the making of stories, the stringing together of episodes.

Here it is impossible to ignore the importance of a work's title in grounding interpretation. From the very beginning, it presents us with two distinct protagonists, without whom we would struggle to fix any meaning. The word 'Epic' is likewise significant, and not a little surprising. After all, given the references to geese and swords and spiders and poison, a more obvious title might have been 'Hero and Bad Mother in Fairy Tale' or 'in Folk Story', or, for that matter, simply 'in Fiction'. Instead, the choice of 'Epic' raises a range of themes, plots and structures of feeling, which are then partially disappointed. The poem thereby becomes something of a joke at the expense of literary pretensions.

'Epic', however, is also an acknowledgement that the poem is at once an instance and exploration of storytelling; it signals not only an elevated tone, or certain themes, but also, following its use by aesthetic philosophers from Aristotle to Hegel, through to Lukács and Bertolt Brecht, an orientation towards narrative. Indeed, Fredric Jameson, in his book on Brecht, feels that 'it is always necessary to remind the English language reader, and perhaps the German one as well, that the crucial term – epic – by no means involves the lofty and classical associations of the Homeric tradition but, rather, something as humdrum and everyday as narrative or "storytelling"'.[22]

Thus 'Hero and Bad Mother in Epic' can be read as a tale of mock-heroic adventure, but also as a story about the resilience of stories, which emerge in spite of obstructions to the referential function of language. In this respect, the poem is related to *In the Heart of the Country*, which, as we have seen, also makes use of repeated and reconfigured textual blocks and a core of significant events. Moreover, if Coetzee's reason for dividing his second novel into numbered passages had indeed to do with pacing, this interest in narrative's structural requirements and possibilities seems also to have animated his poem. For, whatever its opacity, 'Hero and Bad Mother in Epic' is affective, dramatic; indeed, stripped almost entirely of character and setting, it is little other than the distillation of dramatic form: mounting tension, climax and dying fall.

One purpose of this account is to show that, far from being a meaningless joke, 'Hero and Bad Mother in Epic' explores and often mocks at a range of ideas about poetry and figurative language, comparative mythology and archetypal psychoanalysis, storytelling and narrative form, and, indeed, heroism. Not all of these are relevant to the present discussion, but it should at least be clear that these concerns are not wholly divorced from those of Coetzee's fictions and critical writings, and that the poem may therefore be a source of real insight.

This is the case, I think, with narrative rhythm, in which, as we have seen, Coetzee was certainly interested. In *Waiting for the Barbarians*, this interest resurfaces. The work is, after all, very much about rhythm, preoccupied with the contrast, even conflict, between two modes of temporality: on the one hand, historical time of event and action: on the other, pastoral time of day and night, summer and winter, youth and old age. It is the disruption of the latter by the former that constitutes the drama of the novel, which begins with the unfortunate co-incidence of two distinct rhythms, that of the rise and fall of Empire with that of the seasonal migrations of the Barbarians. It is in this sense that, describing the calamity that has befallen both himself and the narrative, the Magistrate laments: 'time has broken, something has fallen in upon me from the sky, at random, from nowhere' (43).

The cyclical time of nature constitutes not only the Magistrate's personal temporality but the background temporality of the narrative itself. The Magistrate, in turn, attempts to limit the intrusion of Empire by construing the anxiety regarding the Barbarians as itself cyclical. From the Magistrate's point of view, Empire, dreaming of an expansion into infinity through successive, progressive and distinct acts and events, has failed to perceive its own particular rhythm (generational) and the rhythm of empires in general ('rise and fall') (133). But the Magistrate is likewise guilty of ignoring the significance of his own acts and omissions. The routine of washing and anointing – the rhythmic repetition of rhythmic repetitions – is his means of escaping into an infinity of sorts, the sleep of oblivion, uninterrupted by dreams, into which he is 'lulled ... by the rhythm of the oiling and rubbing' (44). It is this desire for a kind of wholeness, only partially recognized, that appears to motivate the rhythmic disruption of his sleep.

If *Waiting for the Barbarians* is therefore thematically concerned with rhythm and time, what evidence does it offer of Coetzee's concern for pacing? Having abandoned the numbering of passages, how are the novel's own rhythms controlled? To begin with, by dividing it into six chapters, which gives the narrative a general and overall shape. This can be represented graphically, as in Figure 1, if we use the number of words to measure the chapter lengths.

Several observations follow, the first of which is that chapter 1 comes closest to the mean chapter length (10,932 words), thereby constituting an internal point of reference and measurement. There is, moreover, an initial oscillation between shorter and longer chapters, with an increasing divergence from the mean, but also an upward trend that culminates in the fourth chapter, which is roughly twice the mean length. With the fifth chapter, the oscillation seems to continue, but is abandoned in the sixth, with the result that the final two chapters describe a downward trend. We might then say that the novel builds gradually but in binary alternations towards a climactic point, before subsiding into a kind of coda.

In itself, this movement describes a fairly straightforward dramatic arc, not unlike the one encountered in 'Hero and Bad Mother in Epic',

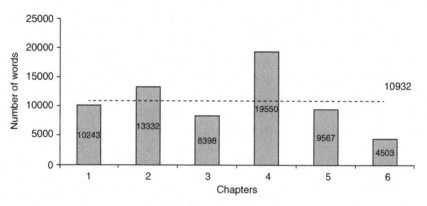

Figure 1 Chapter Length.

particularly as each of the chapters consists of episodes which are so related as to form coherent units: I. Joll's First Visit; II. The Magistrate's Relationship with the Barbarian Girl; III. Expedition to the Barbarians; IV. The Magistrate's Imprisonment; V. Abandonment of the Town and the Magistrate's Return to Society; VI. Preparations for Winter and the Town's Defence. Of course, each of these stages might be described somewhat differently, but what should be clear is that the chapter division obeys a certain logic, which seems also to guide chapter lengths; for the longer chapters, which thereby acquire greater weight, are given over to the captivity first of the barbarian girl and then of the Magistrate.

If this gives some indication that a concern for pacing governs the novel's structure, we should remember that the chapters are themselves divided into sections, typographically distinguished in the Ravan and Secker & Warburg editions by the curious asterisks that occur even in the manuscripts drafts. For it is at the level of these sections – of which there are sixty-one in total – that narrative rhythm is most powerfully shaped. Varying considerably in length, the shortest, 24, contains only 66 words, while the longest, 37, contains 3,941. A comprehensive sense of the pattern they produce across the novel is again made available by graphic representation, as in Figure 2, where the final sections of each chapter are highlighted.

Here too, a number of comments might be made. It should be clear, to begin with, that a certain pattern is repeated at the end of chapters, where section lengths either rise or fall quite steeply, as in chapters I, II,

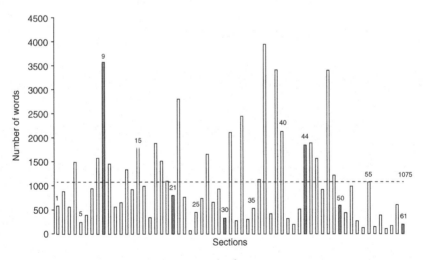

Figure 2 Length of sections.

IV and V. In chapter III, there is instead a binary modulation across the final sections (27 to 30), though one that nevertheless describes a downward trend. The shapes of the gradients, moreover, as well as the occurrence of peaks and troughs, seem to be related to the nature of the events with which sections and chapters are concerned. For example, the final three episodes of chapter IV increase in length as the Magistrate's degradation intensifies, culminating in the hanging scene, which is thereby marked as the climactic point of the novel. In this, the end of the fourth chapter echoes the first, in which there is likewise a gradual building towards scenes of torture, albeit ones from which the Magistrate remains purposefully absent.

In contrast, the movements of decline or deflation that constitute the endings of chapters II and V seem related to a termination of possibilities: in the former, the Magistrate's affair with the barbarian girl draws to its conclusion, and in the latter, the loop that opens with the Magistrate's expedition is closed as he returns to his empty rooms. As for chapter III, any expectation of a rising climax is extinguished abruptly, with the surprise discovery of Joll's return, and in chapter VI, which I have described as a kind of coda, the sections gently rise and fall into silence. Here, their mean length is less than half that of all the sections, as the chapter itself is half the mean length of all the chapters. At both levels, then, there is a gradual closing down, a restriction of vision or scope.

If the shapes of chapter endings therefore appear motivated, evidence of a similar purposiveness is found in the more general distribution of sections: those that constitute climactic points are often associated with events of particular importance. Thus, section 4 gives the account of the Magistrate's visit to the granary hut and his discovery of the injured boy and his dead grandfather; 15, the Magistrate's failed hunt; 27, the encounter with the barbarians; and 37, the Magistrate's escape. In the opposite direction, the culminant sections of downward trends likewise have something in common: 17 describes the Magistrate's sexual encounter with the barbarian girl; 24, the day of rest during the journey; 42, the meaning of torture; and 54, the dream of the grave. In each case, the central event is a troubling one, a cause for discomfort or ill ease, a feeling heightened by the brevity of these sections, which gives a sense of things which are not and perhaps cannot be spoken.

Finally, where the general shape and character of the chapters is concerned, it is of interest that, while the sections of chapter VI are numerous and yet noticeably brief, the sections of chapter V are few in number and noticeably long. This too seems appropriate: there is little action here (save Mandel's departure and the night-time incident prompting the destruction of the fisher-folk huts), and the chapter is given over instead to the Magistrate's gradual return to himself. Following the climactic chapter, with its jagged alternation of sections, we find a steady and ambling progression, very much suited to the Magistrate's night-time wanderings and re-immersion in the dusky beauty of his landscape.

No attempt to characterize narrative rhythms can conceal or entirely surmount the difficulty in ascribing meaning to pattern, sense to sound, not least because, where pacing is concerned, much will depend on the conditions of reading. Nevertheless, though different readers are unlikely to respond identically, their experiences will be determined at least partially by the text, by its actual breaks and divisions and the relative lengths of its parts.

Here again, the real question in any case is of the rhetorical force of a particular strategy, in which regard, it is worth remarking an observation of Paull F. Baum's, whose study of prose rhythm Coetzee knew and cited: 'Though the habits of the reader and the nature of the subject matter play a large part in determining pauses, it seems that the more definitely rhythmical a passage the greater the number and length of the pauses'.[23] Keeping this in mind, alongside Coetzee's comments on the 'remarkable intensity' and 'forward-plunging quality' that certain narrative divisions could achieve, I would suggest that, above all, the segmentation of Coetzee's prose not only aids the novel's pacing, but produces a sense of its acute rhythmicity, and thus an experience of the narrative as something *vivid* and *compelling*, *absorbing* and *gripping*, a narrative that 'plunges' its readers 'into physical ordeals',[24] and 'pulls' them through the novel 'with a gravitational force'.[25]

What I am suggesting here, in other words, is that the very intensity of Coetzee's writing, attested by so many early readers, has something to do with his control of modulation and rhythm, a control explicitly registered in several reviews of *Waiting for the Barbarians*. Jane Kramer, for example, noted the work's interest in rhythms and cycles, as well as the 'odd forms' that Coetzee 'had invented, turning the tensions of the exercise into a kind of choreography'; Irving Howe commented that Coetzee had 'found a narrative strategy for controlling the tensions between subject and author'; and Cherry Clayton insisted that it came 'closest to being the continuous and rhythmical prose experience that one expects of this kind of novel'.[26]

Lyric and Narrative

If the felt intensity of Coetzee's novels has something to do with their rhythmic properties, it has to do also with the affective potential of a lyric narrative mode. That Coetzee's choice of this mode cannot be taken for granted is clear from the manuscripts, which reveal, amidst several false starts, the difficulty of choosing the right perspective.[27]

In the earliest extant drafts, this difficulty is perhaps overshadowed, for these tell an entirely different story, of a man fleeing war in South Africa; but it is a good deal clearer in those versions in which the basic elements of *Waiting for the Barbarians* become recognizable. The first of these begins in epistolary form before shifting to external 'third person' narration, though the central figure remains the letter-writing commander of the garrison, who is first narrator then focalizer. In the version that follows, however, the return to 'first person' character narration is accompanied by a change in emphasis: the commander remains the object of attention, but the narrator is now his adjunct. Only in the draft marked version G are the narrator, focalizer and principal character finally aligned in the person we come to know eventually as the Magistrate.

One effect of this alignment is a sense of closeness to the novel's central consciousness, even of intimacy, which is greater here than in any other of Coetzee's early works. This is primarily because the dramatic irony that ensures distance from Dawn, Jacobus Coetzee and even Magda is diminished in *Waiting for the Barbarians*. But it is also because the Magistrate is a more coherent subject, with an assured sense of self and memories of his past, a consciousness troubled by doubt, but not, it seems, by obvious madness or uncertainty regarding its own existence, and which is thus less alienating, if not less alienated.

For these same reasons, of all Coetzee's early principal characters, the Magistrate comes closest to resembling the proper subject of the lyric. That is, at least, if we take seriously the story implicit in Coetzee's essay on Achterberg, where he notes: 'The hide-and-seek of the *I* in Sterne has become a serious game, with dangers to the psyche, in Eliot's "Love Song of J. Alfred Prufrock" (1917). What has intervened has been the rise and decline of the romantic-liberal notion of the self.'[28] For the allusion here is not only to a changing conception of subjectivity, but also to a development of literary forms that it parallels and affects: the expansion and gradual unravelling of the lyric. It is with this in mind that we might consider also the *kind* of character the Magistrate is: a middle-aged man, educated, possessed of civil and juridical power, with amateur interests in farming, hunting, astronomy, philology and archaeology. A man whose milieu, in other words, echoes that of the nineteenth-century European bourgeois, the very apotheosis of the 'romantic-liberal notion of the self'.

The closer affiliation with the lyric in *Waiting for the Barbarians* is therefore consequent on a number of factors, formal and thematic, which have to do with the kind of narrator and character the Magistrate is. In this way, the novel prompts the question – raised in any case by certain of the revisions to its manuscript drafts – of Coetzee's choice of a lyric narrative mode, not only in this novel, but in each of his early fictions.

This question becomes more pertinent when we consider that, in the South African literary field, a determined anti-lyricism had become increasingly prominent, after more than a century in which, as Coetzee himself suggests, the lyric had prevailed: 'Much of South African poetry in English has applied itself to the salvation of the European soul alienated in Africa through the means of a Romantic projection of consciousness into the alien: into the African himself, into the African fauna or landscape.'[29] By the 1970s, however, a poetics associated with subjectivity and affect had grown suspect and was losing ground.

This is apparent, for example, in the burgeoning of a new kind of performance poetry: paeans and panegyrics dedicated to trade unions and political leaders, disseminated quickly and to large township gatherings where they met with an 'overwhelming response' and gave evidence of a new 'bond between the writers and their audience'.[30] Within the medium of print too, changes were occurring, as attempts were made to establish a black readership and black-controlled means of production. The most radical outcome was *Staffrider*, a seminal literary magazine founded by Ravan Press, the aims of which were clearly stated in its first editorial: to provide an outlet for new creative forces; to include submissions without regard to older notions of literary merit; and to encourage a new community-based literature which would draw on the work of community writing groups.[31]

In each case, the impact of the Black Consciousness Movement was felt. Having emerged in the late 1960s, it placed considerable emphasis on self-reliance and the centrality of community to African conceptions of the self and to revolutionary struggle. Modes of intimate address that prioritized subjective experience therefore stood accused of expressing bourgeois notions of personhood and freedom, and of blocking the authors' and readers' fuller integration in the community. Associated not only with intimacy and interiority, but also with a certain idea of literariness, the lyric was bound to suffer.

The clearest instance of its abandonment is found in the works of the Soweto poets, Mbuyiseni Mtshali, Mongane Serote, Sipho Sepamla and Mafika Gwala. Although committed initially to what David Attwell describes as 'something like the poetry of personal statement', in which the 'individuality and intensity of the speaking voice' came to the fore and 'the isolated, intelligent, contemplative observer-self' was instantiated, these poets began, in the mid-seventies, to seek out different possibilities. What they hoped to achieve was a 'seamless connection … between the self and the nation' and 'an integration of the personal and existential … with the historical and the national'.[32]

Above all, they required 'longer and stronger forms' of the kind that might give access to or even produce collective identity and popular perspective. For this reason, Attwell speaks of a shift 'from lyric to epic' because, in the tradition that builds upon Hegel, epic is not only narrative, but stands to lyric as the public to the personal, the objective to the subjective.[33] It is in this sense that Brecht, for example, decried any resort to lyricism as an appeal to 'feelings', and called for an 'epic theatre' that would instead work on 'the spectator's reason', a theatre set against that kind of drama in which 'the plot leads the hero into situations where he reveals his innermost being' and thereby allows catharsis, 'the spiritual cleansing of the spectator'.[34]

Whether nor not they had read Brecht, certain of Soweto's erstwhile poets certainly developed their practices in line with these arguments, not only in turning to the novel but also in adopting particular narrative strategies. Sepamla, for example, in *A Ride on the Whirlwind*, recounts events following the uprising of 1976 by making use of an external narrator that shifts between different groups: student activists, their elders and supporters, the police, and assorted neighbours, collaborators and drunks. In each group, representative individuals become points of focalization, as is the case with Mandla, the student-leader, Mzi, the militant returned from exile, and Batata, the traitorous warrant officer. But what is most important is that the narrative strives to signal its exteriority, by insisting, for example, on the observability of even psychological features: 'His leadership qualities *could be assessed from the way* he dealt with the other members; 'Her aggressive nature *showed up easily*'; 'whose superior standing *could be read from the way* he held up his neck', '*The way* his creased face suddenly warmed up … *showed* the relief'.[35]

This exteriority is further serviced by a strategy that speaks at the same time of the work's search for a perspective exceeding the individual's: the characterization of Soweto as an agent unto itself, a being constituted of multiple bodies and consciousnesses. We find, for example, 'Soweto laughed at the red shame on the ears of the armed men', 'Soweto went to sleep that night unaware of the nightmare to which it had given rise', 'Soweto began to nudge itself again', 'Soweto sang the comedy of the house of Uncle Ribs', 'Soweto hovered between hope and despair, death and life'.[36]

A similar strategy is found in Mongane Serote's *To Every Birth Its Blood*, though here collective agency is vested elsewhere than in the city. For though Johannesburg and Alexandra, the 'Golden City' and the 'Dark City', are occasionally personified – 'Alexandra met them in song, rallies and demonstrations', 'it was as if Johannesburg ... stood still; just for a second. Then it got into action' – they remain products of serial and even random combination. Thus, Alexandra is figured as 'a terrible stew', and even 'this shit', the membra disjecta of the apartheid state. The role of collective agent is therefore assigned instead to the Movement, a fused group made in praxis, which becomes the subject of a series of extraordinary extended metaphors: 'The Movement is old. It is as old as the grave of the first San or Khoikhoi.... The Movement is as young as the idea of throwing stones.... The Movement is the eyes which see how poverty is akin to a skeleton'; 'Like an old tree, the Movement spreads and spreads its roots. It entrenches itself in the soil, issuing root after root.... The tall tree, spreading its branches all around, gives shade to the weary'; 'The Movement, like the sea, is deep, is vast, is reflective. It can be calm. It can be rough and tough. Like the wind, it moves and moves and moves'.[37]

Nor is it by chance that these metaphors occur towards the novel's conclusion, for communal perspective and objectivity become the principle of its structure: while the novel's first part belongs to the character narrator Tsi, an external narrator takes possession of the second[38]; and each of these narrators corresponds to a moment in time and a form of political awareness and activism. Tsi is a journalist, participates in a township theatre group and then works in a foreign-funded 'research unit', but remains peripheral to any political movement and belongs ultimately to Alexandra's ambiguous urban aggregate. In contrast, the central figures and focalizers of the second narrator are committed youths of the Soweto generation, who take violent action against the state, and whose loyalties are to one another, the community and the Movement. Whereas Tsi's escape into drink, sex or music induces long passages of hallucinatory prose, a more measured account articulates the selfless, even self-sacrificing Oupa, Dikeledi, Mandla and Onalenna, whose only escape is exile or death. Thus, narrative structure serves judgement on a certain kind of being and

a certain kind of art: the affectively charged interiority of the first part –
with its commitment to the lyric 'I' and to lyricism – is condemned as the
proper mode of a selfish, self-enclosed and deficient subjectivity.

It is against this background of local anti-lyricism that Coetzee's choice
of narrative mode acquires much of its charge and signals his rejection of
certain ideas about 'epic'. His reasons are found in an interview conducted
following the publication of *Waiting for the Barbarians*, where he com-
mends *A Ride on the Whirlwind* and *To Every Birth Its Blood* as 'probably
the best novels published by black South Africans in 1981'. Yet he finds
'in both a failure, almost a refusal, to create a structure in which there is
some centre of intelligence', a failure he associates with an adherence to
the central tenets of Naturalism: 'that some kind of transcription of everyday experience into verbal form makes up a novel', and that by transcrib-
ing 'the experience of quite simple people' one might 'say serious things
about the world'. One of the consequences, he observes, is that 'people
in Naturalist novels refuse to act as though they are living inside verbal
artefacts', no matter that 'being in a novel is not the same as being in the
real world (for example, everything you see inside a novel is likely to have
a meaning)'.[39]

These criticisms follow explicitly from Coetzee's comment in his interview with Watson that many black writers were 'working with models'
he regarded as 'dubious'. They also recall Coetzee's critique of La Guma
for denying *A Walk in the Night* 'a central intelligence', and for preferring
'a narrative point of view above the world of his characters, the point of
view of a spectator watching people act out their lives', and which produces, Coetzee says, 'the dullness of a world without consciousness'.[40] As
in the comments on Serote and Sepamla, the argument seems to be that
notionally objective narrative modes often mistake the nature of truth in
art; their commitment to describing observable data shuts them off from
complexities of thought and feeling, and thus of the world; and their outcomes are likely therefore to seem at best simple-minded, at worst boring.

At least some of these views are central to 'Hero and Bad Mother in
Epic', which parodies the desire for distance and the refusal of any centre of
intelligence. It is, after all, a poem that makes automatism a compositional
condition and that instantiates distance at every turn: between the poet
and his poem, between the reader and the poem, between the poem and its
title, and between the events narrated by the poem and the reality of one of
its characters, the dreaming nude whose vision of death is ultimately over-
turned. Yet, for all that, affect cannot be banished because structure itself is

rhetorical; and the consequence of refusing consciousness is only an aban-donment to a story of the simplest kind, borne along by an all too-familiar rhythm, the rhythm of emotional purge; an abandonment, then, to the automatism of Naturalism as much as automatic writing and an 'automa-tized' outmoded realism, each of which blocks access to those most potent means by which narrative might know the world.[41]

At the very least, this allows us to explain one of the oddest things about 'Hero and Bad Mother in Epic', which is its appearance in the first issue of *Staffrider*, set alongside works by such established figures as Douglas Livingstone and Mothobi Mutloatse, and such unknowns as the mem-bers of the Creative Youth Association of Diepkloof, Soweto. For, though Coetzee clearly appreciated the importance of the journal – he described it soon after as 'the most interesting venture on the South African literary scene for years', which 'set itself up' not 'to be an arbiter of the best', but 'in the hope of fostering the growth of relevant, contemporary, mainly black writing, and of building up a readership for it' – he also recognized the need for caution in the rush to embrace epic.[42] Thus, even if Coetzee had not anticipated its inclusion in *Staffrider*, his poem might be read in the context of the journal as a judgement on certain ideas about stories and storytelling. At the very least, this must have seemed relevant to Mike Kirkwood, Ravan's new editor, to whom Coetzee had given the work.

In any case, keeping in mind his several responses to the local shift towards epic, we might begin to understand why Coetzee adopted a form of address grounded in the perspectives of a very limited number of characters (one, for the most part), and that makes substantial use of the present tense, since this allows a sense of proximity, immediacy and direct involvement. In this regard, it is significant that *lyrical* has come recently to signify that someone or something is 'excitedly effusive; highly enthu-siastic, fervent'. Nor does this have to do only with the fact that, as David Lindley observes, the phrase 'lyrical intensity' generally signifies the 'per-sonal expression of feeling'.[43] For this relates only to the kind of thing that the narrative describes, rather than the kind of response it elicits from the reader, and, indeed, the kind of reader that responds, or that is brought into being.

Yet if the lyric 'I' is a personal 'I', a subject characterized by its intensity and emotion and the immediacy of its presence, the kind of 'you' that this 'I' addresses is necessarily different from the 'you' that is addressed, for example, by an external narrator, or indeed by a character narrator who speaks in the present about events in the past.[44] Coetzee's use of a certain kind of 'first person' character narration thus makes available a set of expressive possibilities, which include access to the narrating subject's inner workings, but also to a form of relation between reader and narrator that contributes to the force of the writing, to its *intensity*, *power* and *vividness*. Here, we have only to imagine *Dusklands* or even *Life & Times of Michael K* transposed into the kind of external narration found in *A Ride on the Whirlwind* to understand something of the importance of the lyric situation.

Nor need rhetorical force – which worried Brecht no less than it did Plato – cause concern. A novel is a novel, rather than a poem or a play, and the fear that affective involvement might dull critical engagement in any case seems somewhat simple-minded. But the most important reason for disregarding this anxiety about rhetoric is that novelists in apartheid South Africa faced the problem of how to ensure that the reality of their fictions impinged upon the worlds of readers who always threatened to be too dispassionate, and to refuse any sense of their own complicity. In its very intimacy and intensity, the lyric situation of Coetzee's early novels deprives us of this escape.

For all that, it is necessary to remember that the relation between 'I' and 'you' in Coetzee's novels is always mediated by that measure of dramatic irony required for enjoining the acknowledgment that art's truth – its ability to 'say serious things about the world' – is a function of artistry, not the transcription of reality. Even in *Waiting for the Barbarians*, which abandons the most obvious signals of fictionality, evidence remains that the characters are living inside 'verbal artefacts'. For example, the steadiness and clarity of the present tense narration, above all in moments in which the Magistrate is subjected to violence, ensures not only that a 'centre of intelligence' continues to govern the fiction, but also that we again feel the presence of the implied narrative consciousness.

The Magistrate himself, moreover, seems aware that everything in his world 'is likely to have a meaning' (and that meanings can be multiple and complex). Yet there are meanings he cannot find or see, and he is haunted in his dreams and waking thoughts by that blankness which speaks of the condition of his ignorance: his existence as a character in a novel. The irony is especially great in those moments in which he becomes conscious that the significance of his story eludes him, as when he thinks: 'There has been something staring me in the face, and still I do not see it' (155). It becomes greater still upon discovering that the dreams which trouble the Magistrate are not entirely his own, or that of his text, but trace their origin to a different narrative entirely. For it is in early drafts, relating a very different character's attempted escape from civil war, that one of these dreams – of pubic hair transformed into 'bees clustered densely atop one another' – first comes into existence (13).

At last, we come to the question of why, in *Waiting for the Barbarians*, we encounter not simply the *lyric situation* of each of Coetzee's early novels, but the proper 'I' of the lyric: the romantic-liberal self. In general, this has been explained as having something to do with Coetzee's determination to subvert or deconstruct liberal humanism and all its dogmas, but, while doubtless relevant to an understanding of the novel, this seems to miss or ignore important elements, which, as before, can be drawn out only by attending to particular literary relations. In the present case, it is helpful to address, very briefly, Coetzee's interest in the *nouveau roman*.

Thus far, scholars have made little of this engagement, though there is ample evidence for it in Coetzee's early critical writings and interviews. He cites Claude Mauriac, Alain Robbe-Grillet and Nathalie Sarraute approvingly in his doctoral dissertation, and though these citations disappear from the essays on Beckett and Nabokov, they return in Coetzee's reflections on Yvonne Burgess's *The Strike* and again in his interview with Watson.

Here, the relevance of these authors has to do with their attack on the romantic-liberal notion of the self, and indeed on humanism, conducted at the level of narrative form, in works which remain capable nonetheless of accommodating complexities of thinking and feeling. Thus, in novels such as *The Planetarium* and *Do You Hear Them?*, Sarraute gives voice to what she calls the 'sub-conversation', the train of flickering impressions and barely formulated thoughts that grow and wilt in an instant, and which seem to explode any notion of a coherent, established self.[45] So too, in Mauriac's *The Marquise Went Out at Five*, the narrative shifts bewilderingly from consciousness to consciousness, trying 'to catch this murmur of ordinary life', and yet the central focus is none of these persons, but rather the Carrefour de Buci, through which they pass at greater and lesser speeds.[46] As for Robbe-Grillet, he says explicitly that his novels refuse and refute 'the idea of an interiority', as well as 'the *humanist* point of view'.[47]

What is evident in the works of both Robbe-Grillet and Mauriac is indeed a desire for a kind of scientific rigour and an art of objects, if not an objective art. Thus, Mauriac's novel regards its aims as achievable only by a writing that operates 'like a machine geared to retain one kind of data rather than another', a writing which seeks out 'a truth in which literal exactitude was preferred to literature'.[48] And for Robbe-Grillet, whose *Jealousy* pushes the first person perspective to (and perhaps over) the limits of impersonality, he says that the 'exclusive cult of the "human" has given way to a larger consciousness, one that is less anthropocentric', and calls for a writing 'that contents itself with measuring, locating, limiting, defining'.[49]

Without being anything like a satisfactory overview of the *nouveau roman*, this brief sketch should suggest that there were models available to Coetzee, of which he knew, for a thoroughgoing deformation of narrative modes wedded to liberal-humanist subjectivity. And yet, though he agreed with Robbe-Grillet that the 'novel of character' was defunct, and that it belonged to a preceding 'stage in the history of the middle class', his narrators and indeed characters seem somewhat conservative when compared with those of the *nouveau roman*.[50]

Here, two things seem important. The first has to do with Coetzee's sense of the *nouveau roman*'s achievements, and thus the basis for his own indebtedness. Of Mauriac's *The Marquise Went Out at Five*, he suggests that its aim is more limited than the novel itself claims, that its purpose, faced with the impossibility of escaping illusionism, is simply to decode the codes of fiction. This, certainly, was not Coetzee's objective, as we have suggested already in relation to Beckett. Instead, what Coetzee says he learned from Robbe-Grillet is the lesson repeated in 'Hero and Bad Mother in Epic', a lesson about putting narrative together: 'from the point of view of structuration I think that Robbe-Grillet ... has certainly been an example to me of a certain kind of fluid complexity.'[51]

The second matter of importance, however, relates to what Coetzee does *not* take from the *nouveau roman*, which is, above all, its stance towards humanism, and indeed the human. Thus, in response to Robbe-Grillet's assertion that the 'cult of the "human" has given way to a larger consciousness', Coetzee says that he does not understand what 'larger consciousness' means. Taken in isolation, this may be little more than a quibble with the implicit metaphysics of the statement; but, seen in the context of Coetzee's other writings, it suggests, to me at least, an important point of departure, which has to do precisely with the humanism of Coetzee's novels.[52]

Here again, the divergence in subject matter seems the most pertinent ground on which to clarify this departure, particularly if we set the urban and urbane bourgeois Parisian milieux of Sarraute's and Mauriac's novels against what we find in Coetzee's (though even *Jealousy*, with its colonial setting, does not deal with the peculiar maladies of colonial existence). If we consider the action of *Waiting for the Barbarians*, on the other hand, we might say, in very broad terms, that the novel describes the beginning of a conflict between the Empire and those beyond its borders, the initiation of what we might call a struggle to the death, a manichean conflict in which there are only allies and enemies. Moreover, at the level of interpersonal relations, there is a story of a dwindling and ultimately extinguished possibility of reciprocity. Finally, at the level of the narrator, the novel describes a gradual stripping away of all the accoutrements of the self, a sloughing off of everything that gives the person of the Magistrate social weight and social presence.

In this, we might note, *Waiting for the Barbarians* differs from *Dusklands* and *In the Heart of the Country*, both of which begin and end in the midst of the nightmare that is existence laid bare, where the self is already in thrall to the other. Here, in contrast, we witness the event of the catastrophe, and feel its greater force precisely because we see its gradual effects, which in turn are visible because the figure presented to us is possessed of a personhood from which we are not immediately alienated. Not only that: this personhood and its deepest longings are suffused with a certain poetry. And so we begin to see why it is that the Magistrate must so closely resemble the self of romantic-liberalism.

What am I claiming here? Only that, though the novel may indeed be a critique of the compromises forced on the liberal in times of political crisis and necessity, and though it may well ask questions of a certain notion of the self, it does not and cannot reject completely the possibility of a fuller humanity. For the increasing terror and bareness of a diminishing life, exposed by the narrative's progress, are understood as losses, and not simply as features of an existential human condition, or consequent on the inevitable absence or aporia or différance that conditions and undermines all self-identity and self-presence.

And yet we must be reminded that lyricism, and the fullness of the Magistrate's being, are themselves associated with a position of privilege and power that is from the outset both threatened with decay and anchored in the past and youth of Empire. Thus, the novel's humanism, if that is what we wish to call it, remains available only as utopian possibility, the negation of the badness of an inhuman present. The 'I' of the lyric has indeed been liquidated, but that is a cause for anguish, not celebration, an anguish we come to feel in our own longing for, loss of, and distance from a certain lyrical beauty, however compromised.

CHAPTER 4

Native Traditions and Strange Practices
The Metaphorics of Life & Times of Michael K

Towards a Grammar of Metaphor

In Coetzee's writings of the late 1970s and early 1980s one finds a more concerted engagement with rhetoric and rhetorical features of language. Metaphor, for example, already important in 'Hero and Bad Mother in Epic' and the essay on computer poetry, becomes the principal focus of 'Blood, Flaw, Taint, Degeneration', where Coetzee traces, through the South African novels of Sarah Gertrude Millin, a series of root metaphors that constitute a 'metaphorics of blood degeneration', an 'imagery' and 'poetics of blood'.[1]

This interest in metaphor impacts upon Coetzee's fictions most forcefully in *Life & Times of Michael K*, for reasons that will become evident as this chapter progresses. One might note in the meantime that the various characters and narrators in this novel are perpetually seeking some way of understanding its eponymous protagonist, some conceptual framework into which to translate him. Their quest, in other words, is for an appropriate means by which to figure K. Thus, the novel is concerned thematically with processes fundamental to metaphor.

If Coetzee was clearly preoccupied with metaphor in the period during which both *Life & Times of Michael K* and the essay on Millin were composed, might we identify in his own novels a structure of metaphor as systematic as that which he finds in Millin, if less the product of half-conscious prejudice? Is it possible, in other words, to delineate the metaphorics of Coetzee's early fictions? To answer this, one would need a clearer sense of what a 'metaphorics' is, but there is no comprehensive definition in 'Blood, Flaw, Taint, Degeneration'. Nevertheless, Coetzee's presuppositions regarding metaphor might be gleaned from other writings of the period.

In 'Linguistics and Literature', he noted that linguists working within the framework of transformational grammar had shown little concern for what they considered deviant forms. Indeed, Coetzee observed that in Noam Chomsky's original formulation, there was 'no way of dealing with metaphor except as an infringement of lexical category boundaries'. This state of affairs had since gone un-remedied, for there had not yet been any 'substantial studies of the grammar of metaphor or of the language of individual poets in the transformational tradition'.[2]

In another essay of 1982, on Isaac Newton's scientific language, Coetzee might not have articulated his own 'grammar of metaphor', but he did give clearer expression to his views on the nature and function of figurative language. Intending to test Whorf's hypothesis that language determines thought, Coetzee analysed Newton's *Principia*, making a series of observations on its attitude towards metaphor, and on the role of figurative language in epistemic shifts. For Newton, Coetzee argued, the struggle to describe a reality perceived in mathematics was ultimately the struggle for a 'pure language in which a pure, pared-down, unambiguous translation of the truths of pure mathematics' could be achieved. Seen 'from Newton's own perspective', Coetzee believed that the 'problem of expounding' the theory of gravitational force should be understood as a 'problem of finding words in which to do so, and specifically as a problem of finding matter-of-fact, non-metaphoric words'.[3]

Ultimately, Coetzee notes, this venture was quixotic, for if a metaphor-free language is not wholly chimerical, saying 'anything significant or new' without recourse to metaphor is unlikely to be possible.[4] Indeed, he cites Richard Boyd's observation that the metaphors of scientific discourse are often '*constitutive* of the theories they express, rather than merely exegetical'.[5] Nor does Coetzee believe that a word used figuratively might slowly die into its proper meaning, cleansed of everything obscure, transitory and inessential, coming through its death to register the truth of reality. For Coetzee, 'there is something inherently unsatisfactory about this explanation', which is based on a 'radical idealism' according to which the 'mind gropes' towards pure concepts by means of 'metaphorical thinking', attaining these concepts as the 'impurities of secondary meanings are shed and language becomes transparent, i.e., becomes thought'.[6]

If Coetzee largely accepts its impossibility, he nevertheless believes 'the ideal of a pure language ... deserves a more extended discussion'.[7] This would not be to deny that language determines many 'metaphysical pre-conceptions of the language community'; it would only be to avoid the wholesale adoption of linguistic relativism, and to acknowledge what 'we find in Newton': 'a real struggle ... to bridge the gap between the non-referential symbolism of mathematics and a language too protean to be tied down to single, pure meanings'. A struggle, in other words, to find a means of conveying a truth about reality not yet articulated in natural language.

On the basis of these various comments, we might set down Coetzee's beliefs about metaphor as follows. First, metaphor is neither a function of syntax nor of linguistic deviance, but is instead fundamental to language and the way we perceive the world. Second, figurative and non-figurative language can nevertheless be differentiated, not least because of long-established conventions according to which the former is considered the preserve of literary writing, and the latter is associated with precise and objective descriptions of reality. However, because metaphor is in fact ubiquitous, the difference can only be relative: literary texts will be marked by creative instances, whereas scientific texts will be restricted to metaphors naturalized through heavy use. Third, it is precisely those metaphors that have been naturalized, and which are therefore used without any sense of their metaphoricity, that point to the ideological presuppositions of a language community.

What is striking about Coetzee's conception of metaphor is that it accords in most respects with the grammar of metaphor – the description of its basic units and their laws of combination and inflection – that was being formulated elsewhere and at much the same time. In 1980, George Lakoff first published his seminal *Metaphors We Live By* (co-authored with Mark Johnson), which argued that metaphor was not a deviant use of language, but something fundamental to the perceptual schemas of different speech communities.[8] Though Lakoff was not primarily interested in literature, he and Mark Turner would later outline, in *More than Cool Reason*, the relation between literary uses of metaphor and the basic conceptual metaphors of the English language. By drawing on this work in particular, it is possible to develop Coetzee's notion of a metaphorics.

Metaphor, for Lakoff, always involves a conceptual mapping of source domain onto target domain. For example, in the conceptual metaphor LIFE IS A JOURNEY, the target domain LIFE is understood in terms of the source domain JOURNEY.[9] There is an important distinction in Lakoff's early work between this kind of conceptual metaphor and its linguistic instances: 'Linguistic expressions – mere sequences of words – are not metaphors in themselves. Metaphors are conceptual mappings. They are a matter of thought, not merely language.' It is in any case necessary that every basic conceptual metaphor depends on thought that is simple and precise, a proposition Lakoff and Turner refer to as the 'grounding hypothesis': 'metaphorical understanding is grounded in semantically autonomous conceptual structure'.[10]

Whatever the shortcomings of this theory, it enables the systematic classification of a literary work's metaphorical instances on the basis of shared source and target domains. These instances can then be further divided among (a) unconscious uses of basic conceptual metaphors; (b) uses that extend, elaborate or combine basic metaphors; and (c) the invention of entirely new conceptual mappings. Where the focus is on literary style, instances of the first kind are of little interest, for they provide insight only into structures of thought inherent in a language. Instances of the third category, on the other hand, will likely be found only in the most radical works, because entirely new mappings tend to be characteristic of 'the avant-garde in any age'.[11] As such, stylistic analysis will concern itself primarily with the extension and combination of basic metaphors, whether such instances have become conventional by long use, or are marked by an inventive freshness of thought and expression.

With these distinctions in mind, we might begin to analyse Coetzee's own metaphorics. One matter, however, requires further elucidation: the syntactical differences between varieties of metaphor. Neither Lakoff nor Coetzee gives much weight to these, and in the analysis to follow, *metaphor* likewise signifies a whole range of forms, including those traditionally described as similes, personifications and comparisons, as well as the kinds of clause introduced by 'as if'. What therefore constitutes an instance of metaphor is a mapping of source onto target domains, regardless of how this mapping occurs, though each linguistic form undoubtedly has its own connotations.[12]

Rather than give an exhaustive account of metaphor across Coetzee's early novels, the focus here will be on the metaphorics of *Life & Times of Michael K*, and specifically on those conceptual mappings foregrounded through repetition, reflexive use and inventiveness. When these factors are combined, we encounter mappings that contribute most to the work's stylistic distinctiveness. Elsewhere, repetition and reflexivity draw our attention to otherwise conventional instances, which we might thus consider more summarily.

In *Life & Times of Michael K*, the majority of such conventional instances can be identified with a single fundamental mapping, which we might call the concretization metaphor because things that are relatively abstract or immaterial are figured as things that are more palpable and solid. By and large, the specific source and target domains of such mappings are not repeated, though certain basic metaphors do recur, as is the case with TIME IS A FLUID, instances of which include: 'time was poured out upon him in such an unending stream'; 'time flowing slowly like oil ... washing over his body, circulating in his armpits and his groin, stirring his eyelids'; 'all that was moving was time, bearing him onward in its flow'; and 'currents of time swirling and eddying'.[13] Other recurrent examples of the concretization metaphor include IDEAS ARE SEEDS, of which an instance is 'he watched the thought begin to unfold itself in his head, like a plant growing' (129); and BODIES ARE CONTAINERS and EMOTIONS ARE FLUIDS, which are often compounded: 'his body was overflowing with vigour' (133); 'felt his heart suddenly flow over' (156); 'it was exactly as they had described it, like a gush of warm water' (156); 'Irritation overflowed in me' (189).

None of these instances or their basic mappings is very unusual. Indeed, one might say of concretization metaphors in general that, if they are not fundamental to the English language, they certainly have an important place in the rhetorical repertoire of English-language novelists, not least because they lend immediacy to things that are otherwise diffuse or difficult to imagine. In any case, it is with this effect that instances of the concretization metaphor are deployed in *Life & Times of Michael K*, as in all of Coetzee's early novels, though this is not done without a degree of reflexivity, such as is evident when K registers the truth of the simile that says love is like warm water gushing.

Understood in this way, the concretization metaphor is clearly related to instances of personification, for the description of non-human entities in human terms imbues with familiarity the relatively alien natural and animal worlds. Although personification is not an especially large category in the metaphorics of *Life & Times of Michael K*, a particular cluster of instances is worth remarking. These figure the earth and the pumpkins and melons K coaxes into life in terms of the human family: 'once that cord was broken, the earth would grow hard and forget her children' (150); 'he loved these two, which he thought of as two sisters' (155); 'The first fruit, the firstborn' (155); 'he ate these two children' (162); 'We are all the children of the earth' (190).

Within the narrative, these particular instances are grounded in the thoroughly conventional EARTH IS MOTHER metaphor, which suggests itself once Anna K has been buried on the farm, and thereafter becomes the basis for the more expansive THINGS OF THE EARTH ARE FAMILY. However conventional, the rhetorical force of these personifications should not be underestimated, for they lend to K's gardening a peculiar charge, which is especially evident when K comes to harvest the first of his pumpkins.

Because we repeatedly read that K thinks of these fruits as his own children, the detailed description of his preparation and feast is at once joyous, compelling and unsettling, a moment of great tenderness but also horror. When we read, for example, that 'the knife sank in without a struggle', the prior identification of pumpkin with 'first fruit' and 'firstborn' allows this to mean both the ease with which K slices and the firstborn's lack of resistance (155).

A premonition of precisely this double meaning is found in the specific mapping of 'first fruit' with 'firstborn', an allusion to Numbers 18:13–15, in which both terms appear in the context of sacrifice and specifically burnt-offerings. The web of associations that links these terms and K's actions with the Binding of Isaac (Genesis 22:1–24) becomes, in turn, a means of re-enlivening the dulled metaphoricity of 'skin' and 'flesh' in such descriptive sentences as 'The fragrance of the burning flesh rose into the sky' (155) and 'Beneath the crisply charred skin the flesh was soft and juicy' (156).

Given that concretization and personification allow the novelist to produce effects of immediacy and force, the substantial presence of these metaphors in Coetzee's novels may help to explain why his literary prose has been so often described as something *vivid*, *hard* and *sharp*. These mappings do not, however, account for the most inventive instances of Coetzee's metaphorics.

For these, we must consider two more of the basic metaphors in *Life & Times of Michael K*, PEOPLE ARE ANIMALS and PEOPLE ARE THINGS, which together account for almost half the novel's metaphorical instances, and a far greater proportion of those that are inventive. In its general form, however, PEOPLE ARE ANIMALS is itself fairly conventional. It is common, for example, to speak of someone who acts like an ass, eats like a pig, sleeps like a dog, sings like a bird, laughs like a horse, dances like a monkey, and even lives like an animal.

There are certainly examples of such conventional mappings in *Life & Times of Michael K*. These include such properly idiomatic expressions as 'the sheep from the goats' (151) and 'at odds like hawk and mouse' (227), where the ground of correspondence is the hierarchical relation between two kinds of animal, a relation which has become proverbial. In cases such as 'I feel like a toad under a stone living here' (12), and 'I'm just a little fish in a big ocean' (89), the ground of correspondence is, instead, the relation between an animal and its environment.

The following examples all occur as similes, and likewise involve familiar mappings: 'He stole his mother's tea … gulping it down like a guilty dog' (41); 'He baulked, like a beast at the shambles' (55); 'He coughed, and gave a little hoot like an owl' (77); 'He thinks I am an idiot who sleeps on the floor like an animal' (85); 'Where would you rather sleep, out in the veld under a bush like an animal' (110); 'From being shut up like animals in a cage' (121); 'the rest of the squad moved like a swarm of locusts' (124); 'a man must be ready to live like a beast' (135); 'gone off like a sick dog to die' (212).

These similes can be distinguished from examples that take the form of what is usually understood by the word *metaphor*, where the source domain is less explicit: 'Michael sat with his ears pricked' (16); 'K was driven to the railway yards ... and herded into a lone carriage' (55–6); 'Herded back into the carriage at last' (58); 'Hunger had turned them into animals' (94); 'Whatever the nature of the beast that had howled inside him, it was starved into stillness' (94); 'A nest of vice, men and women all together' (112); 'men, women and children were herded on to the open terrain' (123–4); 'fix up that kennel of his' (173); 'pricking his ears' (186); 'driven back to the railway yards and herded' (218).

Given that these instances are taken largely from narrative moments in which the police, military or institutional authorities interact with groups of inmates or enemies, it is unsurprising that there is no necessity even to specify the animals of the source domain, but simply to gesture to the general category of the beast (understood here to include large domesticated animals, either livestock or beasts of burden) or to the general category of the parasite. The ground of these metaphors, in other words, is not so much behaviour or appearance, but rather a particular relation between social strata, that is, between classes of human dominant and dominated.

At this point, it is worth making two remarks concerning the instances of PEOPLE ARE ANIMALS noted thus far. The first relates to their narrative origin, and the second has to do with the conventionality of their particular source domains. With regard to the first, it should be remembered that several distinct voices constitute the narrative of *Life & Times of Michael K*. There are, of course, the two narrators (the external narrator of the first and third parts of the novel and the medical officer who is the character narrator of the second part), but there are also the mediated voices of the midwife, Anna K, Michael K, the Visagie grandson, Robert, Captain Oosthuizen, Noël, December, and a few others. It is significant that many of the instances of PEOPLE ARE ANIMALS cited previously originate not with K, but with these other characters.

It is Anna K, for example, who compares her situation with that of a toad under a stone, while it is the Visagie grandson who feels himself as insignificant as a small fish in a big ocean, and in whose thoughts K sees himself reflected as an idiot animal who sleeps on the floor. As for the notion of the camp as a nest of parasites, this originates with Captain Oosthuizen, before being taken up by the people of the camp and K himself. In the case of those instances in which the inmates of Huis Norenius and Jakkalsdrif are figured as beasts, their origin, for the most part, is the first narrator.

If we turn now to the second matter, it should be noted that, where humans are figured as animals, these tend to be of kinds familiar through either domestication or a perceived physiological or behavioural proximity. This explains the prevalence of both mammals and farmyard animals in the most commonplace expressions of this basic metaphor, as well as those proverbs and idioms that are themselves a means of domestication. For it is those creatures upon which we most rely, or with which we most closely interact, that most obviously remind us of our own animality, or that we most easily view in human terms. In the instances cited previously, the animals used as source domains tend to be of this kind, and on this basis these mappings are deemed relatively conventional.

However, though such instances of PEOPLE ARE ANIMALS occur quite often, their number is far exceeded by mappings of a more inventive kind. For *Life & Times of Michael K* frequently uses a range of stranger animals in its metaphors' source domains, invoking the insect world especially to figure human behaviours, appearances and modes of being. The first thing that the midwife, or anyone, notices about K is that that his lip is 'curled like a snail's foot' (3). There is nothing unusual in mapping animal onto human features: one might have a beak for a nose, the eyes of an owl, the ears of a monkey or, less commonly, the torso of a gorilla. It is odd, however, to use the anatomy of a creature so alien to human beings to figure the shape of a hare lip; and this oddness is further emphasized by the corresponding use of human anatomy ('foot') to describe part of a snail.

Treated in isolation, this instance might be understood as nothing more than an arresting means of describing K's appearance, one that produces in a reader, quite subtly, the discomfort characteristic of responses to both physical disfigurement and the world of earth and dirt and damp to which the snail belongs. But the creatures of this world – snails, lizards, stick insects, ants, termites, worms – are repeatedly used to figure K, as in the following: 'He thought of himself as a termite boring its way through a rock' (91); 'I am like an ant that does not know where its hole is' (114); 'Like a worm he began to slither toward his hole' (147); 'He crouched ...

feeling like a snail without its shell' (154); 'Like a parasite dozing in the gut' (159); 'like a lizard under a stone' (159).

In each of these mappings, K is not only target domain but also narrative origin, as he is in the great majority of such instances, though notable exceptions do occur in the novel's second part. Here, many of those mappings initially introduced by K are repeated by the medical officer, and the specific targeting of the central protagonist as a creature of earth and rock therefore becomes emphatic. The striking resonances, moreover, suggest that the real source of these metaphors is in any case the work's implied narrative consciousness, or indeed its style.

To begin with, the medical officer sees in K a harmless old man who needs care, and so thinks of him alternately in terms of the gentlest creatures, the ones for which it is easiest to feel sympathy, and of the less familiar creatures, the ones to which K himself is drawn. Thus, K is at once an injured pet, 'A mouse who quit an overcrowded, foundering ship' (187), 'a squirrel or an ant or a bee' (188), 'the weakest pet duckling ... or the runt of the cat's litter, or a fledgling expelled from the nest' (195); and also something more alien, even threatening, 'holding his face up to the sun like a lizard basking' (181), 'waving an arm like an insect's claw' (186), 'He moistened his lips with his lizard-tongue' (190).

There is, however, a particular moment at which the medical officer, whose ministrations are refused time and again, comes to view K more resentfully and aggressively: 'you have become an albatross around my neck. Your bony arms are knotted behind my head' (199). From this point onwards, the language of the narrative shifts, and K is now figured consistently as something belonging to a different order of existence. To this sequence belong such observations as 'his smile was repulsive, sharklike' (201), and 'you are the last of your kind, a creature left over from an earlier age, like the coelacanth or the last man to speak Yanqui' (207). Perhaps the most striking example is found in the passage in which the narrator develops one of his earlier comparisons:

> You are like a stick insect, Michaels, whose sole defence against a universe of predators is its bizarre shape. You are like a stick insect that has landed, God knows how, in the middle of a great wide flat bare concrete plain. You raise your slow fragile stick-legs one at a time, you inch about looking for something to merge with, and there is nothing. Why did you ever leave the bushes, Michaels? That was where you belonged. You should have stayed all your life clinging to a nondescript bush in a quiet corner of an obscure garden in a peaceful suburb, doing whatever it is that stick insects do to maintain life, nibbling a leaf here and there, eating the odd aphid, drinking dew. (204–5)

K, it is true, has never considered himself a stick insect, but the creature belongs in the same domain as the ant, the termite, the worm, the snail and the lizard, creatures low to the ground.

Towards the very end of the second section, in a moment of reflection, the narrative makes explicit the ground for all these mappings: a scale of animal being that begins with humans and moves from domestic animals and familiar mammals to the reptilian and, ultimately, the insectoid. The medical officer observes: 'putting you through the motions of rehabilitation would have been like trying to teach a rat or a mouse or (dare I say it?) a lizard to bark and beg and catch a ball' (223). Something as familiar as a dog is no longer considered a suitable point of comparison for K, and, ultimately, the lizard seems more appropriate than the rat or mouse. This scale of being is similarly invoked in the fairly disquieting notion of K as 'like a bunny-rabbit sewn up in the carcase of an ox' (225). The initial desire to see in K a fledgling or foundling or injured pet is confounded in this grotesque imagining, in which K's strangeness becomes manifest.

K himself recognizes the desire of others to view him as a creature needing help. In the novel's third part, he observes: 'They want me to open my heart and tell them the story of a life lived in cages. They want to hear all about the cages I have lived in, as if I were a budgie or a white mouse or a monkey' (247). But the manner in which K sees himself is quite different, and certainly has nothing to do with household pets, no matter how exotic: 'I am more like an earthworm, he thought. Which is also a kind of gardener. Or a mole, also a gardener, that does not tell stories because it lives in silence. But a mole or an earthworm on a cement floor?' (248).

This discussion leads to another of the basic metaphors of *Life & Times of Michael K*, indeed, its most inventive: PEOPLE ARE THINGS. For in one of K's earlier meditations on his own nature, there is an illustration of the difference between this basic metaphor and PEOPLE ARE ANIMALS: 'He thought of himself not as something heavy that left tracks behind it, but if anything as a speck upon the surface of an earth too deeply asleep to notice the scratch of ant-feet, the rasp of butterfly teeth, the tumbling of dust' (133). Here, K understands himself as something which is not a beast or large animal, human or otherwise, that might easily be noticed. On the contrary, if he is any kind of animal, it is something minute and insignificant, an ant or butterfly. But then, perhaps not even animals such as these properly describe K's being in the world. Perhaps, after all, he is nothing more than dust, or, at most, a plant, 'turning his face up like a flower' (136).

This is not the first time K has figured himself as something that has no capacity to think or feel, or, at least, that has no brain or nervous system. Much earlier in the narrative he wonders if he is perhaps 'the stony ground', and once he has begun his regime of idleness, he observes himself 'becoming smaller and harder and drier every day' (65, 93). In the camp at Jakkalsdrif, others – the children of the camp – seem to sense his affinity with the hard, dry stonescape of the Karoo: 'They clambered over him and fell upon him as if he were part of the earth' (116).

The medical officer too, from time to time, sees K not as a lizard or insect, but as some kind of automaton: 'He is like one of those toys made of sticks held together with rubber bands' (182). It is not long, however, before he realizes that K may be less (or more) than a cheap puppet, and again, he echoes K's thoughts:

> He is like a stone, a pebble that, having lain around quietly minding its own business since the dawn of time, is now suddenly picked up and tossed randomly from hand to hand. A hard little stone, barely aware of its surroundings, enveloped in itself and its interior life. He passes through these institutions and camps and hospitals and God knows what else like a stone. Through the intestines of war. An unbearing, unborn creature. I cannot really think of him as a man. (185)

K's stoniness is remarked by the medical officer in other moments – 'His face closed like a stone' (191), 'he stared stonily back' (192) – and in another of the extended similes of the novel's second section, the notion that K is a being of dust, earth and stone is combined with the notion of him as stick-man:

> With Michaels it always seemed to me that someone had scuffled together a handful of dust, spat on it, and patted it into the shape of a rudimentary man, making one or two mistakes ... but coming up nevertheless in the end with a genuine little man of earth, the kind of little man one sees in peasant art emerging into the world from between the squat thighs of its mother-host with fingers ready hooked and back ready bent for a life of burrowing, a creature that spends its waking life stooped over the soil. (220)

What remains to be said of instances of the metaphor PEOPLE ARE THINGS – which are in fact always instances of K IS A THING – is that they are often very strange, without being entirely alien. It is not unusual to figure someone as a plant or tree, or to remark a person's steely determination, iron will, craggy features or stony stare. Even the notion that man is dust is at least as old as the Book of Genesis.

On the other hand, though the source domains of these instances are not wholly unconventional, the grounds of their mappings very often are, for K is likened to stone and dust not because of his physical or psychological attributes, but because something about his mode of existence is reminiscent of these things. To the medical officer, the stone that is Michael K is not simply a dead, inanimate object, but an entity with its own kind of being, even its own inner world. Likewise, in K's imaginings, though the earth may be too sleepy to be aware of his miniscule existence, it is nevertheless something with the potential for such awareness. One might say, therefore, that a kind of personification precedes all these mappings. But this would only obscure what makes them so distinctive, which is that they imply modes of being in the world that are specifically non-human.

Nadine Gordimer and the Ideal of Totality

Thus far, the discussion of Coetzee's metaphorics has been largely descriptive, and necessarily so, because an understanding of its stylistic value requires a point of comparison, a relational literary context. To proceed to an interpretation of the use of metaphor in *Life & Times of Michael K*, one would need more than a general sense of the relative conventionality and inventiveness of its particular conceptual mappings. Here, Coetzee's essay on Millin is again helpful.

Early in the piece, Coetzee comments that Millin was a 'writer of considerable achievements, certainly the most considerable novelist writing in English in South Africa between Olive Schreiner and Nadine Gordimer'.[14] What Coetzee identifies in this moment is not only a particular literary tradition – that of the South African novel in English – but also its prominent position-takings, associated with established authors. Of these, Gordimer was undoubtedly pre-eminent, something of which Coetzee was more than aware.

In the interview of 1978, Stephen Watson asked Coetzee whether he admired any particular South African writers or saw himself as having any local literary forebears. Coetzee responded: 'This is not a great literature and there are no really gigantic figures in it.' As for his contemporaries, Coetzee had the following to say: 'I read mostly the stuff that, crudely speaking, I can cannibalize. There aren't many South African writers I feel like cannibalizing. If I want a good meal I go elsewhere. I read Nadine Gordimer because I think she's extraordinarily accomplished.'[15] The opinion expressed here of Gordimer's novels, that they are at least significant achievements, continues to surface elsewhere in this period.

From Coetzee's later review of Michael Wade's critical study, it is clear he had read Gordimer's novels thoroughly but thought them fairly conventional: 'Whatever she is, Gordimer is not an innovator in narrative method. *The Conservationist*, technically her most complex novel, does not use any technique that had not been used by 1930.' This does not mean Coetzee now believed Gordimer's achievements irrelevant, for, in rejecting Wade's claim that her novels had subverted 'the European mode of realist fiction', Coetzee noted: 'By trying to turn Gordimer into the kind of novelist she is not, Wade only damages the case for her as an important novelist in her own right, though of a fairly traditional cast.'[16] When interviewed by his French translator, Sophie Mayoux, and asked to situate himself in relation to Breytenbach, Brink and Gordimer, Coetzee again acknowledged the accomplishment of these writers while distancing himself from them. 'Je les admire tous' says Coetzee, 'Ce sont tous des êtres courageux et intègres. Ce sont tous de bons écrivains.... Mais en fin de compte, nous faisons tous des choses différentes.'[17]

These exact themes re-emerge more explicitly in a 1983 magazine article where Coetzee asks: 'if we are thinking of a Great South African Novelist, is there anyone past or present who has approached as near as Gordimer to being that mythical beast?' Indeed, Coetzee says here that he 'cannot imagine an informed literary jury anywhere in the world that would not place Gordimer among the top 25, or top 12, novelists at work today'. However, even more so than with Beckett or Robbe-Grillet, Coetzee's admiration need not indicate an identity of practice and orientation: 'As for writers like Etienne Leroux and myself who in our different ways work in modes less committedly realistic than Gordimer or Brink, I think (for reasons I will set out below) that our products are less likely to fall into the Great Novels class.'[18]

What one finds repeated across these several texts, then, is a double movement: on the one hand, Coetzee believes Gordimer is an important novelist of global stature; on the other hand, he asserts the difference between their literary practices. From the point of view of a relational stylistics, it is precisely this double movement that indicates the paramount importance of Gordimer's novels to an understanding of Coetzee's bare prose, for she was not only the most critically acclaimed South African novelist of the period, but also the greatest of Coetzee's local rivals.

It is therefore no surprise that comparisons with Gordimer began surfacing early in Coetzee's career.[19] Where technique has been taken into account, however, these have seldom done more than insist on Gordimer's realism and Coetzee's anti-realism. Yet the claims for Coetzee's anti-realism are overstated, and often beside the point, as I have been suggesting throughout, and Gordimer's fictions of the 1970s and early 1980s had period, its most comprehensive articulation found again in 'SA Authors Must Learn Modesty', where Coetzee observes that, 'as a practising writer', one is 'involved in a daily problem of wedding subject matter, or content' to '*form*'. In fact, Coetzee says, finding subject matter is not difficult, so long as one has some sense of 'what the world is like'. The real problem is that 'what you can say, what you can think, what you can feel, are always limited and defined by the forms in which they can be expressed.... And these forms, literary and linguistic, are not easily changed, much less invented.'[24] This problem is a most pressing one, because, as Coetzee suggests in 'Idleness in South Africa', whatever is most important or challenging about one's subject will remain obscured without some work on form.

With this in mind, we might consider more closely Coetzee's suggestion that the metaphorics of Millin's novels was not simply the product of her 'interest in race and blood', but also a response to the peculiar demands of writing about South Africa. According to Coetzee, Millin faced the dilemma of deciding which 'elements of the European novel' were 'relevant to the colonial situation'. Lacking the craft for the kind of 'adventurous response' that might have led her to a 'radical rethinking of the novel as a form', Millin simply 'takes over traditional European forms but adapts them in such a way that the field of conflict they exploit is a mixed field of race, caste and class rather than the difficult field of class alone'. In other words, responding to 'the problem of finding a social field rich enough to bear the transplanted European novel', Millin supplements the typology of class with an 'ethnic' typology that allows her to establish a 'system of characterological oppositions out of which to generate writing'.[25]

The metaphorics of blood can be understood to function in much the same way, that is, as an attempt to meet the technical challenges posed by the 'thinness' of settler-colonial society, by its lack of those intricate hierarchies and networks that characterize the European social milieux of the nineteenth and early twentieth centuries. Millin, Coetzee argues, redefines 'destiny' in terms of 'physiology and psychology', as the Naturalists had done, in order 'to exploit the themes and emotions of tragedy'.[26] By means of her metaphorics, blood becomes fate, for its various conceptual mappings constitute a framework within which miscegenation – the weakening or poisoning of the blood – is both a sin and a guarantee of doom. Observing that Millin's sympathies often 'flow against the deterministic scheme in whose terms she has chosen to see human evolution', Coetzee notes that this also is 'to Millin's advantage as a writer', for precisely 'This

already distanced her from the mode identified by Georg I
geois realism'.[20] Nevertheless, there *are* important differend
literary practices of Coetzee and Gordimer, some of whic
trated if we continue to focus on metaphor. First, however,
make some general observations about the tradition of the
novel in English, and about the challenges of subject matter.

It is a theme of Coetzee's essays of the period 1980 to 198;
the difficulties for South African authors – and colonial aut
eral – was the 'thinness' of settler society. At least, this is how
the problem in his essay on Millin, as well as 'Idleness in So
where it is implied that eighteenth-century travellers, nineteei
American novelists and early twentieth-century South Afric
shared a frustration with a local way of living that failed to pi
as proper subject matter. Instead, the societies they encounter
too coarse, too much lacking in nuance, too brutal and o
to be accommodated by the refined discursive forms elaborai
metropolis.[21]

Clearly, the situation of the novelist in apartheid South Afric;
much different. Here also, one confronted a society that, howe
and complex, yet remained too coarse, if not for its lack of sul
distinctions, then certainly for its manichean brutality. That this
in any case Coetzee's is intimated in 'SA Authors Must Learn N
where he recalls a 'British colleague' admiring the position of the v
South Africa, where there was '"a great subject staring you in the
Coetzee's only comment is that 'great subjects do not make gre;
els. Oppression and exploitation on a massive scale, the struggle
oppression and exploitation – these are certainly not a new subject.

This observation is striking precisely because it warns South A
authors against complacency, and against the belief that they might ;
the demands of their craft simply by recording apartheid's realities as
appeared in immediacy. To a similar end, Coetzee reminds his cou
men that they exist not at 'the cutting edge of history', but 'in the [
inces'. For this reason, 'the South African writer may have to learn t
modest, to accept that his historical destiny, and the destiny of his soc
are in no way special, that ... his relationship to the metropolis, like
of other African writers in English, is not all that different from wha
was seventy years ago.'[23]

In any event, the problem of subject matter will always be tied to t
struggle for new forms. This is another theme of Coetzee's writings of th

conflict of sympathy with system ... generates most of what we can loosely call the tragic interest of her novels'.[27]

If the metaphorics of blood was part of Millin's response to the thinness of settler society, what might we say about Gordimer's novels? How might they be understood to have met the challenges of a brute subject matter? The answer is to some extent obvious, since Gordimer's novels are remarkable for their detail, the range of their technical vocabularies, their capacity and desire to catalogue the world. From *The Lying Days* to *Burger's Daughter*, the descriptions are of such depth and breadth that they suggest a desire to sketch an entire field of class and race relations, to reproduce, at the level of character, as wide a range as possible of the subject-positions constituting the South African social totality.

In *The Conservationist*, for example, because the central figure Mehring avoids any extreme ideological position, he can be brought into contact with black farm labourers, Indian store-holders, black urban poor, white Anglo bourgeoisie, Afrikaans highveld farmers, white activists and bohemians, and coloured urban petit bourgeoisie. Not every one of these sociopolitical positions is accorded the privilege of focalized narrative, but the place of each is staked out nonetheless in a novel that is otherwise concerned with the progressive alienation of its chief protagonist and the dissolution of the idyll of the *plaasroman*. In *Burger's Daughter* too, Rosa Burger exists in a position sufficiently unattached to allow her interaction with communists, black nationalists, black petit bourgeoisie, Afrikaner nationalists, Afrikaner petit bourgeoisie, young bohemians, expatriates and exiles.

The characterology of these fictions therefore suggests a concern to map social totality, one that is no less evident in *July's People*.[28] Published in 1981 and depicting a South Africa of the near future in which revolution is under way, this novel of Gordimer's, more than any other, invites comparisons with Coetzee's work, and with *Life & Times of Michael K* in particular, on the basis both of a shared subject matter and certain formal similarities: *July's People* was remarkable in the context of Gordimer's oeuvre for its brevity, for the restricted time span of its action and for its focus on a very limited set of individuals in a highly localized context.

In spite of this restricted focus, however, *July's People* resonates with Gordimer's earlier novels in attempting an expansive invocation of South African reality. This aim is nowhere more purposefully pursued – and nowhere more evident – than in the novel's metaphorics. For through its figurative mappings, the narrative is able to transcend the limitations of scale and, in spite of the extreme and properly marginal position of its protagonists, sketch the shape of South Africa's socio-historical totality.

In some respects, the metaphorics of *July's People* remains close to that of *Life & Times of Michael K.* For example, metaphors of concretization and personification likewise account for almost half the novel's figurative mappings. On the other hand, instances of PEOPLE ARE ANIMALS constitute less than a tenth of the total number, and in the majority of cases the animal of the source domain is either mammalian or avian. As for PEOPLE ARE THINGS, this metaphor is hardly to be found, though there are cases in which the target is a human body part.

This relative lack, however, is compensated for by the proliferation of a very different set of mappings, by means of which one sphere of race or class existence is described in terms of another. The prevalence of this kind of figuration gives rise to the marked category of what we might for the time being call trans-social metaphor, instances of which account for more than a quarter of the total number in *July's People*. For the purposes of analysis, it is helpful to divide these instances into distinct sub-categories.

To begin with, there are several moments in which individuals are figured in terms of particular behavioural or occupational groups which are not in reality their own. So, for example, we read that July's 'head moved from side to side like a foreman's inspecting his workshop or a farmer's noting work to be done on the lands'.[29] Not long afterwards, Bam reflects that he is 'A butcher like any other in rubber boots among the slush of guts, urine and blood at the abattoir' (78), and, when Maureen stands naked before him, he thinks of her as 'like a man stripped in a factory shower or a woman in the ablution block of an institution' (90).

This manner of figuring individuals in terms of socio-economic identities is found throughout the novel. When the members of the Smales family are ordered to visit July's chief, for example, they encounter someone whose 'gait was suddenly recognizable as that of a city doorman or (to her, certainly) an *induna* who would sit on his fruit-crate outside the compound where the shift boss's labourers lived' (112). As in the previous instances, the source domain is expanded to include details of social existence that cannot be directly represented because they do not belong to the time or place of the narrative's action.

In instances such as these, moreover, Gordimer draws not on universal social types, but instead on particular milieux in a particular society, that of apartheid South Africa. In fact, for the most part, the source domains of such trans-social mappings are restricted to spheres of life with which the various characters are directly familiar. This is evident in the last example insofar as the narrator distinguishes between the 'city doorman' that each member of the Smales family can recognize, and the *induna* familiar only to Maureen because she has been raised on the mines. There are other moments in which this aspect of Gordimer's metaphorics is more explicit still, such as when Bam recalls that 'Before an operation for piles he had waited like this on a trolley in the hospital corridor' (114). Here, the narrative reveals the specific source domain of several earlier mappings: 'He did not read but did not put out the light: people in a hospital waiting-room in the small hours, not looking at one another' (48); 'talking over him as people talk over the supine man in his hospital bed' (110).

A more pervasive sub-category of trans-social mappings is one in which both source and target domains are particular realms of social existence. This kind of figuration frequently establishes a connection between the suburban life-world of the Smales family and the rural life-world of July, such that the former becomes a means of interpreting the latter, as in the following instances: 'the woman rested on the earth floor as among cushions' (15); 'the mats used as table-tops' (24); 'The headman of all the headmen. A personal assistant, adviser ... to the chief' (112); 'The red flags of religious sects and those that were the professional plates put up by *sangomas* ... stood out in bright, store colours' (113); 'beer-drink familiarity was of the order of pub acquaintance between men who never invited each other to their houses' (121); 'the concourse that was to these people newspaper, library, archives and theatre' (124–5).

The mapping involved here might be said to serve a number of purposes. On the one hand, it signals the cultural shock to which the Smales family is exposed, while providing Gordimer's middle-class readers with a means of understanding unfamiliar social practices and institutions. On the other hand, it operates in the manner of the instances of social typing discussed previously, allowing the narrator to describe aspects of the South African social field that are absent from the setting of the narrative itself.

This last function becomes especially evident when one considers instances in which the source domain is not the suburban life-world that Bam and Maureen have left behind, but some other, quite different sphere of South African existence. When Maureen joins the 'women in the fields', she recognizes, for example, that a few of them 'remarked on her to each other as they would of someone come to remark upon them – a photographer, an overseer' (91). If this is a glancing reference to the world of white farms on which these women occasionally work, an earlier meditation on the weekend routine in July's village leads to a comparison with the cultural practices of urbanized black workers: 'some kind of circling with little white flags like the green-and-white flags carried by the Zionist Church zealots to their services on vacant lots in the city' (34).

As a consequence of such mappings, the reader of *July's People* is allowed to glimpse whole vistas of social experience, which one is otherwise hurried past. Certain of these vistas, of course, are more easily and more often revealed than others. There are a great many instances, for example, in which the present situation of the Smales family allows for reference to previous experiences, so that events of the time of narration become keys to unlock the vault in which an entire social totality lies hidden. The mapping in these cases, which is always between 'this here' and 'back there', offers a fuller picture of their abandoned suburban lives.

Many of these instances draw attention to the concrete details of domestic existence. In their interactions with July, Bam and Maureen hear 'the echo of those visitors who came to stay in her house and tipped him when they left' (10), while the current restriction on their movement is measured in terms of mundane activities of the past: 'Maureen could not walk out into the boundlessness. Not so far as to take the dog around the block or to the box to post a letter' (27). There are several further examples in which present behaviour recalls a former life: 'As if he had been sent round the corner for a pint of milk when the household ran short' (53); 'Eating animated them in the way they attributed to wine, among friends, around a table' (79); 'Leave it, she said of the vehicle, as she had said of her lawn mower' (101); 'Bam was just as he was when the car keys were lost back there' (143). Encountering such instances throughout the novel, the reader easily guesses what 'detail' is meant in the moment that Maureen speaks to her husband 'as she did back there when domestic detail impinged upon the real concerns of her life' (68).

Not that it is the domestic realm alone that is thus remembered. The cultural activities and leisure pursuits of the white middle class also seep in. As Bam waits to kill the 'wart-hog family', the narrator remarks: 'It was a sight for tourists in a game reserve; drink in hand, legs crossed at the picture window of an air-conditioned bungalow' (74). Even the struggle to get the radio working is an opportunity to allude to holidays at the coast, 'The aerial wavered the single antenna of an injured crayfish he had once caught at Gansbaai' (124), while Maureen's momentary appearance, 'naked below the cardigan', suggests trips abroad, for she looks like 'a woman in the Toulouse-Lautrec brothel drawings they had seen together in Europe' (52).

So compulsive is the drive in *July's People* to a comprehensive charting of social existence that even the natural and animal worlds are soon littered with the fragments of human culture: 'scrubby trees pushed through them like limbs of plumbing exposed in a half-demolished building' (12); 'the aerials of raised tails' (74); 'a snout ..., shaped rather like an old steam railway-engine' (74); 'a veil of flies' (93); 'In a tin-bright angle of sunlight drawn by the slide-rule of the doorway' (123); 'The moon in the sky was a circle of gauze pasted up on the afternoon blue' (145); 'Muslin scraps of butterflies' (147); 'thorn-tree ... with its yellow tassels dangling from downy pink and mauve pom-poms' (147); 'wild figs bristled like bunches of hat-pins' (148); 'The gauze round of moon had become opaque and polished with the light of the vanished sun; it began to reflect, a mirror being adjusted' (150). In every one of these instances, the source domain is some tool or material that might be distributed by class and by gender. However, if the professional realm of the architect can be set against the domestic realm of the housewife, what each mapping has in common is an assertive, even aggressive turning from the animal and natural to the human and social. Anything that threatens to belong to a non-human world is thus immediately drawn in and domesticated.

In what I have said of *July's People*, I have been careful to speak more often of mapping than of metaphor, because there is a question as to whether different segments of a social field in fact constitute distinct conceptual domains, or a single such domain. If it is the latter – and the novel itself is an argument in favour of this view – then one should speak of meton-ymy rather than metaphor. For metonymy 'involves only one conceptual domain. A metonymic mapping occurs within a single domain, not across domains'.[30] From the point of view of the present discussion, however, there is little that turns on this distinction. Far more pressing is the ques-tion of how one is to understand the prevalence of trans-social figurations in *July's People*.

One way of answering this question is to read the novel as an attempt to expose the material conditions of South African liberalism. By constantly referring back to white middle-class existence, the narrative characterizes at once its superstructure and base. As such, when Bam and Maureen Smales come into contact with powerfully disorienting forces, what is revealed is the extent to which their ideological views were engendered in and guaranteed by the comfort of a 'master bedroom' (98, 117, 129).

There is undoubtedly a measure of validity in this reading, though it does not account sufficiently for the true variety and scope of trans-social mappings in *July's People* and, indeed, in Gordimer's other novels of the 1970s and early 1980s. A more compelling possibility is that the general purpose of such mappings is to offer as expansive a description as possible of South African social relations. In this way, these instances of metaphor and metonymy might be identified with a broader drive in Gordimer's novels – one equally evident in her characterology – to capture the totality of social existence.

This interpretation is encouraged by the knowledge that Gordimer's understanding of the novel had been substantially shaped by Georg Lukács. In his 1986 study of Gordimer's oeuvre, Stephen Clingman suggested that Lukács's conception of the relations between history, the subject and the literary work was a 'fair encapsulation of the perspective of most of Gordimer's writing'.[31] This closeness to Lukács is further evident in Gordimer's own literary criticism. In 1973, she referred to his critique of 'experimental modernism from Kafka and Joyce to Beckett and Faulkner' before suggesting that 'African English literature's best writers are critical realists'.[32] A decade later, Gordimer admitted to two 'absolutes' in her life: the belief that racism is evil, and the conviction that a 'writer is a being in whose sensibility is fused what Lukács calls "the duality of inwardness and outside world"'.[33]

Very early in his career, Lukács had insisted: 'For the epic' – by which he meant the novel as much as the epic proper – 'the world at any given moment is an ultimate principle; it is empirical at its deepest, most decisive, all-determining transcendent base'. For this reason, he believed that epic works ought to give 'form to the extensive totality of life'.[34] This position, this belief in totality as the defining aim of the novel, remained intact even after Lukács's conversion to Marxism, and in later literary-theoretical works he continued to argue: 'Epic and the novel are distinguished from all other minor varieties of the epic by this idea of totality.' Indeed, in epic, 'life appears in all its breadth and wealth', and 'an enormous part is played by the physical being of men, by the natural world surrounding them, by the things which form their environment, etc.; man is represented via the interaction of all these'.[35] If man was therefore always at the centre of the Lukácsian novel, it was in the first place as social man, for Lukács was convinced that 'The novel ... must represent the struggle of different classes, strata, parties and trends', and that its aim must be 'the portrayal of a total context of social life'.[36]

With this in mind, it is clear that Gordimer's indebtedness to Lukács marks not only her metaphorics, but other of her novels' distinctive features, such as the use of protagonists who are to some extent socially typical, and yet somehow marginal. This certainly accords with the Lukácsian injunction that novelists choose 'central figures who despite their "middle-of-the-road" personalities ... are nevertheless suited to stand at the meeting-point of great social-historical collisions'. Indeed – and here we see the significance of the unattached status of Rosa Burger and Mehring – such 'middle-of-the-road' heroes are fundamentally important because the 'relative lack of contour to their personalities, the absence of passions which would cause them to take up major, decisive, one-sided positions, etc. make them specially suited to express adequately, in their own destinies, the complex ramification of events in a novel'.[37]

By demonstrating the closeness of Gordimer's relation to Lukács, I do not mean to dismiss her work as in some sense derivative, but, on the contrary, to clarify what is most distinctive about her metaphorics, and indeed her literary practice. For in knowing more of Lukács, we see that the density of Gordimer's descriptive prose, the choice of her central characters and the prevalence of her use of trans-social figurative mappings are consequences of a desire to describe the totality of South African existence. Thus we come to understand that Gordimer's response to the thin reality of apartheid society was to fill it out, to pile up details and fragments, no doubt in order to ensure that its problematic complexity could be understood and resolved, but also as compensation for its bareness, for the amplitude that it lacked.

A Metaphorics of Existential Reduction

If it is fair to describe Gordimer as a proponent of the Lukácsian theory of the novel, Coetzee might as easily be portrayed as its antagonist, though the reasons for this are not widely understood. In 'Die skrywer en die teorie', an important yet infrequently cited conference paper delivered in Bloemfontein in 1980, Coetzee complained of what he regarded as the local resistance to literary theory, arguing that a combination of 'vulgar Marxism' and '*Practical Criticism*' held sway in South Africa and encouraged a 'highly anti-theoretical' attitude. Such an attitude was damaging because it prevented writers and critics alike questioning the orthodox view of 'the novel in the realist tradition', according to which 'the most effective manner in which to represent the reality of South African existence is that of realism, the mode of Balzac and Tolstoy, as interpreted in the twentieth century most notably by Georg Lukács'. What was either forgotten or ignored when such a position was adopted was that literary forms and genres always emerge from and give expression to particular 'world-views'. In this case, the kind of realism Lukács championed could not help 'dragging along a nineteenth-century' vision of reality. As Coetzee put it, the failure of those who continued to champion Lukácsian realism was therefore the failure to be 'historical enough'.[38]

It should be clear from what has been said that this attack on Lukács was also an attack on the tradition of the South African novel in English, and certainly on its chief practitioner, Nadine Gordimer. In fact, in the claim that outmoded forms are bound up with calcified modes of vision and division, and therefore insufficiently oriented towards reality, a connection is established here with Coetzee's earlier critique of Alex La Guma's fictions, his brief comments on Serote and Sepamla and also with his later and less polemical piece 'The Great South African Novel', where Coetzee again addressed, at least implicitly, the problems arising from Lukácsian theory.

Coetzee suggests that the Great South African Novel would have to be 'something more than merely a South African novel of very high literary quality'. At the very least, it would have to:

> (a) include a characterization of the society and historical times in which it is set; (b) employ techniques or presentation that make it accessible to most strata of society, and even in some measure to children; and (c) concern itself with themes that are not so local as to render them of marginal interest to readers elsewhere, and deal with these themes in such a way that they have, or seem to have, universal relevance.

The Great National Novel, in other words, would have to be 'characterized by breadth of social canvas, realistic technique, and universality'.[39]

Coetzee may not refer explicitly to him, but it is clear that the Great National Novel is in fact Lukács's novel, not only because of these requirements, but also because of the emphasis on the nation (which Lukács believed should always be the focus and framework of Great Epic) and because Coetzee ultimately identifies this mode with Gordimer. The problems that Coetzee raises with the South African variety of the Great National Novel are therefore of considerable interest. These, to begin with, include the difficulty of finding 'anyone who *knows* South African society well enough to present it in the depth and fullness that we ... would – legitimately – demand from a Great National Novel'.[40] This is a difficulty that Coetzee expressly associates with Gordimer when he observes that, in her writing, 'certain areas of South African experience seem to be known only from the outside or from theory'. The challenge, however, may be greater than finding the ideally positioned author, for there is a question whether 'South African society' in fact lacks 'that degree of organic unity' which would allow it to 'be known and represented from the inside out, as, let us say, Tolstoy does for mid-nineteenth-century Russian society'.[41]

Here again, the shadow of Lukács lingers, as does the spectre of outmoded literary practice, for Tolstoy, at least in Lukács's later work, is the exemplary novelist of bourgeois realism, able to capture in a paradigmatic way the totality of Russian national experience. What makes such a paradigm untenable for the South African novelist, according to Coetzee, is that the totality at which the Great National Novel aims may be impossible simply because South Africa is 'merely an agglomeration of people within a more or less unitary economic organization', a society 'marked by disunity, fragmentation, internal antagonisms, anomie, and above all by a multiplicity of languages'. At the very least, such incoherence denies the South African author the kind of knowledge necessary to produce a Great National Novel, the 'knowledge of the intimate and petty variety that the realist novel thrives on'. Coetzee is therefore led to warn his fellow authors and readers that they should not 'stare so intently at the horizon searching for the Great South African Novel' that they are blinded 'to other possibilities'.[42]

But what might these other possibilities be? And how are they related to Coetzee's own novels? These questions can be dealt with more easily if we consider the earlier discussion of form and subject matter, on which basis we might say that Coetzee's response to the problem of South African material was something very different from Gordimer's. Here I wish to stress again that this difference is not satisfactorily articulated simply by referring to Coetzee's anti-realism and Gordimer's realism. On the contrary, to understand precisely how Coetzee's novels distinguished themselves from the dominant tradition of the South African novel in English, it is necessary to situate Gordimer's metaphorics, and her literary practice more broadly, in relation to a particular set of European authors of the nineteenth century, a particular kind of realism, and a particular theory of the novel. In this way, Gordimer's fictions of the 1970s and early 1980s can be characterized with greater clarity in terms of a project not simply to confront the real, but to do so by representing the extensive totality of a nation's life-worlds.

Set against this project, distinct from it but necessarily defined in relation to it, is a literary practice that I have identified throughout with a process of paring down, stripping away, laying bare. When its specificities and peculiar qualities are brought to the fore, what is remarkable about this practice is not its anti-realism, but the manner in which it is oriented towards the real, and, more concretely, the way it refuses to aim at totality. In its approach to South African subject matter, this is therefore a style that seeks neither to evade, nor to compensate for, the brutishness of reality, but to encounter such aspects of existence plainly.

Here we might return to 'Idleness in South Africa', in which Coetzee concludes that even the best-meaning anthropologists are unlikely to meet the challenge posed by the Hottentots of the Cape; unlikely, that is, to see idleness in any other terms than those of production, or to overcome the 'temptation to claim that there is something *at work* where there is nothing'. The hope that Coetzee invests in his essay is that it might open 'a way for the reading of idleness since 1652 as an authentically native response to a foreign way of life'.[43] With this hope in mind, it is not unreasonable to suggest that Coetzee's literary practice aimed likewise not to constitute South African reality as a kind of fullness, in the mode advocated by Lukács and adopted by Gordimer, but rather to confront what it was about the local subject matter that most frustrated writers, that is, its 'thinness'.

It is in this way that we can read *Life & Times of Michael K* as a work that intervenes at a very particular moment and in response to a very specific configuration of the South African literary field. This is a novel, after all, in which very little in fact happens, and whose hero is marginal in the extreme, something explicitly outlawed by Lukács. This is a novel, moreover, that repeatedly and in a number of different ways stages the difficulty of trying to tell new stories with old forms and paltry material.

This difficulty is nowhere clearer than in K's struggle to understand the meaning of his existence, for his own story here becomes a burden to him. In this regard, it is important to recognize that, while he may fear those who wish to know the story of his life, this fear is associated in the narrative – at least in its first and third parts – with K's belief that his story is uninteresting, even boring (92, 240), and that he in any case lacks the capacity to tell this story well (108, 240). On the other hand, there is something about his life that K himself does not understand, some piece that remains obscure and therefore denies him the experience of his own meaning, the completion of his own story (122, 151, 240).

What needs to be emphasized here, however, and in spite of what the narrator of the novel's second part might believe, is that there are moments in which K *does* in fact wish to tell his story, or at least finds the idea of having an interesting story appealing. He thinks enviously, for example, of the tales the guerrillas will have, which will be different from those K has 'heard in the camp, because the camp was for those left behind, the women and children, the old men, the blind, the crippled, the idiots, people who have nothing to tell but stories of how they have endured' (150). K, in other words, is neither unaware of, nor insensitive to, the fact that the guerrillas will have 'adventures, victories and defeats and escapes. They will have stories to tell long after the war is over, stories for a lifetime, stories for their grandchildren to listen to open-mouthed' (150).

By remaining with his farm, or rather his garden, K simply chooses to have a different kind of story, a narrative that is neither of adventure nor of patient suffering. Nor is it a narrative of the enduring prisoner, to which K is particularly averse, though he knows that others wish to hear it from him:

> They want me to open my heart and tell them the story of a life lived in cages. They want to hear about all the cages I have lived in, as if I were a budgie or a white mouse or a monkey. And if I had learned storytelling at Huis Norenius instead of potato-peeling and sums, if they had made me practise the story of my life every day, standing over me with a cane till I could perform without stumbling, I might have known how to please them. I would have told the story of a life passed in prisons where I stood day after day, year after year with my forehead pressed to the wire, gazing into the distance, dreaming of experiences I would never have, and where guards called me names and kicked my backside and sent me off to scrub the floor. When my story was finished, people would have shaken their heads and been sorry and angry and plied me with food and drink; women would have taken me into their beds and mothered me in the dark. (247)

Thus, K does not so much reject out of hand the desire to structure his life by narrative, as resist attempts to give it a shape he does not properly recognize. In this regard, it is of interest that, by 1983, both the stories K refuses – that of adventurer and that of prisoner – had become well established and even conventional in the South African literary field.

If the difficulty of thin subject matter is thus staged in Michael K's struggle to make of the paltry material of his life a story of a different kind, it is likewise dramatized in the novel's second part. Although the medical officer who narrates this part is by no means the only figure afflicted by the desire to find K's story and thereby his meaning, he is certainly the most persistent, and indeed imaginative, of K's would-be interpreters.[44]

In the first story that the medical officer tells of K, he is an insurgent, a member and supplier of the guerrilla forces operating in the mountains close to Prince Albert (177). When this story is discarded, the one that takes its place casts K instead as an idiot, a sport of nature, too stupid to manage anything but the simplest tasks, certainly incapable of gardening on his own, and probably coerced or tricked into helping the guerrillas (179–80). In a different version, the most radical, the medical officer suggests that '*There is nothing there*, ... no story of the slightest interest to rational people' (194). Ultimately, the frustration born of K's silence engenders narratives that are more obviously analogical or metaphorical.

K becomes a prodigy, and also a meaning that can 'take up residence in a system without becoming a term in it' (228).

It is not at all surprising that the last of these stories about K is often regarded as the key to understanding Coetzee's novel, at least by critics who wish to make of it an allegory of deconstruction. What is often ignored, however, is the dramatic irony generated by these different versions of K's life and dependent on the fact that the reader, unlike the medical officer, has the privilege of knowing a great deal of K's story, which, after all, occupies the whole of the narrative's first part. The reader is therefore in a position to see that each of the medical officer's attempts to assign meaning to K comes up short, gets things wrong, mistakes crucial elements. The medical officer, in other words, is here not unlike Eugene Dawn and Magda, for the stories that he describes are not exactly those that we read.

At the very least, the medical officer remains blind throughout to K's own desire for a story. I would therefore suggest that *Life & Times of Michael K* is not a novel about the absolute impossibility of telling stories and assigning meaning. Rather, it is a story in search of itself, of its particular shape, what it is and what it is about. The novel thus tells an unusual kind of story, a paltry story, a story not easily told, and, in this way, confronts thematically the thinness of its subject matter.

For all its failures, the medical officer's struggle to narrate K does yield an insight into the nature and function of metaphor, because, as we have noted already, K's intransigence requires that his would-be amanuensis resort to less prosaic modes of storytelling. This leads to the analogical accounts mentioned previously, but also to a version of K's life that is best described as metaphysical, and that begins to emerge when the medical officer wonders whether K thought himself 'a spirit invisible, a visitor on our planet, a creature beyond the reach of the laws of nation' (206).

It is the first of these possibilities that is elaborated as the medical officer laments 'There is no home left for universal souls, except perhaps in Antarctica or on the high seas' (207). The lament grows very quickly into a reprimand and a plea, couched in a meditation on the progress of the soul:

> And do not think you are simply going to waste away, grow more and more insubstantial till you are all soul and can fly away into the aether … I am the only one who sees you for the original soul you are. I am the only one who cares for you. I alone see you as neither a soft case for a soft camp nor a hard case for a hard camp but a human soul above and beneath classification, a soul blessedly untouched by doctrine, untouched by history, a soul stirring its wings within that stiff sarcophagus, murmuring behind that clownish mask. (207)

The passage is a striking one, not least because it raises a number of difficult questions concerning the identification and analysis of metaphor. The most pressing of these is whether this conception of K as a universal soul should not in fact be treated as an instance of figurative mapping. The novel itself seems to imply that it should, at least insofar as 'spirit invisible' is roughly equated with the spacemen and monsters of comic book fantasy. Perhaps more significant, the language used to describe the soul seems purposefully archaic, even arcane, not only because it includes such words as *aether* and *sarcophagus*, but also because it recalls both the teachings of the Church Fathers and ancient metaphysicians, and in particular Plato, whose *Phaedrus* contains an explicitly figurative account of the winged soul.

What we encounter in this passage then is a way of speaking about the world that may no longer be accorded the truth value associated with, for example, scientific discourse, but that yet retains a certain resonance and remains available for quasi-figurative description. As such, it is related to another way of speaking that we encounter often in Coetzee's early fictions, one that is concerned with being, and which we might therefore call ontological. Without entering into a discussion of the various philosophical accounts of being, we might simply note that these metaphysical and ontological ways of speaking are instantiations of what Lakoff and Turner refer to as 'cultural models', sets of commonplace suppositions about the ordering of existence that may or may not accord with empirical fact. Lakoff and Turner discuss such models because, as they argue, the capacity of members of a language community to understand inventive metaphorical instances lies in shared systems of belief about reality, in customary ways of seeing it and dividing it up into distinct but nevertheless corresponding domains.

The insight that mapping between conceptual domains necessarily implies a particular ordering of reality is not entirely new. Indeed, Aristotle's *De Anima* suggests that the ultimate basis for comparison between things in the world is the soul: it is because all things have souls that they can be related to one another. The different kinds of souls are like different geometric shapes; with them too there is a progression from simplicity to complexity such that the more complex exceed the simpler by incorporating them. 'It is clear then', says Aristotle, 'that there will be one account of the soul in the same way that there will be one account of shape. For in the case of shape there is no shape in addition to the triangle and those in series from it, and in this case there will be no soul in addition to the ones we have mentioned. Yet even in the case of the figures there would be a general account, which will fit all but be peculiar to no one figure. And so it is also with the souls that we have mentioned'.[45]

Aristotle's discussion of the soul is relevant here not only because of the references to ancient metaphysics in the medical officer's narrative, but also because Lakoff and Turner argue that an understanding similar to that articulated in *De Anima* continues to operate as a powerful cultural model, a hierarchical arrangement of various modes of existence that produces 'a certain sense of the order of things', a knowledge, generally taken for granted 'about man's place in the universe'. Lakoff and Turner call this model the 'Great Chain of Being', and insist that 'a highly articulated version' of it 'still exists as a contemporary unconscious cultural model indispensable to our understanding of ourselves, our world, and our language'.[46]

Indeed, it is on the basis of this model that there exists 'a vertical scale with "higher" beings and properties above "lower" beings and properties', for the 'Great Chain is a scale of forms of being – human, animal, plant, inanimate object – and consequently a scale of the properties that characterize forms of being – reason, instinctual behavior, biological function, physical attributes, and so on'.[47] It should be emphasized that this kind of cultural model is neither a matter of empirical knowledge, nor properly universal, but is rather a manner of speaking about the world common to particular groups and periods. Nor should it be a surprise that postmodernist and poststructuralist critiques have striven to break this chain, though whether they have had much substantive success is open to question.

Certainly, the Great Chain of Being appears to be operative in Coetzee's early fictions not only as a way of speaking, but as the ultimate ground of their metaphorics, the means by which different entities are both separated into distinct conceptual domains and compared. After all, even the notion that there is a graded relation between the tangible and the intangible is dependent on this kind of ordering of the world. More important, the Great Chain of Being is the necessary condition for all instances of PEOPLE ARE ANIMALS and PEOPLE ARE THINGS. This is especially true of the most inventive mappings, for, if we can say that K is a stone, or that K is like an ant, without needing to specify any further the particular qualities that might ground such a mapping, this is because, within the framework of the narrative, each of these things – K, stone and ant – has a kind of being.

Not that Coetzee invokes the Great Chain of Being without in some way modifying it, for he would then be guilty of the kind of half-conscious deployment of a cultural model that one finds in the metaphorics of Sarah Gertrude Millin, and, indeed, those conventional mappings between animal and human which intend only the debasement of the latter. On the contrary, in *Life & Times of Michael K*, the most inventive mappings require that certain of the boundaries between modes of being are blurred. This is most apparent wherever inwardness or consciousness is attributed not simply to animals, but to non-living entities, in this case to pebbles and stones, but in the earlier novels to bushes and plants also. It is from this that an understanding of the world emerges which flows against the tide of most articulations of the Great Chain of Being, according to which man is distinct in having reflexive consciousness, animals in general are distinct in having sense perception and all living things are distinct in requiring nourishment and having the capacity to reproduce.

As such, the metaphorics of *Life & Times of Michael K*, and, indeed, all Coetzee's early novels, both relies on and reconfigures the model of the Great Chain of Being, and does so in a way that allows us to characterize it, finally, as a metaphorics of diminution, of existential reduction. For what is common to the most inventive and unusual instances of PEOPLE ARE ANIMALS and PEOPLE ARE THINGS is that, in being cast as insect, pebble, earth and dust, K is figured in terms of the lowliest, the most humble forms of existence. It is, moreover, precisely because source domains vary that this metaphorics privileges not a particular entity or essence, but rather a kind of lowly being in general, and a motion towards that being. None of the creatures or things used to describe K proves to be the perfect match; each is picked up and discarded in turn. What remains consistent is a movement of reduction, which begins with K and ends with something possessed of its own, more elemental mode of existence, one that is not, for all that, inferior.

Insofar as reduction might be understood also as a stripping away, or paring down, the semantics of Coetzee's metaphorics coheres with his literary practice more broadly. In certain formal respects too, Coetzee's use of metaphor accords with principles of economy and precision, for it is sparing, and there is a restriction on the number both of source and target domains. Coetzee's metaphorics, in other words, is both agent and object of reduction.

This characterization allows us more readily to perceive the most salient points of divergence between Coetzee's literary practice and Gordimer's, that is, between a literary practice concerned with bare necessity, and one that aims at totality. In this regard, it is worth observing briefly that there

are four times as many metaphorical instances in *July's People* as in *Life &
Times of Michael K*, though the novels are of roughly equivalent length;
and also that the trans-social mappings prevalent in *The Conservationist*,
Burger's Daughter and *July's People* depend for the most part on explicitly
sociological or anthropological models, rather than metaphysical or ontological orderings of the world.

If the analysis of metaphor thus allows us to understand more precisely
the manner in which Coetzee's style was positioned against Gordimer's,
there is something still to be said about the particular significance of
Life & Times of Michael K. My discussion of Coetzee's metaphorics has
focussed on this novel not only because his interest in metaphor intensified during the period of its composition, but also because the narrative
itself finally stages, or rather figures, the stylistic principles by which it is
shaped. K, after all, is a character who makes of himself an object to be
stripped down, whose primary activity is aimed at reduction.

This point can be clarified if we consider the manner in which stones
and pebbles are used by the narrative of *In the Heart of the Country* to figure
a hard, bare language, and by the narrative of *Life & Times of Michael K* to
figure the central character, who seeks out a bare form of life. On the basis
of this intertextual echo, one might then argue that K is a personification
of Coetzee's poetics of reduction. Another way of putting this would be
to say that, in his fourth novel, Coetzee topicalizes the action of paring
down, so that it is not bareness itself that is foregrounded, as is the case
with *In the Heart of the Country*, but rather an attitude to the world, a
certain kind of practice or activity. Thus, in K, Coetzee finds a character
proper to a bare prose, as much as to a paltry story. Even before his days
of idleness begin, Michael K is a product of paring down: the language
through which he exists awaits him.

However speculative these claims, they seem justified not only by the
narrative of *Life & Times of Michael K* and the analysis of style that I have
undertaken, but also by Coetzee's preoccupation, increasingly noticeable in the critical essays of the 1980s, with the peculiar challenges faced by
South African authors. It is, moreover, by understanding K as a figure of
Coetzee's prose style, that it is possible to argue that Coetzee had begun to
attach a particular social value to his literary practice. For K is not, as the
medical officer believes, a being unaware of his surroundings. Rather, he
is an agent who desires to escape the manichean struggle between oppres-
sor and oppressed; who wishes not so much to transcend his situation as
to live in a way that does not deliver him up to the compromises of either
faction. His sympathies may lie ultimately with the freedom fighters, but

he no more chooses the stories of adventure than he does the stories of imprisonment.

On the contrary, as an agent in a fictional field of power relations, K seeks to live and act in a manner that might seem eccentric, in the sense given the term by Lukács, but which also involves a struggle to identify a new form of existence. That this existence is characterized chiefly by reduction is one indication that, by 1983 at least, Coetzee had come to associate his own literary practice with a mode of being in and relating to the world that might bring with it some hope for the future. Reduction has thus become its own value.

CHAPTER 5

From Bare Life to Soul Language

The Old-Fashioned Speech of Coetzee's Middle Fictions

The story I have been telling thus far is a story not so much of an evolving aesthetic mode, as of an evolving understanding of this mode. The simple, spare and sometimes lyrical prose that, in *Dusklands*, is a means of producing a brute reality, has come to seem, with the publication of *Life & Times of Michael K*, something different. To be precise: Coetzee's literary practice – stripping down, paring away, laying bare – has come to be identified with a way of being in the world that might, in turn, constitute a means of overcoming the manichean reality that called forth such a practice. If the thinness of apartheid is at first a challenge to the novelist, the poetics of reduction that issues from Coetzee's response to this challenge seems ultimately to be assigned a social value.

This claim gives rise to a host of vexed questions about the relation between our experiences of art and our actions in and on the world. Rather than venture too far onto this terrain, we need only note that, if there is a principle of composition that governs Coetzee's poetics of reduction, it is that of necessity, and if Coetzee's novels are concerned with that which is needed for the sake of writing, they are clearly also concerned with that which is needed for the sake of living. They are concerned, in other words, not with the good life, but with subsistence, with what is required simply to stand in the world.

Some notion of necessity might therefore be said to orbit about all of Coetzee's early novels and to emerge most clearly into view in *Life & Times of Michael K*. In this novel, not only the mode of composition, but also the central thematic turns on the questions: What is necessary? What is the bare minimum required to tell a story? What is needed for a new kind of life? To these questions, Coetzee's early novels give no definitive answers, but only intimate that from subsistence may come other ways to stand: persistence, possibly resistance.

In South Africa of the mid-1980s, to have posed and left unanswered the question of necessity seems especially pertinent, because the struggle for and against apartheid had become so thoroughly entangled in ethnic-nationalism, outside of which lay only a liberal discourse of the autonomous subject and its universal human rights. This situation, with its several bad choices, has not gone unremarked: many of Coetzee's critics consider it the justification for a mode of writing grounded in poststructuralist critiques of all claims to truth, identity and presence. My contention is, and has been, that this understanding amounts to a misrecognition of Coetzee's early novels.

In any case, the question of need remains a valid and valuable one in the context of late apartheid South Africa, precisely because it is neither a question of essence, nor a question that begins with some already-accepted notion of what it is or means to be human. This point has been developed and argued in far greater detail by the South African philosopher Lawrence Hamilton, in *The Political Philosophy of Needs*.[1] Nor has there been sufficient change in South Africa to make the question of necessity redundant or to deprive the bareness of Coetzee's early novels of its force.

One cannot, however, ignore significant transformations in the materials of life and art. The question with which we are therefore faced is how our efforts to discern the emergence and consolidation of Coetzee's bare style will impact upon readings of his middle and later fictions. What is the relevance, in other words, of the previous chapters, and the model of relational stylistic analysis they propose, to understanding Coetzee's broader oeuvre? It is this question that the present chapter explores, initially by considering *Foe* in greater detail, and thereafter by addressing Coetzee's adoption of what we might for the time being call a language of the soul.

Foe's Antique Tongue

In the introduction to this study, I suggested that *Foe* was an idiosyncratic novel, rather than the culmination of Coetzee's attempts to shape a literary practice. If it is necessary to insist on this again, it is because *Foe* has so often been taken as the signal work of Coetzee's apartheid-era fictions. Prior to the publication of *Disgrace*, it was certainly the most written about, in all likelihood for precisely those reasons it disappointed its first reviewers: the greater opacity of its relation to its social and political contexts; its more apparent concern with the history of the novel; and, above all, its deeper engagement with ideas about writing, language and authorship identified with poststructuralism broadly and with the works of Roland Barthes, Jacques Derrida and Michel Foucault in particular.

There is no reason to deny *Foe*'s indebtedness to these thinkers, in spite of my previous assertion that Coetzee's early novels neither could nor should be aligned with a project of poststructuralism. On the contrary, the fact that *Foe* drew so openly on Derridean ideas of language and alterity, both for its themes and narrative strategies, is one of the causes of its idiosyncrasy. Nevertheless, I would question whether even *Foe* is the exemplary allegory of deconstructive metafiction it has so often been taken to be. Certainly, there are other ways of reading the novel.

From the point of view of style, what obviously distinguishes *Foe* from Coetzee's other fictions is the subtle inflection of its language by an older variety of Standard English, that of the eighteenth century. If such a prose appears briefly in *Life & Times of Michael K*, particularly in those moments in which the picaresque novel is invoked (for example, when K and his mother, on their journey, are 'accosted by a pair of passers-by'), it becomes thoroughly pervasive in *Foe*.[2] To give a full account of the linguistic features grounding this stylistic shift must go way beyond the scope of this chapter, but it should be possible to sketch at least some of them and to outline certain of the implications of this shift, both for interpreting *Foe* and for understanding the novels it preceded.

The most obvious means of producing the air of the past in *Foe*'s principal narrative is by invoking places, practices and beliefs that have ceased to exist. It may take us some time to notice these signs, and we may even resist them, imagining that there remains undiscovered 'an island of cannibals', or that a community lives on of 'readers reared on travellers' tales'. Eventually, however, references to 'watermen … on the Thames', 'persecutions in Flanders', the 'carrying trade' and 'monsters of the deep' must convince us that the world of the novel cannot belong to the present.[3]

This conviction will be only strengthened as the details of a very particular past accrue. There are the unfamiliar smells of the 'tanner's storehouse' and 'tar' (16, 39); the unfamiliar words of an outdated medical terminology, of 'cupping and bloodletting', 'the plague' and 'the pox' (38, 27, 22); the sight and feel of unfamiliar clothes, of a 'petticoat' (5, 19), 'watch-coat' (45, 55), 'breeches' (99, 102), 'underlinen', 'a drayer's woolen jerkin' and 'woolen hose' and a 'sailor's blouse and pantaloons' (49, 55). There is also an antiquated currency: payments of 'three guineas' and 'five shillings', 'in the day of the twopenny post', and 'a threepenny loaf' (49, 47, 94, 129). And there is travel, on sea by means of 'merchantman' and 'Indiaman', carrying cargoes of 'cotton and indigo', 'parakeets and golden idols and ... skins of panthers' (10, 109, 38, 150–1); and on land, by foot and by 'coach', where one is in danger of encountering 'footpads', 'thieves or highwaymen' or of being mistaken for 'strollers or gipsies' (90, 100, 123, 102). In these words, and others like them, the novel makes present a past in which there is still hanging at Tyburn, imprisonment at Newgate, 'waifs and orphans who sleep in the ash-pits at the glassworks', a seaport at Bristol, plantations in the New World and a refreshment station at the Cape of Good Hope (128).

By invoking elements of eighteenth-century British life, Coetzee's fifth novel insinuates its readers into the world of an historical past. Had it done only this, the texture of this world might nonetheless have felt oddly contemporary; but the narrative does a good deal more than name antique places and practices. For it is uttered in a voice that itself belongs to this past, a voice characterized by words and phrases that, where not wholly obsolete, continue to be used today only in prose that is purposefully archaic or at least knowingly literary. For a certain 'brown seaweed' continues to stink, though we are unlikely to describe its stench as *noisome* (7); and if we no longer travel the sea by Indiamen, there are still sailors, though we do not call them *mariners* or *seafarers* (18, 28, 55); nor, in speaking of their shore leave, do we describe them as *libertines* or mention their visits to *courtesans* and *alehouses* (120, 52, 101). *Prostitutes* and *bars* are what we speak of today, and if we do not, if we use words like *garb* and *livery* where we might use words like *clothes* and *uniform*, or if we say that someone is *chary* and *woebegone* instead of *cautious* and *miserable*, then we are choosing to speak in a tongue made dusty by the passage of years (93, 118, 19, 135).

It is precisely this tongue that constitutes the world of *Foe*, and to it belong words of all classes: we find nouns such as *fixity*, *slumber* (26), *victuals* (52), *burgesses* (70), *tidings*, *spyglass* (71), *freebooters* (81), *consort* (97), *boon* (100) and *blackfellow* (100, 106, 110); adjectives such as *abed* (14, 57, 78), *flitten* (71), *straitened* (93), *blithe* (99), *higgledy-piggledy* (108), *a-bustle* (114), *unbidden* (120), *be-mazed* (136), *fantastical* (141) and *benighted* (146); and adverbs such as *by and by* (6), *yonder* (9), *hither and thither* (11), *mightily* (20), *whereupon* (22, 25, 113), *willy-nilly* (12, 57), *anew* (68), *of a sudden* (74), *perchance* (97), *in a trice* (135) and *all unwitting* (141). More telling still is the slew of such verbs and verbal phrases as *to slay* (10, 38, 84), *to beseech* (39), *to harry* (61), *to behold* (79, 127), *to heed* or *to pay heed* (39, 7, 28, 95), *to befall* (41, 97), *to hold one's peace* (18, 140), *to steal about* (20), *to ask pardon* (20), *to yield up* (39), *to take ship* (44), *to decamp* (63), *to quail* (82), *to hale* (105), *to foreswear* (106) and *to cavil* (150).

The use of obsolete or archaic words may be the surest, but it is hardly the only means of producing the texture of the past. Far more pervasive are words that remain familiar to us in appearance, but not in meaning. For example, early in the novel we meet with the sentence: 'I would gladly now recount to you the history of this singular Cruso' (11). The adverb *gladly* and verb *recount* have today at least a formal resonance, but even if we rewrote the sentence *I would happily now tell you the history of this singular Cruso*, *history* and *singular* would continue to seem out of place. For the former is used here to mean something like *life story*, or even *true life story*, and the latter to mean something like *unique person*, as it does again in the phrase 'singular saviour' (13). Both words then are given meanings they no longer possess, producing a semantic dissonance that we find again where *to quit* means to depart from (12, 75); *to retire* means to go to sleep (14, 27); *to rave*, whether in 'fits' or 'bouts' or 'with fever', means to be delirious (27, 28, 29, 35); and *to go abroad*, or *to be abroad*, means to be away from the home, as in 'he is free to wander as he pleases. But he rarely goes abroad', or 'A woman who goes abroad freely is thought a whore' (55, 115).

These examples are only verbs and verb phrases, and hardly all that might have been cited. To produce a catalogue of every noun and adjective used in a manner that registers semantic change would be no more helpful than it is desirable. It is enough to understand what effect is produced when *to hold* means to believe, as it does in Cruso's suggestion that 'the slavers, who are Moors, hold the tongue to be a delicacy' (23); or when *relation* means narrative and *situation* means job or position (12, 48); or when *all* appears where today we would expect *every* or *everything*, as in 'he follows me in all things' and 'giving voice to all that lay in my heart' (37, 70). It is enough to understand, in other words, that what is manifested in the dissonance of phrasing and word choice is a shift in semantic field that occurs in every language exposed to the currents of time.

Nor is the reach of these currents restricted: closed class words are likewise exposed, as is evident if we consider *but*, which appears frequently in *Foe* where today we would use *only*: 'though he was but a child' (56–7), 'trusting it was but a shower' (101), 'a woman has but three occasions to leave the house' (115), 'Speech is but a means through which the word may be uttered' (143). Likewise, we find *about* used instead of *around*, as in 'my long hair floating about me' (5), 'a bag that hung about his neck' (31), 'with a rope tied about his middle' (32) and 'wrapped itself about Friday' (140). We also find *near*, used as an adverb, where today we would use *nearly*, as in 'We found the garden near washed away' (29); and *save*, used instead of *except*, as in: 'nothing left to talk of save the weather' (34), 'the cellar is bare save for his cot' (55), and 'Save that we do not die when a knife pierces the tongue' (85).

In several ways then, *Foe*'s language is marked by an attempt to give the novel an antiquated sound. Without citing every instance, it should be clear that Coetzee adopts a number of strategies, including: (a) reference to historical places, practices and objects; (b) the use of archaic words and phrases; and (c) the exploitation of dissonance created by the processes of semantic shift. To these properly lexical strategies of antiquation, we might add a range of syntactical ones.

Here, the most obvious examples are: the frequent inversion of the subject and verb in the indicator of reported speech (*said he, said she, said I*); the use of determiners as pre-modifiers of present participles ('worth the remembering' (17), 'worth the saving' (32), 'in the writing down' (40)); the lack of the conjunction *that* in such appositive clauses as 'He saw I shook my head' (23), 'I believe it is I who have become the slave' (87) and 'thus rudely teach him he was not alone on this earth' (98); the related and pervasive use of the zero relative pronoun, as in 'there was not a tree did not grow twisted' (55); and the use of the verb *to be* in perfect constructions, as in 'he *is fled* among the crags' (39), 'I *am new-returned* from far-off parts' (48), 'He *is become* a great lover of oatmeal' (57), 'you *are widowed* many years' (62), 'It *is* only a poor mad girl *come* to join us' (77), 'we *are become* musicians together' (96) and 'the old apeskin sandals *are fallen* apart' (99).[4]

A particularly rich antiquarian vein is struck in the form of negative sentences, which occur in at least two varieties. In the first, we find *no* used as a kind of negative article, in sentences in which we would today make use of *not a*. Thus, we find 'no bad place to be cast away' (20), rather than *not a bad place to cast away*, and 'I am no slave-owner' (150) rather than *I am not a slave-owner*. In the other variety, the lack of the dummy operator *do* causes the main verb to be fronted, as in 'It mattered not who came' (35), and 'I had not the temperament to love such emptiness' (38), where we might have expected *It did not matter who came*, and *I did not have the temperament to love such emptiness*. This absence is similarly marked in a great many of the novel's interrogative sentences, which include: 'Have you a woman to cook your meals and wash your linen?' (61), 'Have you no other books?' (100), 'Have you his papers of manumission?' (110) and 'why need I argue my case?' (126).

Elsewhere, Coetzee achieves the desired effect by adjusting word order. So, for example, instead of *I was so befuddled that I thought myself still aboard the ship*, we find a sentence in which the subject and subject complement are transposed: 'So befuddled was I that I thought myself still aboard the ship' (29). A similar inversion of subject and object is found in the sentence '*Firewood* is the word I have taught him' (21), while in several other instances it is simply the object that is fronted: 'Wood he does not know' (21), 'Timbers too we might loosen' (32), 'Many strengths you have' (72), 'This I have sewn into a little bag' (99), 'These I would not accept' (121) and 'This too I reject' (121). By these and several other adjustments in word order – including the fronting of prepositional phrases and unusual placement of adverbs – the language of the novel is made to seem as if it comes to us from a past not so long distant as to have been forgotten, but all the same obdurately remote.

I hope by now to have shown that there is, in *Foe*, a considerable, even programmatic effort to achieve the effect of an antiquated language. If the examples cited give some of the flavour of this language it is so much the better because it is a synthetic flavour, concocted by its author, rather than copied strictly from any particular eighteenth-century model. If one were to return to the novels of Daniel Defoe, for instance, it would soon be evident that the language in which they are composed is quite unlike that I have been describing. Nevertheless, *Foe*'s prose style differs from that of Coetzee's previous novels; although its sentences remain relatively short and simple, and there is hardly any diminution in clarity, a subtle yet substantial transformation has undoubtedly taken place.

Nor is this a function only of lexis and syntax: *Foe* marks a departure for Coetzee also in its subject matter. To begin with, its focus is less the manichean character of the colonial situation and more the conditions of speech and silence. It thus lacks those scenes of disturbing brutality that characterize the earlier fictions (though the spectre of violence continues to hover), and, while a forestalled reciprocity remains a concern, *Foe* explores this, for the most part, by posing questions about authorship and its institutions, voice and truth, and the silences and occlusions that speech inevitably produces. The question then is whether this shift in subject matter might in some way be related to the shift in grammar. If so, this would help to explain the novel's stylistic antiquarianism.

In tackling this question we should note that it is precisely these new preoccupations that resonate most with the ideas of Barthes, Foucault and Derrida. Indeed, in moments such as the following, Susan Barton might be reading aloud from *Of Grammatology*: 'When I reflect on my story, I seem to exist only as the one who came, the one who witnessed, the one who longed to be gone: a being without substance, a ghost beside the true body of Cruso. Is that the fate of all storytellers?' (51). In the face of such allusions to Derrida's circulating thoughts regarding writing-as-trace, Coetzee's engagement with deconstruction can hardly be denied.

Nevertheless, much as *Foe* may be concerned with the always already absent figure of the author, it seems a good deal more interested in modalities and varieties of presence, in the ways one might feel sufficiently or insufficiently substantial. Above all, it seems interested in the ways words on the page, however much they operate by processes of difference and deferral, produce impressions, indeed worlds, that are themselves effectual, perhaps even substantial, not only because they have an existence for readers, but because this existence gives shape to a world beyond the fiction.

In this regard it is telling that, in the passage just cited, Susan Barton's worry is not that she is absent from the story she narrates, but that, in her narration, and in her mode of being present, she lacks Cruso's solidity and self-sufficient existence. It is telling, moreover, that *substance* becomes one of the novel's key terms, a word that attains increasing resonance as the narrative progresses. To begin with, it is a feeling of insubstantiality that sends Susan Barton in search of the writer Foe: 'Return to me the substance I have lost, Mr Foe: that is my entreaty. For though my story gives the truth, it does not give the substance of the truth' (51). There are stories, we learn from this, that may be truthful without being substantial; stories, however accurate, that therefore deprive their tellers, and even their subjects, of something they desire. But what is this something, this *substance*, that may be missing from both truth-teller and truth?

From the novel itself, it seems *substance* has to do with corporeality, for Barton insists she 'was as much a body as Cruso', a being who 'ate and drank, … woke and slept, … longed' (51). In other words, it is insofar as she has been a body performing bodily functions that Barton is dismayed to find that she and her story have become insubstantial. Yet the novel also hints that this *substance* may have to do with something else, even something more, by its reference, almost blasphemous, to the 'true body of Cruso', and, indeed, to 'the substance of the truth'; for both cases imply a kind of super-substantiality, a way of being abundantly present.

As the narrative advances, the tension between these two understandings persists, even as *substance* enters into new phrasal and semantic contexts. For example, Susan Barton early on associates the capacity to 'tell the truth in all its substance' with imaginative power and a feeling for language: 'you must have quiet, and a comfortable chair away from all distraction, and a window to stare through; and the knack of seeing waves when there are fields before your eyes, and of feeling the tropic sun when it is cold; and at your fingertips the words with which to capture the vision before it fades' (51–2). *Substance*, then, is what comes when one can conjure, feel and communicate the texture of an experience not one's own. Yet even here there is a sense in which the imagination must be restricted by fact, by the presence of what simply is, for in her guise as a muse, Barton promises no more than a form of clear-sightedness: 'I gather my strength and send out a vision of the island to hang before you like a substantial body … : so that it will be there for you to draw on whenever you have need' (53).

This version of *substance* is again prominent when Barton responds to Foe's attempts to provide the 'substantial and varied middle' that her story lacks (121), for she argues that the substance she wishes saved would be wholly eradicated if the writer simply invented the material he desired: 'if I were a mere receptacle ready to accommodate whatever story is stuffed in me, … surely you would say to yourself, "This is no woman but a house of words, hollow, without substance"' (130–1). Being substantial therefore means that, whatever invention may be required to tell the truth in its proper manner, the facts of one's existence cannot be transmuted freely; it means, moreover, a form of self-sufficient presence: 'to no one, not even to you, do I owe proof that I am a substantial being with a substantial history in the world' (131).

Yet Barton herself refuses to accept that 'Friday is Friday', that the 'mere names' given to him 'do not touch his essence' because 'he is a substantial body, he is himself' (121–2). Instead she insists: 'No matter what he is to himself … what he is to the world is what I make of him' (122). It would seem then that the simple presence of a body waking and sleeping, consuming, longing and labouring, remains somehow insufficient, a point driven home in Barton's subsequent assertion of the body's paltriness: 'I could return in every respect to the life of a substantial body, the life you recommend. But such a life is abject. It is the life of a thing. A whore used by men is used as a substantial body' (125–6). What Susan wants must therefore be something more than corporeality; it must be 'the true story of that year, the story as it should be seen in God's great scheme of things' (126).

Substance therefore continues to be what Barton has and yet lacks, what her story needs but cannot accommodate. It is sometimes simple presence, the being of the body and of fact, and sometimes an essential or super reality. And if it has been used in moments to indicate a mode of being opposed to whatever existence is given to ghosts and verbal constructs, these too ultimately come to possess a form of substantiality. In the passage describing Susan's journey into 'the darkest heart of the forest' with the girl who claims to be her daughter, we read: 'In a sea of fallen leaves we sit, she and I, two substantial beings' (90). Side by side, seated together, embraced by the forest's gloom and mulch, two beings of substance; and yet, as we discover, figments of fantasy. For Susan has been sleeping, and she and the girl are both products of dream work.

This strange girl nevertheless becomes the very focus of questions about the meaning of *substance*. She clearly *is*, and yet cannot be what she says: 'this child, who calls herself by my name, is a ghost, a substantial ghost, if such beings exist' (132). And when, on the final page of the novel's third part, Foe asks Susan for 'the truth about your own child, the daughter lost in Bahia? Did you truly give birth to her? Is she substantial or is she a story too?', Susan responds by questioning again whether 'the girl you send, the girl who calls herself by my name' is herself 'substantial'. In the dialogue that follows, the test of substantiality that Foe offers is once more a test only of bodily presence: 'You touch her; you embrace her; you kiss her', says Foe of this girl, 'Would you dare to say she is not substantial?' To which Susan can only reply: 'No, she is substantial, as my daughter is substantial and I am substantial; and you too are substantial, no less and no more than any of us. We are all alive, we are all substantial, we are all in the same world' (152).

It is quite correct, of course, that these several beings are 'all substantial ... all in the same world'. For, whether they are true bodies, simple presences or substantial ghosts, each of these personages shares the same sphere of fictional reality occupied by Barton. This sphere is already a complex one: it includes historical figures, such as Foe; literary-historical figures such as Cruso and Friday; and figures concocted by the narrative itself, such as Susan Barton. If it should also include personages created by one of these characters, this is not to make the fictional reality more fictional, but to make it more complex, insofar as it consists of a greater range of modalities of being. What needs to be stressed is that, within the narrative, each personage has a substantial presence because he or she has an existence for the other personages within the fiction and, more important, an existence for us, the readers of this fiction.

Indeed, there are moments in the novel in which the weight and significance of something rests less on its permanent presence in the world, or even on its truth, and more on the effects it produces. Such a moment arrives with the narrative's meditation on love and lovemaking: 'Are not both music and conversation like love? Who would venture to say that what passes between lovers is of substance (I refer to their lovemaking, not their talk), yet is it not true that something is passed between them, back and forth, and they come away refreshed and healed for a while of their loneliness?' (97). This is a point to which the novel returns, in the form of another of the combative dialogues between Foe and Susan Barton, which begins with Foe's story of a story, his story of an encounter, either dreamed or real, between a man and one of the 'souls of the dead', a weeping soul who chides the visitor: "'Do not suppose, mortal," said this soul, addressing him, "that because I am not substantial these tears you behold are not the tears of true grief"' (138). To which Susan responds: 'True grief, certainly, but whose? … The ghost's or the Italian's?' (138). Though Foe does not do so, we may be prompted to ask in turn: does the origin of this 'true grief' in the end matter? For, however it is achieved, something passes between novel and reader, which cannot be touched or embraced, but which seems all the same to have effects with a substantiality of their own.

In this respect, the final meaning of *substance* becomes as little important as it is impossible to resolve. The interest of the narrative's circling around the word lies not in its capacity to offer strict definitions, or even, by a process of deconstruction, to leave such definitions in irresolvable play. Its interest lies rather in the novel's capacity to imbue the word with a special texture and weight, a greater solidity and mass. And with this greater mass comes a gravitational field of relative proportions, pulling the reader in, so that the meaning of *substance* becomes a question on which the novel itself seems to turn, and thus a question in relation to which the novel's formal qualities might, or even should, be addressed.

Here we might note that a consequence of *Foe*'s antiquated language is that the narrator who speaks it, largely on her own behalf, but also on behalf of others, thereby acquires a substantiality that Coetzee's other character narrators lack. I do not mean by this that Jacobus Coetzee, Magda and the Magistrate are entirely without substance, when, on the contrary, their worlds are communicated with such visceral intensity. But what seems striking is the peculiar presence of which Susan Barton is possessed, which has everything to do with the fact that she, more than the narrators of Coetzee's early fictions, is constituted in the use of her own syntax, turn of phrase, choice of terms: speaking in an antiquated tongue, Susan Barton acquires a voice all her own.

What does it mean if Susan Barton's voice should seem substantial, when its substance, from the outset, belongs to the past? It means, first of all, that the reader is immersed in a vision of the world that is alien, but nevertheless coherent, understandable in its context. It means, moreover, that entry is granted to fate, the knowledge of what has been already determined, and thus of pathos, a feeling with and for the suffering of this wholly fictional being, though the desires that engender this suffering – especially for substance and truth – belong to a sense of the world, indeed a metaphysics, that is itself outmoded. This is the strange effect, and indeed achievement, of *Foe*'s use of an antiquated language: it lends and guarantees a distinct being to the voice of its narrator, enabling the reader's closeness to and feeling for concerns that are nevertheless bracketed simultaneously as those of the past.

It is in this way that *Foe* might be said to differ most from Coetzee's earlier fictions, where the voices we encounter and the desires they articulate are often undercut by rival voices or subjected to a corrosive irony, even satire. Certainly, it is more difficult to take very seriously the wants and needs of Eugene Dawn and Jacobus Coetzee, or that unnamed functionary the medical officer, for they are uttered in a language more contemporary to our own and so subject to a different form of scrutiny. Even Magda and the Magistrate, who seek reciprocity, do so in a manner that instantiates distance and doubt. In *Foe*, the motion is otherwise: rather than a movement from proximity to distance, there is a movement from distance to proximity, which makes it possible gradually to imbue Susan Barton's desires with a weight of their own, encouraging readers to treat them seriously, on their own ground, as desires sincerely expressed, however archaic or naïve they appear.

Indeed, it may well be their naïveté and archaism that allow us to forgive these concerns, in a manner that we could not were they the products of Jacobus Coetzee's manichean vision or of the lyrical liberalism of the Magistrate. This is not, of course, to suggest that irony disappears altogether from *Foe*. On the contrary, a potent form of its dramatic variety subtends the entire novel, insofar as the reader knows from the outset what the principal narrator does not: the truth of her ultimate erasure. But even here, the effect is only to heighten the pathos that the novel's antiquated language has permitted, which is further intensified when we realize Susan Barton's terror of insubstantiality is wholly justified.

It is precisely in relation to this realization that the antiquated language of *Foe* might be understood as a dramatic requirement arising from the logic of the novel. For, if its central conceit is to have any purchase, what is erased must indeed seem significant. It must be clear, in other words, that something substantial will have been lost once Susan Barton's tale is re-organized and made more palatable. For this reason, Barton herself must have a voice at once palpable and anchored in the past. If, in contrast, she were nothing more than a further effect of Coetzee's bare prose, this would hardly ask the question of Defoe, and of the origin of the novel itself, that seems intended, the question of those voices and stories that must be left out of account. Nor can the attempt to signal this institutional occlusion seem too easily accomplished: again, the logic of the novel itself requires that some considerable effort is made to respond to the effacement with which it is concerned, an effort that is not only imaginative, but may entail the invention of a wholly idiosyncratic tongue.

Ultimately, the significance of Susan Barton's substantiality may exceed even these dramatic requirements. Here we might return to *Foe*'s debts to Derrida, and note that, in making a question of the meaning of *substance*, and in thereby drawing attention to the substantiality of fictional worlds and personages, Coetzee is concerned with a matter that, without being incongruent with deconstruction, escapes its ambit, at least to some extent. What is at stake here is neither the author's relation to his or her writing, nor the absence that writing requires and from which it follows; but rather the kinds of substantiality, indeed the kinds of presence, that survive this absence, in particular the presence of the narrative voice.

In fact, it is on the very ground of presence that one might distinguish between author and narrator; for if, as Derrida suggests, the former is always already absent in any writing, the latter can be present only through that writing. The narrator, in other words, is only ever an effect of the text, though one that is itself subject to modification, so that we can distinguish between narrators whose presence seems immediate, such as Susan Barton or *Lolita*'s Humbert Humbert, and narrators who seem more distant and difficult to identify, such as the impersonal narrator of Robbe-Grillet's *Les Gommes*, or, indeed, the narrators of Coetzee's *Life & Times of Michael K* and *Disgrace*.

Before concluding this section on *Foe*, it is necessary to reflect on the novel's fourth and final part, in which one is confronted, all of a sudden, by a narrative voice quite different from that of the previous parts; a narrative voice that arrives without the signals of quotation and that seems somehow closer to us; a narrative voice, speaking in its own person, that is estranged by what precedes it, and yet familiar, at least to those who have read Coetzee's earlier fictions. For, in considering this final part of *Foe*, we might qualify and confirm certain of the claims made thus far, and, in addressing what seems a weakness in the novel's design, perhaps explain the disappointment of some early readers.

To begin with, the arrival of this new voice further defines and affirms Susan Barton's distinct presence. Although she is suddenly silenced, we are made aware by this shift in language how accustomed we have become to the cadences of her tongue, how familiar we have grown to its phrases and words, however foreign these seemed at first. It is by this shift, then, that *Foe* confirms to its readers that while Susan Barton may lack the kind of being in the world associated with what can be touched, embraced and kissed, she yet has her own kind of substance and effectuality.

What is also affirmed is the origin of this substance in the past, for, not long into *Foe*'s final pages, we receive proof that its new narrative voice belongs to a time closer to our own. The blue plaque with white lettering, located 'At one corner of the house, above head-height', naming the illustrious former tenant, now attributed his full name and occupation – '*Daniel Defoe, Author*' – assures us we have moved into a near-contemporary London, in which the local authorities are concerned more with the writer's literary estate and reputation than his bad debts (155). But this is only confirmation: before this plaque is reached, the language has already altered, shedding many of its lexical and grammatical oddities. 'It does not stir', we read, and 'they are quietly composed'; not *quietly they are composed* and *It stirs not* (153).

This narrative shift may come as a shock – of recognition but also of sudden immediacy – as if the reader had likewise slipped overboard into an icier medium, a world somehow clearer and more intensely felt precisely because it is a world of the present. Of course, the semantic clarity and resolution promised by this plunge into greater immediacy fails to materialize. Instead, it becomes increasingly difficult to understand what is being described, and one is unsettled, finally, by the impression that one ought now to see more clearly, but cannot yet see clearly enough.

Contributing to this dissonance is the sense of being all at once cut off from a voice that has sounded throughout the novel. It is a sense of separation and of a loss, which is not ours alone but also that of Susan Barton, whose narrative ends abruptly, unresolved, as the novel performs the movement from substance to insubstantiality that has been one of its principal concerns. Our sudden distance from Susan Barton is further amplified as we discover, along with the new narrator, the desiccated remains of the woman who has only recently been speaking to us.

But if we come, in these final pages, to feel Susan Barton's loss more acutely, the introduction of this new narrative voice has several further consequences. To begin with, we may grow to suspect that, in seeking out these figures of dust and straw, this voice of the present has been, all along, the real source of the narrative's vitality; that though it quotes and refers to what Susan Barton says, it has simply been giving a ventriloquist's performance, and will now cast off its disguise.

In fact, the impression may begin to form, as this new voice proceeds, that it is not only the true source of the novel's vitality, but also somehow closer to the ground. For, in a series of passages, the narrative describes some kind of lowering or sinking, first onto the floor beside Friday, and next through the floor, by way of the dispatch box that has stood upon it, and into those waters in which Susan Barton has swum and over which Friday has floated; a lowering and sinking that ends in complete submersion, and then descent to the ocean bed, where the sand is 'soft, dank, slimy, outside the circulation of the waters' (156).

Being closer to the ground means being closer also to the truth – at least the truth Susan Barton has sought throughout, which will give to her story and self the substance both lack – although this new narrative persona will initially achieve no more than Barton has imagined: in opening Friday's mouth, it only hears the roar of which she has spoken and feels the 'slow stream' of Friday's syllables, 'caught and filled with water and diffused' (157). Nonetheless, the repeated approach to Friday enacted in *Foe*'s final part creates the impression that the search for substance has concealed another, more important quest: its closing pages and paragraphs reveal that it is indeed Friday who is guardian of the novel's truth, the black heart or hole around which the story spins and spins, knowingly and yet without comprehension. After all, in his silence, Friday remains living and breathing whilst Susan Barton and her companions lie parched and entombed, or sodden and floating.

Nor is the truth of Friday, and hence of the novel, simply a matter of unclenching his jaw and parting his teeth and finding his tongue, a fascination inherited from Susan Barton. For, in these strange primal scenes animated by the living body of Friday, guardian of secret meaning, things 'not observed ... before' are newly discovered: there is, to begin with, the scar around Friday's neck, 'like a necklace, left by a rope or chain' (155), which confirms what Susan has only suspected; then, in the final part's second section, the scar is replaced with 'the chain about his throat': this, it seems, is what has kept Friday under, submerged, buried in 'the last corner, under the transoms' (157).

Thus, the fact of enslavement, which has passed as a shadow through the novel's earlier parts, becomes suddenly substantial, inscribed on and about Friday, rather than concealed behind his lips. What thereby rises to the surface is historical truth: a violent subjugation that has previously been spoken only in figures, or intimated in anxious concerns for the fate of Friday's tongue. And it is this truth, the structure of the novel suggests, that has caused Susan Barton's twin stories (of the search for substance and of erasure from the island) ultimately to founder. For its horror is so great that it keeps Friday alive in a deadened world, and so ponderous and massy that it pulls the narrative in, sucking it under.

In this way, *Foe* returns us to the concerns of Coetzee's previous fictions. Of course, in experiencing a lack she wishes to overcome by conjuring a more complex reality, Susan Barton has in any case echoed, from time to time, certain of the character narrators who precede her. But its final part confirms that the novel itself is somehow lacking and troubled by this lack, by the paltriness of its own story. More important, we here begin to understand that Susan Barton has been deprived of her substance not by the lassitude or stubborn silence of a man who either cannot speak or wishes to keep his tongue; but rather because the possibilities of communication and thus reciprocity have been foreclosed by that manichean order with which we have become all too familiar. To restore this substance, teaching Friday to read and write could never be sufficient; instead, one would need to discover a means of speaking with the dead. Beyond institutional silences, in other words, there are silences of a simpler, more brutal kind.

It is telling that in returning to the subject matter of his earlier fictions, Coetzee's fifth novel also reverts to a prose style reminiscent of them. Forced, it would seem, to abandon its artifice, its mimicry of an antiquated language, it must now embrace a prose of greater simplicity. Thus, the voice of the present appears to be won by stripping away and paring down, as the language of *Foe*'s final part comes to glitter again with that cold hardness found in the previous fictions. Indeed, in spite of the novel's entry here into murky waters, the writing has all the lucidity and spare intensity otherwise largely absent from *Foe*. The effect is not unlike that produced in the previous novels, where one finds the prose of greatest clarity, tension and vigour in moments that lay bare the violent truth of the colonial situation. However, this is not without consequences for the narrative's earlier parts, since it suggests that the story the novel has set out to tell, though valuable in its own terms, must ultimately give way to a truth of far greater import.

In being thus reframed, Susan Barton's narrative is by no means subjected to the kind of satiric irony meted out to S. J. Coetzee, largely because her blindness is understood as the consequence not of wilful bad faith, but of precisely those structures of speaking, writing and thinking that will eventually cause her own erasure from the castaway narrative. Nevertheless, bracketing Susan Barton's concerns as matters of lesser urgency may in the end unbalance the novel, by withdrawing from its earlier parts some of the weight they had sought so determinedly to acquire. This return to the prose of the present, in other words, may amount to a betrayal of that immense effort it has taken to give Susan Barton substance. For her narrative is thus made to seem a cover for a more fundamental story, whilst her language – exposed to the sudden glare of a more immediate and energetic manner of speech – grows more obscure, more *static*; perhaps even more *anaemic*.[5] Thus, in the intensity of the novel's final pages, Susan Barton's narrative, desires and difficulties, seem to be overwhelmed and washed away.

At the very last, then, in spite of the enormous lengths to which Coetzee has gone to revitalize a voice silenced and erased, to animate its needs and desires, he seems to withdraw. In doing so, the vitality given to the quest for substance ebbs, not only because the narrative of this quest is made to appear naïve or old-fashioned, but also because it inevitably misrecognizes the truth it has attempted to tell. Thus, while it begins to pose a series of important questions – about the losses entailed by the struggle for survival and in the aftermath of a wreck, about the possibilities that remain after rescue or salvation, about the difficulties of returning to a fuller life – *Foe* ultimately retreats from them, and so from asking how one might live otherwise than by killing time.

A Theological Lexicon: On Learning to Speak of Soul, Spirit and Heart

However much *Foe* may ultimately withdraw from its initial concern with *substance*, its attempt to re-energize an antiquated language is of real importance to Coetzee's oeuvre. If it remains a transitional work, this is only because the bracketing of Susan Barton's world is ultimately too whole-hearted: having created a space in which her longing for substance acquires weight and resonance, Coetzee seals it off from the present. His later novels, however, will refrain from this act of enclosure, as they return to the question of salvation – of that which is required for a new life to emerge – without depriving it of urgency.

Before turning to these novels, we might dwell a while longer on *Foe* and on *substance*, considering the word from the point of view of its own history, rather than the novel's semantic economy. This history begins, according to the OED, in the fourteenth century, at which time *substance* has a theological dimension, which survives well into the nineteenth century. Thus, in *Foe*, *substance* might be grouped with words and phrases belonging to a religious and specifically Christian lexicon, such as *Providence* (23), *salvation* (14, 82), *resurrection* (19), *confession* (61, 89), *the path of righteousness* (36), *choirs of angels* (114) and, indeed, *the true body* (51). Within this lexicon, it might further be associated with words suggestive of an essential or metaphysical nature, such as *soul* and *spirit*.

One effect of this lexicon is of course to contribute to the local colour of eighteenth-century London. Speaking of God's writing and God's creatures is not unlike speaking of cannibals and the kraken: beliefs prevalent in a particular time and place that belong to a world of the past. But these particular words and phrases achieve something more, a metaphysical expansion of the narrative and its fictional world. Precisely this movement is ultimately curtailed in *Foe*, but it will become a distinctive feature of Coetzee's later novels: in *Age of Iron*, *The Master of Petersburg* and *Disgrace* we again find an opening into metaphysical dimensions by means of a theological lexicon. This lexicon, it is true, shifts from novel to novel, so that, in place of *substance*, emphasis is given to *charity* and *mercy* in *Age of Iron*, and to *possession* in *The Master of Petersburg*. Certain words, however, remain significant in all Coetzee's middle fictions. Of these, *confession* is especially prominent, though none achieves the effect of expansion as much as *soul* and *spirit*.

In what follows, I detail the use of this theological lexicon in Coetzee's middle fictions in order to explain the claim I am making about the development of his literary practice. What must be reiterated at the outset is that this expansive strain emerges against the background of what continues to be a bare prose style: it remains very much a minor motif, pulsing always through and over a spareness hardly relieved by its presence, and often only intensified. Nevertheless, it is a strain that constitutes an important element in Coetzee's middle and later works, a language of the spirit and soul that enables them to pose new questions about salvation and the transformation of subjectivity, and to produce worlds and realities qualitatively different from those of *Dusklands*, *In the Heart of the Country*, *Waiting for the Barbarians* and *Life & Times of Michael K*.

Perhaps the most important point to make about the orchestration of this expansive strain is that it entails a shift less in the use of particular words and more in their frequency and semantic range. For in each of Coetzee's early fictions one finds instances of this theological lexicon. More often than not, however, its terms are deprived of any properly metaphysical content. For example, *soul* often occurs in plainly idiomatic phrases ('commit myself body and soul to some fiction', 'the captain of my soul',[6] 'commit herself body and soul to the first willing fellow'[7]), or as a synonym for *individual* ('Marilyn is a trusting soul', 'a pretty child was the only soul about',[8] 'a town of three thousand souls', 'these few souls here', 'there is not a soul in the town who approves'[9]). Likewise, *spirit* often means mood or emotional state ('my spirits have been low', 'in a spirit of evil', 'in good spirit',[10] 'a spirit of courage'[11]).

Used non-idiomatically, these words occur infrequently and in restricted narrative and semantic contexts. Five of the six non-idiomatic instances of *soul* in *Life & Times of Michael K* are thus found in the passage cited in the previous chapter, where the medical officer gropes for a metaphysical language in a moment of frustration. Likewise, in *Waiting for the Barbarians*, seven of eight non-idiomatic instances of *soul* are found within an eleven-page segment, primarily in passages concerned with the mechanics of torture, as when the Magistrate imagines Mandel's operation on his spirit as a kind of surgery on the heart: 'He deals with my soul: every day he folds the flesh aside and exposes my soul to the light'.[12]

Narrative and semantic restriction is operative in *Dusklands* also: it is primarily in his delirium that Jacobus Coetzee becomes aware of 'the flexings of the soul's wings'. However, a more potent means of depriving *soul* and *spirit* of any serious purpose is by ironic detachment and comic deflation, a distance and bathos engendered in the misapplication of theological terminology. Thus, Eugene Dawn, blind to his own madness, speaks of the 'insights into man's soul' he has acquired from thinking 'about Vietnam', and construes his professional troubles as spiritual self-sacrifice: 'Not without joy, I have girded myself for purgatory. If I must be a martyr to the cause of obedience, I am prepared to suffer.'[13]

As for Jacobus Coetzee, his descendant thinks him 'a humble man who did not play God', but he is easily enough convinced of his own apparent divinity: 'Perhaps ... I looked like a god, a god of the kind they did not yet have.' Whatever kind this may be, to himself Jacobus Coetzee is God of the Old Testament, whether attacking a child ('Jehovah I fell upon his back'), or the Lord's own animal ('Like God in a whirlwind I fell upon a lamb'). In such acts, however, and in every other moment in which he aims to clothe himself in borrowed majesty – including the *meditationes* of his illness-induced delirium – a petty cruelty pokes through the mis-woven fabric.[14]

As in *Dusklands*, the presiding godhead of *In the Heart of the Country* is the absent Father: 'God has forgotten us and we have forgotten God'; and yet, as in *Dusklands*, the scriptures of this withdrawn divinity continue to make themselves available as a means of endowing both fantasy and reality with a certain splendour, albeit with consequences that are frequently comic. This is only too evident to Magda herself in her vision of motherhood, cradling the 'Antichrist of the desert', surrounded by 'The brown folk, cowed servitors, kneeling to offer a trussed lamb, first fruits, wild honey, sniggering at the miracle of the virgin birth'. Unable to embrace the language, or indeed the pathos and grandeur of godly things, she is compelled to undercut its terms: having considered her capacity for 'redemption ... from loneliness, from loneness, by marriage ... to another lone soul', she must immediately recant, dismissing the notion as 'bucolic comedy'.[15]

Elsewhere, the language of the soul slides over into gasping melodrama: 'With the story coming to its end, all one's last bad poetry finds release. I ... exhale the last beloved breath (goodbye, spirit!), and dive for the abyss'; or teeters on the brink of farce: 'All morning I have lain waiting for her discreet tap at the door. I think of tea and rusks and my saliva flows. There is no doubt about it, I am not pure spirit.' Even as the novel draws to a close and Magda feels a final urge to 'yield to the spectre of reason' by offering some kind of confession, the reader is reminded that this is only a quaint manner of speaking: 'To die an enigma with a full soul or to die emptied of my secrets, that is how I picturesquely put the question to myself.'[16]

In Coetzee's third and fourth novels, this comic deflation becomes less pointed, but even in *Life & Times of Michael K*, the language of the soul is exposed to a kind of mockery and made to seem excessive, another outlandish means of describing someone who may as well be a 'coelacanth' or 'a visitor on our planet' as a 'spirit invisible' or an 'original soul'.[17] At best, *soul* belongs to a cultural model that has become superannuated, and that, within the context of Coetzee's early fictions, is largely subordinated to one in which existence trumps essence and the privileged terms are *being* and *consciousness*.

Of these fictions, it is perhaps only *Waiting for the Barbarians* in which the language of the soul is used without being rendered somehow absurd (although, again, it occurs infrequently, and cannot wholly escape the suspicion generated by the Magistrate's own desire to pierce the interiority of others). If this seems significant, an explanation may lie in the fact that the world of the novel, in a fairly straightforward sense, is non-Christian.

Words of the Old and New Testaments might therefore be used without freighting them with an irony made necessary by history itself; used, that is, in a manner which is sincere and yet entails a certain distance. It may also be relevant that *Waiting for the Barbarians* begins to pose the question of how to recover from the damage manichean violence causes to both its perpetrators and victims. What we would then find in this novel are the first signs of a strategy that will be thoroughly explored in *Foe* and that will become increasingly central to the literary practice of Coetzee's middle fictions.

The words *soul* and *spirit* do not appear often in *Foe*. Nor are they accorded much weight by the narrative, though Susan Barton's soul does takes flight in pursuit of substance, and Friday elicits her concern insofar as he possesses 'a spirit or a soul – call it what you will' (50, 32). Nevertheless, what we witness in *Foe* is the abandonment of that ontological or existential cultural model deployed in Coetzee's previous novels, where its terms are granted a purchase denied to an amusingly 'picturesque' theological manner of speaking. With this rival lexicon supplanted, the language of the soul seems restored to roles from which it had been disqualified, including that of cultural model for a metaphorics of reduction.

Of still greater consequence, at least from the point of view of developing practice, is the manner in which *Foe* summons antiquated terms and grants them a kind of second life, however provisionally. For it is this technique of parenthetic sincerity that will be taken up and modified in Coetzee's subsequent fictions, where one finds a complementary shift from a concern with the bareness of life to a concern with how this bareness might be remedied, which revolves increasingly around questions of confession, salvation and the transformation of subjectivity.

Whether or not by design, the modifications to this technique of parenthetic sincerity address the shortcomings of its use in *Foe*, for the means of bracketing become less dramatic and restrictive. One therefore encounters, in *Age of Iron*, *The Master of Petersburg* and *Disgrace*, a language of the soul that is not repeatedly undercut by its narrative and semantic contexts. Instead, it is made prominent and used with that sincerity found previously in *Foe*, and, to a very limited extent, *Waiting for the Barbarians*. In this, a commitment is implied less to the particular words used than to a region of existence and experience they create and describe. It is a commitment, above all, to the kind of truth that is produced by art's negation of what-is for the sake of what-may-be.

We can begin to substantiate these claims by turning to *Age of Iron*, which marks a pronounced shift in literary practice insofar as Coetzee for the first time locates his narrative in his present and place of writing. Published in 1990, the novel's end is punctuated by the dates '1986–1989', which suggest both the period of composition and the period during which the events narrated run their course, a reading prompted by the work itself: Mr Thabane, born in 1943, tells Mrs Curren that he is forty-three years old.[18] Thus, we find ourselves placed squarely in the final years of apartheid, and must therefore take for granted an existence in which human relation has been almost completely liquidated.

This world is not wholly unlike that of Coetzee's previous fictions, but, whereas the processes and effects of reduction and brutalization constitute the very subject of those works, they are, in *Age of Iron*, that which is already given, the starting point for thoughts about remediation and recovery, which open out into questions about the nature of education, about the kind of learning that may be required of the old as much as the young, and about the distance that separates one generation from another. If these thoughts and questions have continued to occupy Coetzee, their appearance in *Age of Iron* marks something of a shift in subject matter, to which we will need to return to explain the language of the soul in Coetzee's middle fictions. First, however, we ought to sketch some of the ways this language and its parenthetical sincerity are articulated.

In *Age of Iron*, the word *soul* becomes prolific: within the novel's 181 pages it occurs at least thirty-seven times. More important, only three instances seem idiomatic, and its range of semantic and narrative contexts has been significantly broadened. Of these, one of the more frequent and familiar is the transition from life to death, where *soul* identifies that part of the self that survives. It is with this *soul* that Mrs Curren is increasingly concerned. Indeed, as her cancer runs its course, she returns several times to the scene of life's aftermath, which early on in the narrative resembles 'A hotel lobby full of old people dozing, listening to music, while souls pass and repass before them like vapors, the souls of all. A place dense with souls' (22). Later, this afterlife will become more sinister, more like the underworld visited by Aeneas in which the dead wait on either bank of oblivion. Towards the novel's end, however, as she lies beneath the overpass, something of the initial scene returns. Listening to the 'air dense with noise', Mrs Curren thinks of the 'Thousands of wings passing and repassing without touching', wondering: 'How is there space in the skies for the souls of all the departed? Because, says Marcus Aurelius, they fuse one with another: they burn and fuse and so are returned to the great cycle' (144).

Used to mean the immortal part of the self, *soul* is still more frequently encountered in passages that envision the moments before and after death. In one such passage, Mrs Curren thinks of herself as a cocoon, and her 'soul readying itself for further flight' as being 'Like a moth from its case emerging, fanning its wings.... A white moth, a ghost emerging from the mouth of the figure on the deathbed' (118). Having thus imagined her end, Mrs Curren hastens to assure her daughter and reader that there will be no haunting, 'no need to close the windows and seal the chimney to keep the white moth from flapping in', for 'It is not my soul that will remain with you but the spirit of my soul, the breath, the stirring of the air about these words' (118–9).

The idea of the soul emerging from the body as from a chrysalis, slough-ing off the tired and brittle part of the self in a transfigurative death, is a familiar one. Yet it becomes peculiarly visceral in Coetzee's recasting, as, for example, when Mrs Curren gives 'thanks for this mercy ... : for the sick body stunned, for the soul drowsy, half out of its casing, beginning to float' (167); or when she thinks of 'Vercueil and his dog' beside her, 'wait-ing for the soul to emerge. The soul, neophyte, wet, blind, ignorant' (170); or, finally, when she considers the meaning of 'Decency: the inexplicable: the ground of all ethics', and defines it as that which 'we do not do', espe-cially in the presence of death: 'We do not stare when the soul leaves the body, but veil our eyes with tears or cover them with our hands. We do not stare at scars, which are places where the soul has struggled to leave and been forced back, closed up, sewn in' (180).

However prominent, the end of life is by no means the only semantic context in which *soul* appears. For it is not simply that which survives death, but also a part of the self that enables a special kind of commu-nication. Sometimes, it is true, this capacity is linked with the soul's immortality, as is the case with the words flowing from Mrs Curren to her daughter: 'you are with me not as you are today in America ... but as you are in some deeper and unchanging form: as the beloved, as that which does not die. It is the soul of you that I address, as it is the soul of me that will be left with you when this letter is over' (118).

Earlier though, when Mrs Curren and Vercueil listen, transfixed, to the Goldberg Variations, they are bound together not because they have immortal parts, but insofar as each has the capacity for a pleasure of an intense, spiritual kind: 'Two souls, his and mine, twined together, ravished. Like insects mating tail to tail, facing away from each other, still except for a pulsing of the thorax that might be mistaken for mere breath-ing. Stillness and ecstasy' (27). In fact, it is this capacity that ensures some memory of life will survive death: 'But the music I will take with me ... for it is wound into my soul. The ariosos from the Matthew Passion, wound in and knotted a thousand times' (119).

The *soul* thus enables communication and pleasure of the most intense kind, but the narrative suggests it may also be that on which every mood and feeling depends, no matter how inconsequential. It is in this sense that Mrs Curren speaks of 'the motions of the soul' in relation to Vercueil's ignorance of love (180); that she speaks of the 'peace of mind, ... peace of soul' that comes with having children (22); and that she remarks the 'light, fickle sadness' that brings her to tears, 'the blues, but not the dark blues: the pale blues, rather, of far skies, clear winter days. A private matter, a disturbance of the pool of the soul' (64–5).

In addition to functioning as seat of emotions and means of intense connection, the soul plays a still more vital role. In it reside those qualities that are associated with a kind of moral life. Thus, Mrs Curren thinks how she 'strove always for honour', a 'notion' to which she has clung 'through thick and thin', and how she once believed 'that in his soul the honourable man can suffer no harm' (150). If this now seems doubtful, if she has come to know that, far from being immune, the soul itself might be damaged by brutality, she yet holds fast to her sense of it as the lodestone of moral qualities, as that which is required to realize the full richness of human life.

In fact, it is in this sense, as that on which remediation depends and which a manichean life may yet have irreparably damaged, that *soul* is used for the first time in *Age of Iron*. Speaking of her anxiety for future generations, and of the fear she has come to feel for 'the sullen-mouthed boys, rapacious as sharks, on whom the first shade of the prison-house is already beginning to close', Mrs Curren describes them as 'Children scorning childhood, the time of wonder, the growing-time of the soul.' They are children, moreover, whose 'souls, their organs of wonder' have been 'stunted, petrified' by the life to which they have been subjected (6).

Nor are these boys the only victims of the soul's petrifaction: 'on the other side of the great divide their white cousins' have become, Mrs Curren believes, 'soul-stunted too, spinning themselves tighter and tighter into their sleepy cocoons.' Leading lives 'within walled gardens', these pupae are 'children of paradise, blond, innocent, shining with angelic light, soft as *putti*', yet they reside not in Eden, but in 'the limbo of the unborn, their innocence the innocence of bee-grubs, plump and white, drenched in honey, absorbing the sweetness through their soft skins. Slumbrous their souls, bliss-filled, abstracted' (6–7).

Given the concerns central to Coetzee's middle fictions, this aspect of *soul* seems especially important, an impression to which the novel contributes, not least by repeating the word so often on its first occurrence, in a passage foregrounded by relative metaphoric density. The predicate *organ of wonder* is itself arresting, and explicitly constitutes the soul as that part of the self required for an orientation towards the world. In precisely this sense, the word occurs in another of the novel's significant moments. For when Mrs Curren confronts the military overseers of the township's internecine conflict, she is clearly worried about the soul as something other than that which survives death, or through which one is moved: "'Why don't you just put down your guns and go home, all of you?' I said. "Because surely nothing can be worse than what you are doing here. Worse for your souls, I mean'" (98).

Simply going home will not, of course, alleviate those conditions of existence to which Mrs Curren later alludes when she explains that by placing her trust in Vercueil she is 'trying to keep a soul alive in times not hospitable to the soul' (119). Merely by living through these times she and her compatriots grow ugly 'from being unable to think well of ourselves! ... Ugliness: what is it but the soul showing through the flesh?' (121). Nor can Mrs Curren console herself that things might once have been different. She has found evidence of the soul's petrifaction in her own generation, and now believes that even these 'children of that bygone age', who enjoyed 'A childhood of sleep, prelude to what was meant to be a life without trouble and a smooth passage to Nirvana', are rightly condemned to the limbo she has earlier envisioned:

> If justice reigns at all, we will find ourselves barred at the first threshold of the underworld. White as grubs in our swaddling bands, we will be dispatched to join those infant souls whose eternal whining Aeneas mistook for weeping. White our color, the color of limbo: white sands, white rocks, a white light pouring down from all sides. Like an eternity of lying on the beach, an endless Sunday among thousands of our own kind, sluggish, half asleep, in earshot of the comfortable lap of the waves. *In limine primo*: on the threshold of death, the threshold of life. (85)

It should be clear from these passages that *soul*, in *Age of Iron*, is used not only more widely than in Coetzee's previous novels, but also in a manner that protects the word from the evisceration of irony, thereby allowing signification to accrue around it. Thus, sense is made of Mrs Curren's late assertion: 'This was never meant to be the story of a body, but of the soul it houses' (170).

Meaning is accreted, moreover, by the narrative itself, and does not depend on any particular religion or system of belief. Instead, as it is put to work in *Age of Iron*, *soul* draws its resonance from a variety of such frameworks, sometimes all at once. In a passage cited previously, for example, Mrs Curren speaks first of Nirvana, the end of suffering promised by the Dharmic faiths, and then of a liminal afterlife that is a mélange of Virgilian underworld, holiday resort, the limbo of infants discussed by medieval theologians and a beehive of grotesque proportions; an afterlife, in other words, that is nothing so much as a highly literary confection.

This particular confection may be the product of an especially dense set of allusions, but Judeo-Christian and Graeco-Roman understandings are intertwined throughout the novel: Mrs Curren refers as easily to Marcus Aurelius as to heaven and angels and the Matthew Passion wound into her soul; and Vercueil can strike her as a Charon-like boatman or an escorting angel whose visitation follows the annunciation that has confirmed her cancer. Thus, we know long before it is confirmed that Mrs Curren is not a woman of any church, that she does 'not call for help, call to God' because it is clear to her that God cannot help her: 'God is looking for me but he cannot reach me. God is another dog in another maze.... Up and down the branches he bounds, scratching at the mesh. But he is lost as I am lost' (126).

No less significant are the several unusual figurations of the soul – as, for example, a giant white moth, or an insect caught in a coital embrace, or a newly born child – which seem to belong primarily to the world of meanings and associations generated by Coetzee's own fictions. Doubtless, it may be possible to trace even these references further, but this would leave undisclosed the broader effects of these mingled multiple sources: first, the sense that the narrative itself is constituting, or perhaps reconstituting, the meaning of *soul*; second, that it does so because it aims at something that cannot else be hit, that *soul* is used, in other words, not to name a particular metaphysical entity, but to evoke an otherwise occluded zone of existence.

In *Age of Iron*, then, the meaning of *soul*, which is important to the novel's broader concerns, is neither circumscribed by anything external to the narrative nor impinged upon by the operations of satire or irony. Nevertheless, the impression of sincerity that arises is somehow compromised or bracketed: we are made to feel that, in spite of its vitality, the word belongs to the past and is used provisionally. This bracketing is achieved, however, not by means of an antiquated tongue, but by the subtle and repeated association of the ideas on behalf of which the narrator speaks with the youth of a woman no longer young.

In fact, it is explicitly the youth of a woman who remembers a time known by none of her interlocutors: her daughter, Vercueil, the policemen, the soldiers, the boy John. And so, sitting at her piano, she must explain her search for a particular chord, 'the one chord I would recognize, when I came upon it, as my chord, as what in the old days we used to call the lost chord, the heart's chord. (I speak of a time before your time, … the maiden of the household groping among the keys for that yearned-for, elusive resonance. Days of charm and sorrow and mystery too! Days of innocence!)' (21). These days may prove less innocent than Mrs Curren initially imagines, but what remains significant here is the notion of a way of speaking – about the world and about the self – that has no place in the present.

Precisely this notion is repeated when Mrs Curren berates several policemen for their rudeness, in a fashion she knows is long out of date: '"In my day," I said, enunciating clearly each old, discredited, comical word, "a policeman did not speak to a lady like that"' (49). For though, like Magda, she seems to signal a detachment from the words she uses, unlike Magda, in uttering them, she risks everything in a confrontation with the ugliness in which she is immersed, an ugliness which has to do with far more than impolite behaviour. While the terms of her protest may seem old and comical, whatever irony they convey is therefore not at her expense, but at the expense of a world deprived of even pretended decency, and so, as 'dotty' as she may appear, Mrs Curren will not refrain from telling those around her that she has 'cancer of the heart', caught 'by drinking from the cup of bitterness' (142).

If these moments of reflexivity constitute one means of ensuring that Mrs Curren's language of the soul is bracketed as old-fashioned, this effect is more dramatically achieved towards the novel's conclusion, where it is revealed that Mrs Curren, once upon a time, was a professor of Greek and of Latin, lecturing in a 'dead language, … a language spoken by the dead' (176). At the last, Mrs Curren is thus a woman old and tired, worn out, who speaks for and on behalf of languages that have fallen out of use.[19] Yet, in several important passages, the words of these languages have 'substance … worldly weight', a significance for her, and sometimes even for those who seem to have closed their ears to her entirely (101). Such is the case with the boy-soldiers manning the barricades. When Mrs Curren urges them to go home, she is surprised to find that one, at least, has heard her admonition: '"No," he said. I had expected incomprehension, but no, he understood exactly what I meant. "We will see it through now"' (98).

In other moments, however, she is met with the misunderstanding she anticipates, as when informed that she makes a mistake about '*comrade-ship*' if she can think only of the 'killing' and 'bloodletting' committed in its name (136). Nevertheless, though she is always ready to concede that her auditors and readers 'do not believe in words', and certainly not in the words she tries to use, she remains convinced it is important to continue speaking them: 'You think only blows are real, blows and bullets. But listen to me: can't you hear that the words I speak are real? Listen! They may only be air but they come from my heart, from my womb. They are not Yes, they are not No. What is living inside me is something else, another word. And I am fighting for it, in my manner, fighting for it not to be stifled' (133).

Here, the narrative as much as the narrator seeks out a language through which to address a particular reality, struggling against a suspicion of words themselves, trying to resuscitate a way of describing the world that may well have been discredited. Trying, in fact, to do more than this, for the truth that Mrs Curren readily acknowledges – to Vercueil at least, and in the hesitant manner that again marks her use of a theological lexicon – is that it is never a matter only of describing: 'I wondered whether you were or not, if you will excuse the word, an angel come to show me the way. Of course you were not, are not, cannot be – I see that. But that is only half the story, isn't it? We half perceive but we also half create' (153).

Nor, in this Wordsworthian effort to half perceive and half create, does Mrs Curren rely only upon *spirit* and *soul, angel* and *heaven, God* and *afterlife*. Added to her discredited lexicon are several other words that prompt a kind of speculative etymological meditation, which in itself becomes a distinctive feature of Coetzee's later novels, complete with its peculiar syntax: clauses and phrases stacked beside one another in apposition, transmitting meanings across commas, allowing sense to brew. For example, early in the novel, Mrs Curren crossly insists that, if she does not turn her home into a 'soup kitchen and a dormitory', it is 'Because the spirit of charity has perished in this country. Because those who accept charity despise it, while those who give give with a despairing heart' (19). From this wound to the heart, charity has died; 'What is the point of charity,' Mrs Curren asks, 'when it does not go from heart to heart? What do you think charity is? Soup? Money? *Charity*: from the Latin word for the heart. It is as hard to receive as to give' (19–20).

Of course, as she will admit, this lesson of hers rests 'on false etymologies', since 'charity, *caritas*, has nothing to do with the heart' (20). But this hardly seems to matter, and not only because there is a truth about charity that Mrs Curren half perceives: the effect of this passage is to mark *charity* as a key term, derived from a way of speaking and acting that is, if not dead, then certainly in a morbid state. Elsewhere, this technique of rhetorical etymology is used to similar ends, as when Mrs Curren is led from the recognition that Vercueil is not 'a nurse, a *nourrice*, a nourisher', to the further realization that 'He is dry. His drink is not water but fire. Perhaps that is why I cannot imagine children of his: because his semen would be dry, dry and brown, like pollen or like the dust of this country' (179–80). In much the same way, she comes to understand that a consequence of abstinence and puritanical zeal is a hardening of the heart against life: 'Alcohol, that softens, preserves. *Mollificans*. That helps us to forgive. He drinks and makes allowances' (75).

More important still are those words on which the narrative catches several times, and which are thereby constituted as the lexicon to which *soul* and *spirit* properly belong, and as the elements in a system of meaning that the novel itself produces, a meaning that may well rest on false etymologies, but that yet remains substantial, full of worldly weight. For, in each case, what attracts her attention and ours is a word related somehow to that *organ of wonder* with which she is, from the very outset, concerned. Thus she reflects on something as simple and difficult as 'gratitude, unbounded, heartfelt gratitude': '*Gratitude*: ... What does it mean? Before my eyes it grows dense, dark, mysterious. Then something happens. Slowly, like a pomegranate, my heart bursts with gratitude; like a fruit splitting open to reveal the seeds of love. *Gratitude, pomegranate*: sister words' (51).

Later, she will have cause to reflect also on the meaning of *shame*, 'The name for the way in which people live who would prefer to be dead. Shame. Mortification. Death in life' (78). What seems truly to confound her is the related 'feat' of those who govern South Africa, which is, 'after years of etymological meditation on the word, to have raised stupidity to a virtue'. They have done this, it seems, by fully enacting the word's meanings, and those of its cognates, all of which derive, she suggests 'From *stupere*, to be stunned, astounded. A gradient from *stupid* to *stunned* to *astonished*, to be turned to stone'; and through doing, Mrs Curren's catalogue suggests, we come in the end to being, action leads to condition: 'To stupefy: to deprive of feeling; to benumb, deaden; to stun with amazement. Stupor: insensibility, apathy, torpor of mind. Stupid: dulled in the faculties, indifferent, destitute of thought or feeling' (26).

The process Mrs Curren describes in meditating on *gratitude* is reflexive insofar as it resonates with the experience of readers of Coetzee's middle fictions, who are so often invited to look carefully at particular words, to reflect on their meanings and allow them to gather and grow and spill out, seeping into the narrative and the world. Sometimes they are words freighted with the baggage of a moribund metaphysics or morality, though they may be words hollowed out simply by familiarity. In both cases, they must be restored, re-glossed, made newly effectual.

Early in *The Master of Petersburg* we encounter an example, as Fyodor Mikhailovich reflects on his motionless vigil at the window of his dead son's room: '*Pondering*, he thinks – that is the word. This heavy head, these heavy eyes: lead settling into the soul.'[20] Here again, by an unarticulated etymology and the cascade of meaning set off by apposition – not to mention the four beat rhythm and internal rhyme of the second sentence – the narrative moves via its English cognates to the Latin root of *ponder*, in order to perceive and create a motion of the soul, the particularities of which require a particular word, the right word.

Italicized in this way, words such as *pondering* appear elsewhere in the narrative, though they do not in every case require reflection to bring out their meanings. 'The word *omen*', for example, simply presents itself to Fyodor Mikhailovich, crossing his 'mind in all its dark, ominous weight', bearing with it a premonition of disaster: 'The dawning sun is there not for itself but to undergo eclipse; joy shines out only to reveal what the annihilation of joy will be like' (68). There are, however, several further moments in which some concerted effort is required to restore words to a fuller significance. Thus it is with '*Master of life*', a 'strange term', though Fyodor Mikhailovich is 'prepared to reflect on it. He will give a home to any word, no matter how strange, no matter how stray, if there is a chance it is an anagram for Pavel' (141); thus it is with '*Believe*: another word. What does it mean, to believe? I believe in the body on the pavement below. I believe in the blood and the bones. To gather up the broken body and embrace it: that is what it means to believe. To believe and to love – the same thing' (122).

Although these later words do not in themselves refer to or characterize motions of the soul, they arrive encased in the language and phrasing of bible and liturgy, having to do with death and resurrection, and with the need of the narrative's central figure to communicate with the son he has lost and whose ghost he struggles to conjure. These concerns on their own explain the continued presence of *soul*, which, though less frequently encountered than in *Age of Iron*, occurs twenty-eight times across the novel's 250 pages. For in *The Master of Petersburg* too there are visions of a life after death, whether the Graeco-Roman 'eternity on a river-bank

with armies of other dead souls, waiting for a barge that will never arrive'
(17), or the Christian 'eternity' guaranteed by 'Baptism: the union of a
soul with a name' (5).

Soul itself is amongst the words for which Fyodor Mikhailovich listens
in his quest to establish contact with Pavel. It comes to him, for example,
as he explains himself, not for the first time, to Anna Sergeyevna:

> His mind is quite blank. Out of that blankness he begins to speak, surren-
> dering to the words that come, going where they take him.
> 'On the ferry, when you took me to see Pavel's grave,' he says, ' ... I
> said to myself, "She will bring him back. She is'" – he takes another deep
> breath – '"she is a conductress of souls." That was not the word that came
> to me at the time, but I know now it is the right word.' (139)

This may well be a moment of madness, as Fyodor Mikhailovich suspects,
but he nevertheless both 'believes and does not believe what he is saying'
(140).

These attempts to envision or make contact with the world of the
dead are hardly the only contexts in which *soul* survives in *The Master
of Petersburg*. For it is elsewhere used again to mean that interior part of
the self which may be convulsed by epileptic fits (118), or into which one
might withdraw, insect-like: 'He thinks of himself as going back into the
egg, or at least into something smooth and cool and grey. Perhaps it is not
just an egg: perhaps it is the soul, perhaps that is how the soul looks' (19).
More significant, *soul* continues to be that which is endangered by acts of
violence committed on others – 'however scientifically these enemies of
the people are selected, you lack a means of killing them without peril to
your soul' (99) – and which one risks in gambling on one's own salvation,
playing games that leave Fyodor Mikhailovich in particular 'outside himself, perhaps outside his soul' where 'everything is suspended before the
fall' (249).

Thus, *soul* comes to mean in *The Master of Petersburg* largely what it
does in *Age of Iron*, though it is never made the subject of any predicate resembling *organ of wonder*. There are, however, several other words,
peripheral to *Age of Iron*, which attain in *The Master of Petersburg* a resonance more intense than that of *soul*, and which thereby make up for
this lack. One such word is *possession*, a term drawn from Dostoevsky's
own lexicon, which is used in *The Master of Petersburg* to figure: sexual
ecstasy (231); a mode of reading, preached by Fyodor Mikhailovich to
Maximov (47); and that operation by means of which dialectical necessity is bodied forth (44). 'In fact,' as the novel approaches its end, Fyodor

Mikhailovich, who has insisted throughout that Nechaev is like a crea-ture possessed, finds himself wondering 'whether *seizure* is any longer the right word' to describe his own fits, 'whether the word has not all along been *possession* – whether everything that … has gone under the name of seizure has not been a mere presentiment of what is now happening, the quaking and dancing of the body a long-drawn-out prelude to a quaking of the soul' (213).

Related to *possession* is a word of still greater importance, *spirit*, which occurs no fewer than thirty-five times in the novel. There must, after all, be possessor as well as possessed, and if this role is sometimes fulfilled by a kind of devil (231) or species of demon (44), the narrative's principal agent of possession is indeed a spirit, whether 'a spirit of petty evil' of the kind that holds Fyodor Mikhailovich 'in thrall' as he goes 'rummaging … through Anna Sergeyevna's possessions' (71), or the 'spirit of irritation' that keeps him from writing (236), or the 'spirit of justice' with which he believes Nechaev was born, and which 'is not yet stifled' (183–4).

In these examples, we find little more, perhaps, than an elaboration of the kind of idiomatic uses of *spirit* that occur in Coetzee's previous fictions. Elsewhere in the novel, however, *spirit* comes to mean something like the ghostly presence that haunts the living: 'He sits in his son's room … try-ing to evoke a spirit that can surely not yet have left these surroundings' (12); 'has he become not only old but a ghost, an angry, abandoned spirit?' (116). Or else it means the immaterial part of the self: 'the spirit wrestling against its bonds while the body burns away' (63–4); 'the spirit released, the spirit that at present seems knotted to his body at shoulders, hips, and knees' (127); 'Easy to kill the spirit, harder to dispose of what is left after that. The burial service and its incantations directed, if the truth be told, not at the soul but at the obstinate body' (214).

However, in several of the novel's key moments, at the heart of impor-tant confrontations, *spirit* is something closer to an animating sense of and relation to the world. It is with this meaning that Pavel has used it in his story, taking as his 'Theme' the 'spread of the spirit among the serv-ants. First muttering, then anger, rebelliousness, at last a joining of hands' (218). It is in this sense, more importantly, that Fyodor Mikhailovich attempts to explain to Maximov what Nechaev has brought into being: 'Nechaevism is not an idea. It despises ideas, it is outside ideas. It is a spirit, and Nechaev himself is not its embodiment but its host; or rather, he is under possession by it' (43–4). As for the nature of this spirit, 'There is nothing remarkable about' it; on the contrary, 'It is a dull, resentful, and murderous spirit', which has 'elected to reside in this particular young man' (44). Whatever its reasons for doing so, 'it is because of the spirit inside him', Fyodor Mikhailovich assures Maximov, 'that Nechaev has followers. They follow the spirit, not the man' (44). In much the same way, he will later explain the matter to Anna Sergeyevna: 'you will never recruit people to your cause by invoking a spirit that is alien to them, or means nothing to them. Nechaev has disciples among the young because a spirit in them answers to the spirit in him' (112).

Describing the spread of Nechaevism as a form of possession is not the same as using the language of the soul to characterize moral stultification. Nevertheless, several parallels with *Age of Iron* seem suggestive. To begin with, both novels regard their revolutions as movements of the young, struggles against oppressive regimes, but also against the previous generation of revolutionaries and the morality for which they stand. They are struggles, moreover, that refuse any compromise and will use any means necessary to attain their ends; to which words and stories are deemed irrelevant; and which, finally, by countering force with force and death with death, cannot escape the condition of existence from which they have arisen.

For revolutions of this kind remain the products of 'An age of acting ... of disguise', in which words can longer be 'trusted to travel from heart to heart' (195); an age that cannot allow any 'delicate flower' to survive, but asks that each of its children is something tougher, 'a burdock or a dandelion' (73). It is an age that therefore brings about the 'death of innocence' that so frightens Fyodor Mikhailovich when he glimpses it (213); whose harbinger is Nechaev, a man 'without sympathy. Immature in his feelings, stalled, like a midget. A man of the future, of the next century, with a monstrous head and monstrous appetites but nothing else. Lonely, lone. His proper place a throne in a bare room' (196).

Furthermore, in *The Master of Petersburg* as in *Age of Iron*, the language of the soul is deemed suspect not only by the revolutionaries but also their opponents. This must come as a surprise: we expect that Nechaev should treat religiosity with disdain, but not that those who themselves belong to a Christian world would have similar misgivings. Yet Anna Sergeyevna is impatient with Fyodor Mikhailovich's mutterings about ghosts and souls and spirits, and Maximov, though he finds it 'Interesting' that the spirit inhabiting Nechaev should be identified with Baal, must ask: 'how practical is it to talk of spirits and spirit-possession? Is it even practical to talk about ideas going about in the land, as if ideas had arms and legs?' (44). While he is prepared to admit that 'these child conspirators are certainly a different kettle of fish', and that fighting them is, in a sense, 'like fighting demons', Maximov wonders, 'in the end, whether the Nechaev phenomenon is quite as much the aberration of the spirit' that Fyodor Mikhailovich suggests (45).

Moments of doubt trouble Fyodor Mikhailovich too, as when he becomes anxious that his vision of Anna Sergeyevna as a 'conductress of souls' arises from madness. He knows full well that the language he speaks can sound strange and portentous, that it comes across sometimes like the 'language of the heart' in which the hero and heroine of Pavel's story converse, that is, as a 'funny, stammering, old-fashioned language' (196). Facing Nechaev with the command 'Swear it on your immortal soul!', Fyodor Mikhailovich hears only too clearly 'the melodramatic ring to the words', and is led to wonder where there 'are true words to be found, words to which Pavel will give his slow smile, nod his approval' (120). And, though he clearly has not ceased to believe in God, he imagines, like Mrs Curren, that 'God must be very old by now, as old as the world or even older. Perhaps he is hard of hearing and weak of vision too, like any old man' (75).

Nevertheless, though he may seem old-fashioned to his auditors and opponents, Fyodor Mikhailovich holds fast to his conviction that there are words for which he must listen and which he must use. For he needs a way of speaking with and on behalf of Pavel; and about that which communicated to and through Pavel: a voice, most closely identified with Nechaev, animated not by 'the power of life, but the power of death', a voice that articulates 'something dumb and brutal that is sweeping through young Russia' (112). He continues to insist, moreover, that, while Nechaev refuses any talk of the spirit, he yet employs a 'fashionable jargon' of his own, that of materialism; this means he cannot see 'what the Greeks call a demon', which 'speaks to him' all the same and 'is the source of his energy' (112–13).

At the last, Fyodor Mikhailovich is able to conclude his vigil, 'listening for the lost child calling from the dark stream', only when he acknowledges his compulsion to confront the spirit that has taken possession of the present age (235). Then, he can abandon altogether the demands of fidelity and accept 'betrayal – betrayal of love first of all, and then of Pavel and the mother and child and everyone else. *Perversion*: everything and everyone to be turned to another use' (235). For, through this perversion, this turning things and also words to a different use, he encounters the figure who has stalked him and to whom he will now give life. Thus he meets his fate, which is to 'live through the madness of our times' (235).

As for whether this is 'the truth or just a boast', Fyodor Mikhailovich comes to see what Mrs Curren has understood in relation to her false etymologies, which is that 'The answer does not matter, as long as he does not flinch. Nor does it matter that he speaks in figures, making his own sordid and contemptible infirmity into the emblematic sickness of the age' (235). It does not matter, in other words, whether what he follows is 'madness or epilepsy or vengeance or the spirit of the age', because 'Nothing he says is true, nothing is false, nothing is to be trusted, nothing to be dismissed. There is nothing to hold to, nothing to do but fall' (235).

Which brings us to *Disgrace*, a novel in which a theological lexicon drawn from multiple and contradictory sources again provides terms that are central to the unfolding of the narrative, but which, carried over into unfamiliar territory, often encounter resistance. This is most obviously the case with the inquiry into David Lurie's misconduct, during which he objects to the need for confession when a guilty plea should be sufficient, and protests that the repentance demanded of him 'belongs to another world, another universe of discourse.'[21] Yet, when he does confess, David Lurie will himself have recourse to a notion of agency 'beyond the scope of the law' (55), talking of Eros and Aphrodite, invoking 'the god who makes even the small birds quiver', and the older gods of flame (89, 166). To those he addresses, this manner of speaking will seem evasive or at the very least a strange kind of storytelling.

What we find in *Disgrace*, then, is a thematization of that process with which we have been concerned throughout the discussion of *Age of Iron* and *The Master of Petersburg*: the recourse to a theological lexicon in contexts that make it seem odd or misapplied. This thematization continues, moreover, as the novel proceeds. When Lucy Lurie suggests her father has been 'safely expelled' so that his 'colleagues can breathe easy again, while the scapegoat wanders in the wilderness', David Lurie questions the validity of her analogy: 'Scapegoating worked in practice while it still had religious power behind it.... It worked because everyone knew how to read the ritual, including the gods. Then the gods died' (91). Later, in the aftermath of the attack, their roles will be reversed. Refusing 'talk of plagues and fires', Lucy Lurie insists that 'Guilt and salvation are abstractions' (112).

The question of what to do with a theological lexicon once the gods have died is thus a question brought very much to the fore in *Disgrace*. It is, amongst other things, a question about what to do with an inheritance that lacks coherence and is unequally divided, a question that the novel poses broadly of the English language itself. To David Lurie, English has become 'tired, friable, eaten from the inside as if by termites' (129), and might therefore be 'an unfit medium for the truth of South Africa', or, at the very least, for the story of Petrus: 'Stretches of English code whole sentences long have thickened, lost their articulations, their articulateness, their articulatedness. Like a dinosaur expiring and settling in the mud, the language has stiffened. Pressed into the mould of English, Petrus's story would come out arthritic, bygone' (117). Nor does any obvious solution present itself; there is nothing to be done, it seems, or at least 'Nothing that he, the one-time teacher of communications, can see. Nothing short of starting all over again with the ABC' (129).

Of course, were this pessimism well founded, *Disgrace* would be disqualified in advance from communicating anything of the 'truth of South Africa'. In much the same way, a theological lexicon could be used only for the purposes of mystification if a word such as *scapegoat* were completely deprived of its meaning once the divinities underwriting its ritual significance had disappeared. Yet we cannot simply dismiss the possibility that terms of a particular lexicon can be misapplied or inappropriate, that *repentance*, for example, might reside in a 'universe of discourse' different from that in which courts and committees of inquiry operate.

A way beyond this impasse is suggested by the novel itself: instead of a wholesale ban on the transference of terms between domains, some kind of semantic accommodation will be required, such as occurs when Mr Isaacs wishes to speak of God, and David Lurie, who is 'not a believer', must 'translate what you call God and God's wishes into' his 'own terms' (172). For the words of a theological lexicon, even where they seem most out of place, most outrageous, may yet convey a truth otherwise obscured: '*I was a servant of Eros*: that is what he wants to say, but does he have the effrontery? *It was a god who acted through me.* What vanity! Yet not a lie, not entirely' (89).

This is just as well, because *Disgrace* continues to speak in the mixed tongue familiar from *Age of Iron* and *The Master of Petersburg*, in which the writings of the Old and New Testaments mingle with the language of the poets and philosophers of Greece and Rome. And as before, the theological lexicon thereby confected bears the mark of the past. Although deployed by David Lurie and his colleagues, by Lucy Lurie and Mr Isaacs, it makes little sense to the generation of the present, particularly David Lurie's students, whose 'range of ignorance' includes not only 'fallen angels or where Byron might have read of them', but also the identities of 'Byron, Lucifer, Cain' (32, 34). 'Post-Christian, posthistorical, postliterate', those to whom David Lurie professes have ceased even to recognize the terms he uses. Thus, when he speaks to them of the beloved, of the need 'to keep her alive in her archetypal, goddesslike form', their response may be anticipated: '*Archetypes?* They are saying to themselves. *Goddesses? What is he talking about?*' (22–3). Nor is it only his recourse to divinity that separates him from them: 'Do the young still fall in love,' he wonders 'or is that mechanism obsolete by now, unnecessary, quaint, like steam loco-motion? He is out of touch, out of date' (13).

This sense of being out of date, however, is not simply a function of age. Even by his head of department, David Lurie is regarded 'as a hango-ver from the past, the sooner cleared away the better' (40). Within the 'institution of learning' in which he labours, the signs are everywhere that he and 'his colleagues from the old days' find themselves 'burdened with upbringings inappropriate to the tasks they are set to perform; clerks in a post-religious age' (4). Once expelled, David Lurie becomes only more convinced that 'His mind has become a refuge for old thoughts, idle, indi-gent, with nowhere else to go', and so comes to think of himself as 'obscure and growing obscurer. A figure from the margins of history' (72, 167). And when, as happens from time to time, he hears his words 'through another's ears', they seem 'melodramatic, excessive', obliging recourse to a more grounded language, so that he will choose to speak of his 'dream' for example, when 'The word *vision* is suddenly too old-fashioned, too queer' to use in Lucy's presence (66, 103).

As for the language of the soul, it continues to appear throughout *Disgrace*, reprising certain of its earlier roles. It is that, for example, which survives death, in 'the great marsh of Styx, with souls boiling up in it like mushrooms.... Souls overcome with anger, gnawing at each other' (209–10); and it is that part of the self from whence emerge emotions of an intense kind, the 'longings' for immortality that are hurled 'to the skies' (185), or the deepest desires with which, Manas Mathabane assures David Lurie, the committee of inquiry neither is nor can be concerned: 'What goes on in your soul is dark to us, as members of what you call a secular tribunal if not as fellow human beings' (58).

From the novel's beginning, it is clear that talk of souls and spirits belongs to another world. Or, at the very least, another means of conceiv-ing subjectivity and its formation. David Lurie, for example, cannot accept the premise 'enunciated in the Communications 101 handbook', which is that '"Human society has created language in order that we may commu-nicate our thoughts, feelings and intentions to each other"'; to his mind, the true origins of 'speech lie in song, and the origins of song in the need to fill out with sound the overlarge and rather empty human soul' (3–4).

In his classroom, as he struggles to communicate his passions, the language of the soul proves a particular stumbling block. Standing before his students, David Lurie reads from Book 6 of *The Prelude*: 'From a bare ridge we also first beheld / Unveiled the summit of Mont Blanc, and grieved / To have a soulless image on the eye / That had usurped upon a living thought' (21). Later, he will cite Byron's 'Lara': 'He stood a stranger in this breathing world, / An erring spirit from another hurled; / A thing of dark imaginings'. In each case, the terms that prove most difficult to gloss are precisely those we have been following. For David Lurie will invite his class to explain 'soulless image' and, later ask, 'Who is this "erring spirit"? Why does he call himself "a thing"? From what world does he come?' (32). Faced with incomprehension, he will need to answer his own questions: the 'soulless image', he says, is a 'mere image on the retina,' which 'has encroached upon what has hitherto been a living thought', the 'visual image ... disappointing us with its matter-of-fact clarity' (21–2). As for the 'erring spirit', he is none other than Lucifer, and is a 'thing', a 'monster', because he is possessed of a 'mad heart' (33).

Clearly, *soul* and *spirit* belong to a universe of poetry and poetic understanding that has faded from the world, along with ideas about morality and existence that depend on a now moribund distinction between live thought and dead matter. David Lurie will muddle on nonetheless, trying to restore his dying universe, as in a conversation with his daughter, who believes that dogs 'do us the honour of treating us like gods, and we respond by treating them like things':

> 'The Church Fathers had a long debate about them, and decided they don't have proper souls,' he observes. 'Their souls are tied to their bodies and die with them.'
> Lucy shrugs. 'I'm not sure that I have a soul. I wouldn't know a soul if I saw one.'
> 'That's not true. You are a soul. We are all souls. We are souls before we are born.'
> She regards him oddly. (78–9)

Here again, David Lurie and the language of the soul are aligned with a world of thought and learning long expired. Yet, whilst the passage openly stages the faithlessness of the present, it also foregrounds the capacity of a man who assures us there is no 'higher life', that 'this is the only life there is', to assert, all the same, that he, his daughter and all of humanity not only possess spirit but *are* spirit (74).

In the aftermath of the attack, the novel returns to this matter, to the difficulty of using words contrary to belief and reason because one cannot otherwise capture the truth of one's experience. Although he tells himself 'It must be an effect of the pills', and that he encounters 'not a vision, not even a dream, just a chemical hallucination', David Lurie cannot banish the apparition by which he is confronted: 'Nevertheless, the figure of the woman in the field of light stays before him.' And so he is led to ask: 'Is it possible that Lucy's soul did indeed leave her body and come to him? May people who do not believe in souls yet have them, and may their souls lead an independent life?' (104). Of course, he thereby raises questions about his own incredulity: May one speak of souls without believing in God or gods or any kind of 'higher life'? If so, what would one mean? Is it the same as knowing that visions are impossible, whilst experiencing something that, but for *vision*, lacks a name?

The narrative itself seems to encourage this view when it assigns to David Lurie the role of 'dog psychopomp', guide of dog souls, whose task is to ensure that when 'The business of dog-killing is over for the day, the black bags are piled at the door, each with a body and a soul inside' (146, 161). It is he who performs the last rites, breathing in 'the smell of expiration, the soft short smell of the released soul'; it is he who watches over the condemned as 'the soul is yanked out of the body', before 'it is sucked away and is gone' in 'this room that is not a room but a hole where one leaks out of existence'; it is he who packs the bodies away 'when the soul is out' (218–19). This work is not without consequences: though he fears that 'Habit hardens', that 'people from whom cruelty is demanded in the line of duty, people who work in slaughterhouses, for instance, grow carapaces over their souls', he finds, on the contrary, that his task grows ever more difficult (143).

As it had been in *Age of Iron*, the covering over of the soul is one way to speak of the process of moral atrophy, by which we come to treat others as things. But there is another way of describing this process, which, having earlier appeared in *Age of Iron* and *The Master of Petersburg*, becomes increasingly important in *Disgrace*. For, though Mrs Curren has spoken tentatively of something going from heart to heart, and Fyodor Mikhailovich finds an antiquated language of the heart in Pavel's writings, it is in *Disgrace* that this language is a more pervasive and substantive supplement to the theological lexicon.

To begin with, it is true, *heart* appears only in familiar idiomatic phrases: 'What, in her heart, is she trying to be?' (27); 'Despite himself, his heart goes out to her' (32). But, having raised the question of the meaning of the 'mad heart' of Byron's 'erring spirit', the narrative begins to settle more frequently on what would otherwise be stock phrases. Thus, before he has become aware of the cause of his daughter's unhappiness, Mr Isaacs will confide to David Lurie that 'She always takes things so to heart, Professor, that's her nature,' which will come as a surprise to a man who 'would not have guessed' that 'Melanie-Meláni, with her baubles from the Oriental Plaza and her blind spot for Wordsworth, takes things to heart' (37).

Not long after, once the wrongdoer's identity has been revealed, the question of the heart – of one's deepest feelings, thoughts and desires – is raised again in the committee of inquiry, when David Lurie is told that, if his colleagues and accusers are to 'see if it comes from his heart', if it reflects his 'sincere feelings', his statement will have to 'come from him, in his own words'; to which he responds by asking whether they trust themselves 'to divine that, from the words I use – to divine whether it comes from my heart' (54). And when, finally, he seeks out Mr Isaacs, David Lurie will explain his visit by again referring to the heart: '"I thought I would drop in anyway, and say what is on my heart." That much is true. He does want to speak his heart. The question is, what is on his heart?' (165). What is on David Lurie's heart remains opaque to himself and to others; certainly, it will not have been made clear to Mr Isaacs, who pursues the matter: '"Mr Lurie," says Isaacs: "is there something else you want to tell me, besides the story of yourself and Melanie? You mentioned there was something on your heart"' (167). At which David Lurie baulks. He either does not know or does not wish to share: '"On my heart? No. No, I just stopped by to find out how Melanie was"' (167).

Whatever it is that weighs upon him, David Lurie's fall from grace is made to parallel that of the 'erring spirit' of which he has spoken to his class. Since his own heart might therefore be mad, the novel begins to turn on the question of whether a damaged heart, a wrong way of feeling, might be repaired. If nothing else, this has the effect of adding a certain charge to later occurrences of familiar idiomatic phrases: 'You will have to do it out of the goodness of your heart' (77); 'Looking into his heart, he can find only a vague sadness' (127); 'Bev Shaw may be not a liberating angel but a devil, ... beneath her show of compassion may hide a heart as leathery as a butcher's' (144); 'Will an older Teresa engage his heart as his heart is now?' (181); 'Can he find it in his heart to love this plain, ordinary woman?' (182); 'He goes to bed with a heavy heart. Nothing has changed between Lucy and himself, nothing has healed' (200–1). In each case, *heart* returns as that in which one's true feelings reside, however obscure these remain, an organ that, as with *soul*, enables generosity, love and a relation to what is not ourselves. Thus, it is also from the heart that a gratitude not unlike that experienced by Mrs Curren will suddenly well up: '*Enriched.... A stu-pid word to let slip, under the circumstances, yet now, at this moment, he would stand by it. By Melanie, by the girl in Touws Rivier; by Rosalind, Bev Shaw, Soraya: by each of them, even the failures. Like a flower bloom-ing in his breast, his heart floods with thankfulness*' (192).

The notion that David Lurie's heart may indeed be damaged is there-fore significant, and one that the novel encourages in several important moments, particularly those immediately preceding and following the attack. Even before it has begun in earnest, we read of David Lurie that 'In his chest his heart hammers so hard that it too, in its dumb way, must know. How will they stand up to the testing, he and his heart?' (94). And, in its aftermath, we learn that the attack has 'shocked him to the depths.... He has a sense that, inside him, a vital organ has been bruised, abused – perhaps even his heart' (107). If these instances seem to refer in the first place to an organ of valves and pumps and the circulation of blood, the different sense in which *heart* has previously been used continues to lin-ger, colouring even these anatomical references. In any case, it will ultim-ately be confirmed that the heart as organ of gratitude and love has also been bruised: 'Again the feeling washes over him: listlessness, indifference, but also weightlessness, as if he has been eaten away from inside and only the eroded shell of his heart remains' (156).

It is a mistake, of course, to imagine that David Lurie's damaged heart was in good working order before the attack, but it is no less a mistake to believe that this madness of heart is a wholly personal matter, when there is evidence that desire has been more widely corrupted. To begin with, the hollowing of the heart that has affected him seems to David Lurie to be typical also of what Lucy calls 'Country ways', but for which 'He has other words: indifference, hardheartedness' (125). Yet even this urbane judgement on rural life falls short of the mark, because the conversion of people into things has come to seem a fundamental condition for sanity's survival:

> Too many people, too few things. What there is must go into circulation, so that everyone can have a chance to be happy for a day. That is the the-ory; hold to the theory and to the comforts of the theory. Not human evil, just a vast circulatory system, to whose workings pity and terror are irrele-vant. That is how one must see life in this country: in its schematic aspect. Otherwise one could go mad. Cars, shoes; women too. There must be some niche in the system for women and what happens to them. (98)

And what seems to lie behind this theory, to occasion it and require it as explanation, is precisely that kind of simplified existence that David Lurie sometimes desires, and which he has intuited in his and Lucy's attackers: 'He is tired of shadows, of complications, of complicated people. He loves his daughter, but there are times when he wishes she were a simpler being: simpler, neater. The man who raped her, the leader of the gang, was like that. Like a blade cutting the wind' (170–1).

Yet, were he to have his wish, it would mean the end not only of the notion of human evil, but also all talk of heart and spirit and soul. For David Lurie has previously reflected that the residence of the soul is 'perhaps the gall bladder, which no one will eat. Descartes should have thought of that. The soul, suspended in the dark, bitter gall, hiding' (124). And now, thinking of this 'simpler being', he likewise thinks of the consequences of this particular form of simplification:

> He has a vision of himself stretched out on an operating table. A scalpel flashes; from throat to groin he is laid open; he sees it all yet feels no pain. A surgeon, bearded, bends over him, frowning. *What is all this stuff?* growls the surgeon. He pokes at the gall bladder. *What is this?* He cuts it out, tosses it aside. He pokes at the heart. *What is this?* (171)

Clearly, to this simplified man of the future, those organs required for love and gratitude and wonder have become redundant, immaterial. They may as well be cut out and left to one side, cast away as offal.

The Meanings of Coetzee's Theological Lexicon

I have thus far detailed the presence in Coetzee's middle fictions of a lexicon that is characterized as both necessary and inadequate. The characters who use its words, whether as narrators or focalizers, recognize that speaking of souls and spirits, of cancer of the heart and of possession, will make them seem mad, or at least old-fashioned, to those with whom they converse. Yet they persevere.

As to the readers of these fictions, they are likely to find this lexicon somehow odd, prompted by the narratives' moments of reflexivity, if not by the suspicion of misplaced terminology articulated in *Disgrace*. They may also become aware that this language of the soul is a confection, not only of several systems of belief, but also of a range of literary sources. It is thus a highly literary language, and for this reason too, though it is spoken with sincerity by characters and by the narratives themselves, its use will remain circumspect.

What then is the effect of this sincere yet circumspect language? To begin with, it transposes into a secular context a range of terms and ideas which are then re-energized, granted weight and vitality, constituted as relevant to this new environment, and in particular to the matters with which Coetzee's middle fictions are concerned. For if the language of the soul is made to seem necessary for the truth that Mrs Curren and Fyodor Mikhailovich and David Lurie wish to tell – a truth that is as much about the nature of death and being towards death as it is about life, of whatever kind – it becomes necessary also for the truths that the novels themselves attempt to communicate and create.

In this, Coetzee's middle fictions might be compared with works he addresses in 'Confession and Double Thoughts', an essay published during the period in which *Foe* was composed, and which thus gave prior indication of the coming shift in literary practice. Here, Coetzee follows 'the fortunes of a number of secular confessions, fictional and autobiographical, as their authors confront or evade the problem of how to know the truth about the self without being self-deceived, and of how to bring the confession to an end in the spirit of whatever they take to be the secular equivalent of absolution.' At the very outset, he admits that 'A certain looseness is inevitable when one transposes the term *confession* from a religious to a secular context', but he remains convinced that it is possible to speak of confessional narratives, as distinct from *memoirs* and *apologies* 'on the basis of an underlying motive to tell an essential truth about the self', which motive he discerns not only in works of Tolstoy and Dostoevsky, but also in 'the made-up confessions of sinners like Moll Flanders and Roxana'.[22]

The object of this comparison is not to identify Coetzee's own novels as confessional fictions (though *Foe* and *Age of Iron* may well be understood in this light). It is simply to explain their use of the language of the soul as a not dissimilar transposition of related ideas – particularly ideas about the self – from a theological or metaphysical context to the secular context of the novel. As to what such a transposition would entail, and the reasons for attempting it, we have seen already that the novels are thereby enabled to broach, in a manner that may or may not be metaphoric, a range of important matters: dying and death, moods and emotions, the spread of ideas and the struggles between generations, a kind of moral corruption.

It is, moreover, by means of this language of the soul that the self comes to be constituted as the site of adventure, an expanded ground for exploration, and also as something different to the self-sufficient entity it is imagined to be in the discourse of liberalism as much as in those theories that posit the only end of revolutionary struggle as the unrestricted access to resources. For in each of Coetzee's middle fictions, the self can be damaged and stunted, deprived of its capacity to exercise even those freedoms that might be won on its behalf.

It is the language of the soul, therefore, that allows Coetzee to ask about the consequences of manichean struggle without having to resort to notions of the human articulated by psychoanalysis, such as, for example, trauma. Indeed, by transposing this theological lexicon (which is really, as we have seen, a literary lexicon), he confronts the problem of how the self might come to require re-formation and how, indeed, it might come to be reformed. For, regardless of whether we believe in the soul as such – and there is nothing in the novels that compels such a belief – we are invited to consider the self *as if* it had whatever dimensions and qualities we associate with being ensouled.

Of all the middle fictions, this effect is perhaps clearest in *Disgrace*, which is most explicit not only in exploring the aftermath of a life-and-death struggle, but also in conducting this exploration through words and ideas transposed from a religious to a secular context. Needless to say, this transposition may be significant also in reflecting on the mechanism of national confession and absolution inaugurated during the transition from apartheid. But it is all the more significant for allowing Coetzee to pose questions about education, about the formation of subjectivity. For it is only insofar as the self is expanded and understood as something other than that which is simply given, something that might indeed need to be *re*-formed, that we can begin to ask certain questions about transformation, of the subject, and of society itself.

Here we might note that David Lurie arrives in his narrative holding fast to *temperament*, a notion of the self as opaque as those with which we have been concerned. What David Lurie believes is that 'His temperament is not going to change, he is too old for that. His temperament is fixed, set. The skull, followed by the temperament: the two hardest parts of the body' (2). On this basis, he will resist all attempts at 'Re-education. Reformation of the character. The code-word was *counselling*' (66); he will insist: 'I am a grown man. I am not receptive to being counselled. I am beyond the reach of counselling' (49); and even when he agrees to help Bev Shaw he will do so conditionally: 'All right, I'll do it. But only so long as I don't have to become a better person. I am not prepared to be reformed, I want to go on being myself' (77).

But this is before the action of the novel has done its work on him, consuming him, burning him, burning him up, replacing his human charges with animals, making of the scholar and poet a dog-man, a care-taker of sorts, making him question his former conclusions: 'How does she get it right, this communion with animals? Some trick he does not have.... Do I have to change, he thinks? Do I have to become like Bev Shaw?'

(126). And so, repeatedly subjected to versions of his interrogation by Mr Isaacs – 'The question is, what lesson have we learned? The question is, what are we going to do now that we are sorry?' – David Lurie will have to reconsider the truth of what he would normally say, which is 'that after a certain age one is too old to learn lessons' (172).

Until, in the novel's final pages, under the sign of the perfective, David Lurie, in search of a new footing, a new start, has become a man ready to acknowledge his own bad faith: 'The truth is, he has never had much of an eye for rural life, despite all his reading in Wordsworth. Not much of an eye for anything, except pretty girls; and where has that got him? Is it too late to educate the eye?' Is it ever too late for education, for the kind of rearrangement of desires, of the imagination, which is at once aesthetic and ethical? These are the questions that the novel asks; and it is able to do so precisely because the very notion of a fixed temperament has been discarded, replaced by a sense of the self as that which can be formed, deformed, and perhaps even reformed.

A further means of understanding the expansive strain found in Coetzee's middle fictions requires that, instead of focussing on the particular meanings generated by *soul, spirit, substance* and *heart*, we consider the general impression these words create, an impression that is ultimately a function of the novels' prose style, which remains simple, spare and lyrical, but becomes somehow more profound, more resonant. For *Foe, Age of Iron, The Master of Petersburg* and *Disgrace* produce a sense of depth in their probing, which might be mistaken even for richness, were it not for the counterweight of the writing's aridity; a depth, in any case, that signals their engagement with precisely those questions of philosophy, and in particular of ethics, in relation to which Coetzee's works have latterly come to be discussed.

Here it is helpful to introduce the notion of *register*, which belongs properly to the field of sociolinguistics. According to Peter Trudgill, who refers in turn to Michael Halliday, 'register' is a 'technical term … used to describe a language *variety* that is associated with a particular topic, subject or activity'. In English, he proceeds, 'registers are characterized for the most part by vocabulary', although 'grammatical features' are sometimes also involved.[23] A given register, then, is a particular lexicon used in a particular context to refer to or talk about a particular thing or subject matter. It is a skein of associations constituted by convention that ensures that a listener or reader might infer from certain words or even a certain tone corresponding threads of subject matter and context.

Clearly, this might be related to the language of the heart, spirit and soul in Coetzee's middle fictions, because this is marked not only by a specific terminology, but also by a specific set of concerns: with the nature of the self, with the nature of life and the end of life and with the nature of relations between selves. Since these concerns are properly those of ontology and ethics, one might well speak of the adoption in Coetzee's middle fictions of a metaphysical or meta-ethical or indeed spiritual register, a register of the spirit, a register that, at the very least, communicates to Coetzee's readers a certain seriousness, an engagement with matters that are, in the fullest sense, fundamental. If nothing else, this may explain something of the frequency with which Coetzee has recently been taken up by philosophers and philosophically minded literary critics.

Beyond the question of Coetzee's attractiveness to philosophers, however, there remains at least one further means of explaining the properly stylistic effects of the language of the soul, which has more to do with the power of fiction as fiction, art as art. For, though we do not in fact encounter ghosts, demons, angels or gods in any of these novels (except perhaps in *Foe*), we meet with *soul* and *spirit* on page after page, and thus come to inhabit realities in which there seems more than meets the eye. Not that there is anything mysterious about this effect: it is simply because *soul* and *spirit* are comprehended in the worlds of these fictions, or rather, because they are constitutive of these worlds, that one comes to feel the reality thus produced is not only bare and stark, but also profound; that it has, for want of a better word, a spiritual dimension.

It must be reiterated that this dimension does not entail the existence of God or the soul or any other metaphysical entity. Instead, it has to do with the capacity of fiction – indeed, the work of art – to produce the truth content of a particular moment. In other words, if the power of Coetzee's early fictions resides in their manner of confronting readers with the truth of a world laid bare, the spiritual dimension added to his middle fictions might be viewed as productive of another such truth. For, without counteracting the sense of bareness produced by stark economy (which, on the contrary, may seem intensified), the expansive strain found in these fictions makes us feel – makes me feel – that the deprivations of a manichean existence ramify more profoundly than we might otherwise have imagined. And this effect depends precisely on the oddness of this spiritual register, its misalignment with an understanding of existence that is in the very crudest sense materialist, because it is when the language of the soul seems to belong to an alien reality that we begin to see and to know how much of our own world has been liquidated.

In his *Aesthetic Theory*, Theodor Adorno writes: 'By their very existence artworks postulate the existence of what does not exist.'[24] The work of art is a work of negation, in particular a negation of the world as it is taken to be, its badness accepted as given. It is in this light, I believe, that the spiritual register of Coetzee's middle fictions is best understood. In opposition to a vision of the world that embraces and is embraced by an economic rationalism that reduces every question of power to a question of access to resources – as if the damage inflicted by manichean struggle were only ever superficial, skin-deep – *Age of Iron*, *The Master of Petersburg* and *Disgrace* confront us with the absence of a different sense of ourselves, with our inability to treat seriously even the notion of a spiritual dimension, and hence the notion of a world other than a world of things.

Whatever its broader significance, Coetzee's spiritual register has a particular poignance in the context of South Africa during the 1980s and 1990s. In the context, that is, of a struggle between political enemies and generations that has made young radicals into simplified people, figures of pig iron, 'swifter, nimbler, more tireless than real people, without doubts or scruples, without humour, ruthless, innocent', 'Without feeling, without sympathy'.[25] For if, from the point of view of Mrs Curren and Fyodor Mikhailovich, there has been a stunting of the soul or some kind of demonic possession, from the point of view of the novels, something has happened that cannot be grasped in the terms chosen by the 'secular authorities' – who are concerned to 'understand in a material, investigative sense' – or, indeed, in those chosen by their youthful opponents, whose approach is likewise conceived, or rather misconceived, as 'materialist'.[26]

Here it is worth noting again that in each of the middle fictions something has departed from the world, whether this is *charity* or *grace* or even *truth*, which suggests that there is a lack not only of a religiosity but also of what we might call a moral lexicon and indeed a moral sensibility. What I have been trying to suggest is that, as an effect of the style of these novels, we come to feel a lack in our own world, a lack not of religion or God or a tired morality, but rather of a particular sense of the world's depth and of ourselves. Yet it is through this sense that we might begin to grasp the nature of the loss inflicted on us by the violence of manichean conflict. The reality of Coetzee's middle fictions – a reality that we are compelled to take for our own – is not only pared down and stripped of human relation, but resistant to a way of speaking and understanding that might allow us to remediate its badness, to overcome the very brutishness that is the truth content of Coetzee's early fictions.

Conclusion

To leave off with *Disgrace* is of course to end where many studies of Coetzee's fictions now begin. It is also to let pass largely unremarked works that have been extremely important in establishing Coetzee's global reputation, as well as his extra-literary significance, and which are undeniably contiguous with the fictions that preceded them. The conceptual cluster that is powerfully present in both *Age of Iron* and *Disgrace* – love, desire, death and care – seems no less central to *Elizabeth Costello*, *Slow Man* and *Diary of a Bad Year*. In each of these novels, the tired, the sick, the lame and the old seek out strange nurses, secretaries, psychopomps, attendants on death, carers of body and soul.

Nevertheless, in spite of such thematic resonances, I am satisfied to leave matters as they stand. For there is a coherence, on the one hand, of the works I have examined, all composed and published while Coetzee remained resident in South Africa, during apartheid and its immediate aftermath; and, on the other hand, of the later works, which have in common not only their Australian subject matter and place of composition, but also a certain striving against generic limits, an attempt to re-make or even unmake the novel. Whereas the concern of the middle fictions is with finding and using new lexicons and registers, the developments in Coetzee's 'Australian' novels have had to do, by and large, with features and factors beyond the word, phrase and sentence.

There is thus a clear continuity between these works and those I described in the introduction as Coetzee's memorial fictions, *Boyhood*, *Youth* and *Summertime*, which attempt to unfix the boundaries between memoir and confessional novel, much as the Australian novels, in staging encounters with central characters who resemble Coetzee (Elizabeth Costello in *Elizabeth Costello* and *Slow Man*, Señor C. in *Diary of a Bad Year*), invite us to approach them also as kinds of life writing. As such, although the publication date of *Boyhood* places it between *The Master of*

199

Petersburg and *Disgrace*, there seem good enough reasons to view it as a first step in a new direction.

What, then, of Coetzee's most recent novel, *The Childhood of Jesus?* Although it is too early to say whether it marks the beginning of yet another stage, it does seem a departure from the three novels by which it is preceded. This has little to do with its thematics: though it focuses on the very young rather than the old, the narrative is yet concerned with what it means to care and to love, to teach and to learn, and with how a theological lexicon might be transposed to a secular context. But in leaving Australia for a *vita nuova* in a Spain of the mind, and in lacking an obvious stand-in for the author, *The Childhood of Jesus* does appear to enter new territory.

If there is a question we might nevertheless pose, in relation to this novel as well as *Elizabeth Costello, Slow Man* and *Diary of a Bad Year*, it is whether we do not see in them an obvious shift towards metafiction, and thus away from the world and towards art. Does Coetzee, in other words, ultimately reproduce the movement he had described in his earliest critical essays and found so troubling? The answer, it seems to me, is that, while Coetzee's later novels are certainly preoccupied more with elements of fiction writing and storytelling, and less with the violence engendered in the colonial encounter, they persist in asking questions about the formation and transformation of subjectivity, about the meaning of care in the face of age, illness and death, and about the consequences of treating others as if they were things.

Certainly, there has been no diminution in the realism of Coetzee's writing, so long as we keep in mind the manner in which this term was defined in earlier chapters, that is, as an orientation towards the world. Both *Elizabeth Costello* and *Slow Man*, it is true, stage their fictionality quite flagrantly, whilst *Diary of a Bad Year* foregrounds its textuality, and *The Childhood of Jesus* its literary imbrications. Nevertheless, each remains animated by what the philosopher Stephen Mulhall has recently described as the 'realistic spirit'. Though it focuses largely on *Elizabeth Costello* (and takes too seriously literary critical assertions of the irresolvable tension between realism and modernism), Mulhall's compelling account of this novel's 'commitment to represent reality' can, I believe, be generalized to include all of Coetzee's late fictions, in each of which there is an attempt 'rigorously to think through the true nature and consequences of an impossibility', to offer 'an unsentimental articulation of what the impossible embedding of one reality into another might reveal about both'.[1]

In bringing this chapter to a close, and with it this book, there is a temptation – not wholly dissimilar to that which Magda feels at the conclusion of *In the Heart of the Country* – to slip those bonds that have limited its scope, however self-imposed, in order to gesture towards a far territory of meanings and values, theories and ideas; a temptation to fall, in other words, into those 'closing plangencies' proper to literary criticism, and to enact a retreat from whatever may have seemed too dogmatically argued or forcefully proposed.

Of course, what I have offered is only one way of addressing Coetzee's novels. The critical corpus is rapidly expanding, and though I have not quoted widely from it, my understanding of Coetzee's oeuvre has certainly been enriched and made possible by the insights of others. For all that, I remain committed to my initial aims, chief amongst which was to illuminate aspects of Coetzee's fictions that have been central to the experiences of a great many readers, and yet often neglected by literary critics; aspects that are of vital importance, I believe, to a sense of what is both distinctive and meaningful about these works.

To this end, I have tried to show how elements of syntax, lexis, prosody, rhetoric and narrative have contributed to the spare, stark, taut, intense and lyrical style for which Coetzee has come to be known; and how, in his middle fictions, changes in subject matter are paralleled and indeed achieved by other changes in his literary practice, and in particular by the introduction of a theological lexicon and techniques of parenthetical sincerity. To this end also, I have tried to explain how the meanings of Coetzee's fictions depend on a context of intelligibility, a literary field and a literary material substantially made up of the writings of other South African authors.

These aims have in turn been inflected by desires and intentions that, without being often announced, have nonetheless shaped the trajectory of this study. Here it is important to acknowledge that, though the particular approach of each of its chapters has been prompted by Coetzee's own texts, its broader concern has been to demonstrate the need for all critical readers to attend to the complex operations of language by which every literary work achieves its effects. If this need is one that appears self-evident, or is assumed to have been always central to literary critical endeavour, it is necessary now more than ever to give it special emphasis. For grammar seems increasingly to be regarded as the special preserve either of pedants or professional linguists, and students of literature continue to arrive in university classrooms and lecture theatres ill equipped to analyse the language that they and others use.

This is not to insist that every undergraduate commit to learning by rote the figures and tropes catalogued by rhetoricians, or to memorizing the arcane technical terminology employed in discussions of syntax and prosody, morphology and narration. It is rather to suggest that we begin both as teachers and pupils by recognizing that we are each of us affected by those subtle shifts in tense and tone, vocabulary and register that are often the consequence of a writer's groping search for subject matters and forms. If a grounding in the terms of linguistics and narratology helps us articulate more clearly the effects of a work as well as the causes of these effects, so much the better, though we should certainly avoid the slavish application of pre-formulated and supposedly portable methodologies.

What we should further avoid is the kind of belletrism that has tarnished several previous attempts to describe and discuss style. In this regard, it is worth repeating that, by examining Coetzee's prose, my purpose throughout has been not to demonstrate its intrinsic aesthetic qualities and achievements, but to explain how it constitutes the meanings of his fictions, and so to show how Coetzee's literary practice has from the outset been oriented towards the world and about the world. As such, if this book is to be aligned with any particular literary critical discipline or tradition, it should be that of postcolonial studies, for though seldom mentioned in these pages, the tenor of its principal concerns, I hope, is everywhere in evidence.

Indeed, this book has been at least partly conceived as a response to the prospects of postcolonial literary criticism, as well as its shortcomings. If it is to survive its own faddishness, it will need to address its failure to treat literary works as literary works, rather than cultural texts, a failure that, although of a general character, has been all too evident in many of the scholarly articles devoted to Coetzee, and above all in those devoted to his early fictions. This book may therefore be seen as one amongst several recent attempts to reorient postcolonial studies towards questions of craft and technique, so that it is better able to respond to the complex and troubling demands of verbal artefacts that have the capacity to produce and confront us with unsettling truths of our particular realities.

Notes

Introduction

1 Nicholas Shakespeare, 'A Slap Bang Farce Nipped in the Bud', *The Times*, 11 September 1986, p. 11; Neill Darke, 'Coetzee Novel Bewildering and Tortuous', *Argus*, 23 October 1986, p. 29; D. J. Enright, 'Visions and Revisions', *New York Review of Books*, 28 May 1987, pp. 18–20 (p. 20).

2 Isabel Hofmeyr, 'A Bewildering Parable', *Star*, 22 September 1986, p. 14; Heather Mackie, 'Consummate Literary Brilliance of Coetzee Emerges Again', *Cape Times*, 31 December 1986, p. 6; Alexander Johnston, 'Skilful Work on Many Levels', *Sunday Tribune*, 18 January 1987, Today section, p. 8.

3 Peter Wilhelm, 'Vietnam, SA Powerfully Linked', *Star*, 24 April 1974, p. 21; Ursula A. Barnett, 'South Africa', *Books Abroad*, 50.2 (1976), 459–60 (p. 460).

4 Frances Bowers, 'First SA Modern Novel?', *Cape Times*, 5 June 1974, p. 8; Peter Temple, 'The Private World of a Major New SA Talent', *Star*, 14 June 1974, Literary Review section, p. 3.

5 Nicholas Shakespeare, 'Forever Blowing Bubbles', *The Times*, 13 January 1983, p. 8; Victoria Glendinning, 'A Harsh Voice Crying in the Wilderness', *Sunday Times*, 23 January 1983, p. 45.

6 Ronald Harwood, 'An Astonishing First Novel', *Sunday Times*, 12 June 1977, p. 41; T. M., 'Exploring an Inner World', *Sunday Tribune*, 30 July 1978, Insight section, p. 3.

7 Lionel Abrahams, 'Drama of Desperation', *Rand Daily Mail*, 15 May 1978, p. 6; Jaap Boekkooi, 'Injustice for "Society's Sake"', *Star*, 19 February 1981, p. 12.

8 Henry Kratz, review of *Life & Times of Michael K*, *World Literature Today*, 58.3 (1984), 461–2; Charles Barry, 'Compassion Makes Memorable Work', *Star*, 28 October 1983, p. 12.

9 Cherry Clayton, 'Coetzee Blends Fable with Harsh SA Reality', *Rand Daily Mail*, 2 March 1981, p. 8.

10 Irving Howe, 'A Stark Political Fable of South Africa', *New York Times Book Review*, 18 April 1982, pp. 1, 36; Dave Wightman, 'Something Familiar about the Barbarians', *Sunday Tribune*, 22 February 1981, p. 6.

11 Claire Tomalin, 'The Magical Historical Shortlist', *Sunday Times*, 25 September 1983, p. 41; Peter Harris, 'The Art of Being a Survivor', *Cape Times*, 30 November 1983, p. 14; Alexander Johnston, 'Triumphs of the Human

Spirit', *Sunday Tribune*, 25 December 1983, Today section, p. 15; Beryl Roberts, 'Not a Wasted Word in this Major Work', *Sunday Times* [South Africa], 13 November 1983, Lifestyle section, p. 7.

12 Anne Pogrund, 'Survival against Odds Powerfully Portrayed', *Rand Daily Mail*, 12 December 1983, p. 12; Cynthia Ozick, 'A Tale of Heroic Anonymity', *New York Times Book Review*, 11 December 1983, pp. 1, 26, 28 (p. 1); Roberts, 'Not a Wasted Word in this Major Work', p. 7.

13 J. M. Coetzee, 'The English Fiction of Samuel Beckett: An Essay in Stylistic Analysis' (unpublished doctoral dissertation, University of Texas at Austin, 1969), p. 78.

14 Wolfgang Iser, *The Act of Reading: A Theory of Aesthetic Response* (Baltimore, MD: Johns Hopkins University Press, 1978); Stanley Fish, *Is There a Text in This Class? The Authority of Interpretive Communities* (Cambridge, MA: Harvard University Press, 1980); Michael Riffaterre, 'Describing Poetic Structures: Two Approaches to Baudelaire's "Les Chats"', *Yale French Studies*, 36/37 (1966), 200–42.

15 Theodor W. Adorno, *Aesthetic Theory*, ed. by Gretel Adorno and Rolf Tiedemann, trans. by Robert Hullot-Kentor (London: Continuum, 2004), p. 169.

16 Mark Schorer, 'Technique as Discovery', *Hudson Review*, 1.1 (1948), 67–87 (p. 67).

17 Blair Rouse and James R. Bennett, 'Editorial', *Style*, 1.1 (1967), v–vii (p. vii).

18 This understanding of the difference between form and style clearly diverges from that articulated, for example, by Roland Barthes, *Writing Degree Zero*, trans. by Annette Lavers and Colin Smith (New York: Hill and Wang, 1968), pp. 9–18.

19 For an incisive account of this process of aesthetic banalization, see Theodor W. Adorno, 'Punctuation Marks', in *Notes to Literature*, ed. by Rolf Tiedemann, trans. by Shierry Weber Nicholsen, 2 vols. (New York: Columbia University Press, 1991), I, pp. 91–7.

20 For an early critique of this approach, see Louis T. Milic, 'Against the Typology of Styles', in *Essays on the Languages of Literature*, ed. by Seymour Chatman and Samuel R. Levin (Boston, MA: Houghton Mifflin, 1967), pp. 442–50.

21 Geoffrey N. Leech and Michael H. Short, *Style in Fiction: A Linguistic Introduction to English Fictional Prose* (Harlow: Longman, 1981), pp. 38–9. Italics in original.

22 Coetzee, 'The English Fiction of Samuel Beckett', p. 155.

23 Pierre Bourdieu, *The Rules of Art: Genesis and Structure of the Literary Field*, trans. by Susan Emanuel (Cambridge: Polity Press, 1996). The critics who have found Bourdieu helpful in this way include: Bo G. Ekelund, *In the Pathless Forest: John Gardner's Literary Project* (Uppsala: Uppsala University, 1995); Peter D. McDonald, *British Literary Culture and Publishing Practice, 1880–1914* (Cambridge: Cambridge University Press, 1997); Pascale Casanova, *The World Republic of Letters*, trans. by M. B. DeBevoise (Cambridge, MA: Harvard University Press, 2004).

24 Simon Jarvis, *Adorno: A Critical Introduction* (Cambridge: Polity Press, 1998).

25 Adorno, *Aesthetic Theory*, p. 194.

26 Ben Etherington, 'What is Materialism's Material? Thoughts toward (actually against) a Materialism for "World Literature"', *Journal of Postcolonial Writing*, 48.5 (2012), 539–51 (p. 543).

27 Adorno, *Aesthetic Theory*, p. 194.

28 Paul Simpson, *Stylistics: A Resource Book for Students* (London: Routledge, 2004), p. 3.

29 Christopher Heywood, *A History of South African Literature* (Cambridge: Cambridge University Press, 2004), p. vii.

30 Peter D. McDonald, *The Literature Police: Apartheid Censorship and its Cultural Consequences* (Oxford: Oxford University Press, 2009), p. 137.

31 Manfred Nathan, *South African Literature: A General Survey* (Cape Town and Johannesburg: Juta & Co, 1925), p. 14.

32 *English and South Africa*, ed. by Alan Lennox-Short (Cape Town: Nasou, 1973).

33 Stephen Gray, *Southern African Literature: An Introduction* (Cape Town: David Philip; London: Rex Collings, 1979), p. 9. It is worth noting that Gray's approach has in turn been critiqued from a feminist and post-structuralist perspective by Louise Bethlehem in *Skin Tight: Apartheid Literary Culture and its Aftermath* (Pretoria: University of South Africa Press, 2006), pp. 38–54.

34 Gray, *Southern African Literature*, p. 1, p. 14.

35 *Close to the Sun: Stories from Southern Africa*, ed. by G. E. de Villiers (Johannesburg: Macmillan South Africa, 1979), p. 1.

36 Anthony Sampson, 'Introduction', in *South African Writing Today*, ed. by Nadine Gordimer and Lionel Abrahams (Harmondsworth: Penguin, 1967), pp. 11–15 (pp. 11–12).

37 Ibid., pp. 12–13.

38 *A Land Apart: A Contemporary South African Reader*, ed. by André Brink and J. M. Coetzee (New York: Penguin, 1987), p. 7.

39 Gray, *Southern African Literature*, p. 14.

40 Philip Segal, 'On *Waiting for Godot*', in *Essays and Lectures: Selected Literary Criticism*, ed. by Marcia Leveson (Cape Town: David Philip, 1973), pp. 188–92 (188).

41 Jarvis, *Adorno*, p. 6.

42 J. M. Coetzee, *Doubling the Point: Essays and Interviews*, ed. by David Attwell (Cambridge, MA: Harvard University Press, 1992).

43 This is one of the respects in which this study differs from Carrol Clarkson's *J. M. Coetzee: Countervoices* (Basingstoke: Palgrave Macmillan, 2009), which 'offers a series of discussions on linguistico-ethical topics, each of which ranges across Coetzee's entire oeuvre', p. 17.

44 I have also made sparing use of J. C. Kannemeyer's recent biography, which, in its account of the early part of Coetzee's career, relies so heavily on his memorial fictions and on retrospective comments in later interviews. J. C. Kannemeyer, *A Life in Writing*, trans. by Michiel Heyns (Johannesburg and Cape Town: Jonathan Ball, 2013).

45 J. M. Coetzee, 'The Novel Today', *Upstream*, 6.1 (1988), 2–5.

46 The Booker is mentioned in: Roberts, 'Not a Wasted Word in this Major Work', p. 7; Johnston, 'Triumphs of the Human Spirit', p. 15; Neill Darke, 'Coetzee's Prize-Winning Novel Original, Compelling', *Argus*, 23 November 1983, p. 26; Garner Thompson, 'J. M. Coetzee's *Life and Times of Michael K . . .* Not All Praise', *Weekend Argus*, 29 October 1983, p. 13.

47 The most important of these was Nadine Gordimer's review of *Life & Times of Michael K*, 'The Idea of Gardening', *New York Review of Books*, 2 February 1984, pp. 3, 6.

48 McDonald, *The Literature Police*, p. 137. For an account of the relevance of Coetzee's involvement with Ravan, see also Andrew van der Vlies, *South African Textual Cultures: White, Black, Read All Over* (Manchester: Manchester University Press, 2007), Hermann Wittenberg, 'Towards an Archaeology of *Dusklands*', *English in Africa*, 38.3 (2011), 71–89, and Jarad Zimbler, 'Under Local Eyes: The South African Publishing Context of J. M. Coetzee's *Foe*', *English Studies in Africa*, 47.1 (2004), 47–59.

Chapter 1

1 J. M. Coetzee, *Dusklands* (Johannesburg: Ravan Press, 1974), front inside cover. Subsequent references are to this edition and are given after quotations in the text, except where indicated.

2 Jonathan Crewe, '*Dusklands*', *Contrast*, 9.2 (1974), 90–5 (p. 91).

3 Stephen Watson, 'Colonialism and the Novels of J. M. Coetzee', *Research in African Literatures*, 17.3 (1986), 370–92 (p. 372).

4 The term 'late modernism' is used by David Attwell in Coetzee, *Doubling the Point*, p. 198. Critics who have identified *Dusklands* with postmodernism include: Rosemary Gray, 'J. M. Coetzee's *Dusklands*: Of War and War's Alarms', *Commonwealth: Essays and Studies*, 9.1 (1986), 32–43; W. J. B. Wood, '*Dusklands* and "The Impregnable Stronghold of the Intellect"', *Theoria*, 54 (1980), 13–23; and Derek Maus, 'Kneeling before the Father's Wand: Violence, Eroticism and Paternalism in Thomas Pynchon's *V.* and J. M. Coetzee's *Dusklands*', *Journal of Literary Studies*, 15.1/2 (1999), 195–217.

5 Derek Attridge, *J. M. Coetzee and the Ethics of Reading: Literature in the Event* (Chicago, IL: University of Chicago Press, 2005), p. 6.

6 Ibid., p. 4.

7 Gilbert Yeoh, 'J. M. Coetzee and Samuel Beckett: Ethics, Truth-Telling and Self-Deception', *Critique*, 44.4 (2003), 331–48 (p. 332).

8 Paul A. Cantor, 'Happy Days in the Veld: Beckett and Coetzee's *In the Heart of the Country*', *South Atlantic Quarterly*, 93.1 (1994), 83–110 (pp. 82–7).

9 Steven G. Kellman, 'J. M. Coetzee and Samuel Beckett: The Translingual Link', *Comparative Literature Studies*, 33.2 (1996), 161–72.

10 J. M. Coetzee, 'Samuel Beckett and the Temptations of Style', *Theoria*, 41 (1973), 45–50 (p. 45).

11 J. M. Coetzee, 'The Comedy of Point of View in Beckett's *Murphy*', *Critique*, 12.2 (1970), 19–27 (p. 26).

12 J. M. Coetzee, 'The Manuscript Revisions of Beckett's *Watt*', *Journal of Modern Literature*, 2 (1972), 472–80 (p. 477).

13 Coetzee, 'Comedy of Point of View', p. 26.

14 Coetzee, 'Temptations of Style', p. 45, p. 47. Italics in original.

15 The significant recent exception is Patrick Hayes, who likewise traces Coetzee's ambivalence to Beckett's later works. Though he remains primarily interested in explaining the nature of Coetzee's indebtedness to Beckett, his analysis of this matter is certainly one of the most astute. However, since we conceive Coetzee's relationship to Beckett in different ways, we emphasize different aspects of the former's literary practice. *J. M. Coetzee and the Novel: Writing and Politics after Beckett* (Oxford: Oxford University Press, 2010).

16 J. M. Coetzee, 'Samuel Beckett's *Lessness*: An Exercise in Decomposition', *Computers and the Humanities*, 7.4 (1973), 195–8 (pp. 195–6). These two paragraphs are not consecutive in the original.

17 Ibid., pp. 195–6.

18 Ibid., p. 196.

19 Coetzee, 'Temptations of Style', p. 50.

20 Coetzee, 'Comedy of Point of View', p. 22.

21 Coetzee, 'Manuscript Revisions of Beckett's *Watt*', p. 474.

22 J. M. Coetzee, 'Statistical Indices of "Difficulty"', *Language and Style*, 2.3 (1969), 226–32 (p. 226). As a brief indication of the general character of Coetzee's prose we might note that the average length of the roughly 3,145 sentences in *Dusklands* is 15.5 words, and that, based on a random sample analysis, many of these are either simple (39%) or compound (17%).

23 Although I speak here of both *implied author* and *implied narrator*, my preference is for the latter, simply because it gives weight to telling, rather than writing. The point of real significance is that all fictional narratives entail the existence of an external narrative or authorial consciousness, including – indeed, especially – those related in the first person by character narrators. For doubts concerning the usefulness of *implied author*, see Shlomith Rimmon-Kenan, *Narrative Fiction: Contemporary Poetics* (London and New York: Routledge, 1989). On the benefits of the simpler *external narrator* and *character narrator* relative to the more technical *heterodiegetic* and *homodiegetic*, see Mieke Bal, 2nd edn, *Narratology: Introduction to the Theory of Narrative* (Toronto: University of Toronto Press, 1997), and James Phelan, *Living to Tell about It: A Rhetoric and Ethics of Character Narration* (Ithaca, NY and London: Cornell University Press, 2005).

24 Coetzee, *Doubling the Point*, p. 27.

25 J. M. Coetzee, 'Nabokov's *Pale Fire* and the Primacy of Art', *UCT Studies in English*, 5 (1974), 1–7 (p. 6).

26 Ibid., p. 5.

27 Coetzee, 'Temptations of Style', p. 49.
28 Ibid.
29 Coetzee, 'Samuel Beckett's *Lessness*', p. 198.
30 Coetzee, 'Temptations of Style', p. 50.
31 Coetzee, 'Nabokov's *Pale Fire*', p. 5.
32 Ibid.
33 Cantor, 'Happy Days in the Veld', p. 105.
34 J. M. Coetzee, 'Alex La Guma and the Responsibilities of the South African Writer', *Journal of the New African Literature and the Arts*, 9/10 (1971), 5–11 (p. 6, p. 11).
35 Coetzee, *Doubling the Point*, p. 434.
36 Coetzee, 'Responsibilities of the South African Writer', p. 10.
37 J. M. Coetzee, 'La Guma, Alex', in *English and South Africa*, ed. by Alan Lennox-Short (Cape Town: Nasou, 1973), pp. 111–12 (p. 112).
38 J. M. Coetzee, 'Man's Fate in the Novels of Alex La Guma', *Studies in Black Literature*, 5.1 [4.4] (1974), 16–23 (p. 22).
39 Alex La Guma, *A Walk in the Night and Other Stories* (Evanston, IL: Northwestern University Press, 1968), p. 24.
40 Coetzee, 'The Novels of Alex La Guma', p. 23.
41 Ibid., p. 22.
42 Coetzee, 'La Guma, Alex', p. 112.
43 Coetzee, 'The Novels of Alex La Guma', p. 22.
44 Ibid., p. 23.
45 Ibid., p. 20, p. 23.
46 Lionel Abrahams, 'Reflections in a Mirror', *Snarl*, 1.1 (1974), 2–3 (p. 3).
47 Crewe, '*Dusklands*', p. 91; Attridge, *Ethics of Reading*, p. 15.
48 Crewe, '*Dusklands*', p. 91.
49 Attridge, *Ethics of Reading*, p. 22. For Attridge's discussion of creation and invention, see his *The Singularity of Literature* (London: Routledge, 2004), pp. 17–62.
50 Abrahams, 'Reflections in a Mirror', p. 3.
51 For recent discussions of realisms after and beyond modernism, see the special issue *Peripheral Realisms*, *Modern Language Quarterly*, 73.3 (2012), especially Joe Cleary, 'Realism after Modernism and the Literary World-System', 255–68; and Jed Esty and Colleen Lye, 'Peripheral Realisms Now', 269–88.
52 Geoffrey N. Leech and Michael Short, *Style in Fiction: A Linguistic Introduction to Fictional Prose* (Harlow: Longman, 1981), pp. 155–85.
53 Bertolt Brecht, 'Popularity and Realism', in *Aesthetics and Politics*, Theodor Adorno and others (London: Verso, 2007), pp. 79–85 (p. 82).
54 Alain Robbe-Grillet, *For a New Novel: Essays on Fiction*, trans. by Richard Brown (Evanston, IL: Northwestern University Press, 1989), p. 157.
55 Such commonplace notions – assumptions about the way that literary technique works – may or may not be related to the actual operations of language, but, as Coetzee observes in his essay on the rhetoric of the passive, this hardly matters, so long as the author and reader share a belief in such 'grammatical

fictions'. Indeed, Coetzee notes as an avenue for further research the compilation of 'a bestiary of grammar, that is, a taxonomy of grammatical fictions and the rhetorical and poetic uses to which they are put'. J. M. Coetzee, 'The Rhetoric of the Passive in English', *Linguistics*, 18.3/4 (1980), 199–221, (p. 218).

56 Coetzee, 'The Novels of Alex La Guma', p. 22.

57 R. D. Laing, *The Divided Self: An Existential Study in Sanity and Madness* (Harmondsworth: Penguin, 1965).

58 J. M. Coetzee Papers, Cambridge, MA, Houghton Library, Harvard College, MS STOR 343 *94M-85. Coetzee's papers have now been acquired by the Harry Ransom Centre, University of Texas, Austin. As I have not had the opportunity to consult them there, I give the Houghton Library call number.

59 Frantz Fanon, *The Wretched of the Earth*, trans. by Constance Farrington (New York: Grove Press, 1968), pp. 38–43; Frantz Fanon, *Black Skin, White Masks*, trans. by Richard Philcox (New York: Grove Press, 2008), p. 192.

60 John R. Searle, *The Construction of Social Reality* (New York: Free Press, 1995); Giorgio Agamben, *Homo Sacer: Sovereign Power and Bare Life*, trans. by Daniel Heller-Roazen (Stanford, CA: Stanford University Press, 1998).

Chapter 2

1 André P. Brink, ''n Oeserige jaar…', *Die Burger*, 2 December 1977, p. 6.

2 André P. Brink, 'Verbysterende roman van Coetzee dring diep in die hart van die land', *Rapport*, 9 October 1977, pp. 14–15 (p. 14).

3 André P. Brink, 'Is dié "Engelse Sestiger" 'n aanklag teen onsself?', *Rapport*, 19 May 1974, p. 9.

4 Ibid.

5 Abrahams, 'Reflections in a Mirror', p. 3; Ursula A. Barnett, 'South Africa', *Books Abroad*, 50.2 (1976), 459–60.

6 Crewe, '*Dusklands*', p. 90. Italics are mine.

7 N. P. van Wyk Louw, *Vernuwing in die prosa: grepe uit ons Afrikaanse ervaring*, 3rd edn (Pretoria and Cape Town: Academica, 1970), pp. 103–10. All translations in this chapter are my own unless there is an indication to the contrary. In subsequent instances, only the English will be given, except where a particular Afrikaans term is significant.

8 Bartho Smit, 'Ter inleiding', *Sestiger*, 1.1 (1963), 1–2 (p. 1).

9 Louw, *Vernuwing in die prosa*, pp. 110–11.

10 André P. Brink, *Aspekte van die nuwe prosa* (Pretoria and Cape Town: Academica, 1967), p. 13, p. 127.

11 Something of this apparently contradictory movement between rejection and commitment is captured in the discussion of N. P. van Wyk Louw and the notion of 'loyal opposition' in Mark Sanders, *Complicities: The Intellectual and Apartheid* (Pietermaritzburg: University of Natal Press, 2002).

12 Marcellus Emants, *A Posthumous Confession*, ed. by Egbert Krispyn, trans. by J. M. Coetzee (Boston, MA: Twayne, 1975); J. M. Coetzee, 'Achterberg's "Ballade van de gasfitter": The Mystery of I and You', *PMLA*, 92.2 (1977), 285–96.

13 Coetzee, *Doubling the Point*, pp. 341–3.

14 J. M. Coetzee, 'The White Man's Burden', *Speak*, 1.1 (1977), 4–7 (p. 5). The use of an antiquated English to render the speech of Afrikaners would be a matter Coetzee would examine again in his later essay on Pauline Smith. See J. M. Coetzee, 'Pauline Smith and the Afrikaans Language', *English in Africa* 8.1 (1981), 25–32.

15 J. M. Coetzee, 'From *In the Heart of the Country*', *Standpunte*, 124 (1976), 9–16.

16 McDonald, *The Literature Police*, p. 91.

17 It is in this light that we might consider Coetzee's decision to submit the manuscript of 'The Narrative of Jacobus Coetzee' in 1972 to Human & Rousseau, an Afrikaans publisher associated with the Sestigers, as well as his membership of the Afrikaanse Skrywersgilde (Afrikaans Writers' Guild), taken up in 1980. See Kannemeyer, *A Life in Writing*, p. 235, p. 310.

18 J. M. Coetzee, 'An Interview with J. M. Coetzee', with Jean Sévry, *Commonwealth: Essays and Studies*, 9.1 (1986), 1–7 (p. 4).

19 Ibid., pp. 4–5.

20 J. M. Coetzee, 'Lughartig, met erns', *Beeld*, 20 October 1975, p. 10.

21 Louw, *Vernuwing in die prosa*, p. 64. Italics in original.

22 Jan Rabie, 'Nuwe bakens in Afrikaans', *Sestiger*, 1.1 (1963), 43–7 (p. 43).

23 *Die verslag van die Simposium oor die Sestigers*, ed. by Jim Polley (Cape Town and Pretoria: Human & Rousseau, 1973) pp. 7–10 (p. 7).

24 J. D. Miles, 'Om die nate te versit', in *Simposium oor die Sestigers*, pp. 32–41 (p. 32).

25 J. C. Kannemeyer, 'Die toekoms van die Afrikaanse Letterkunde', in *Simposium oor die Sestigers*.

26 Jack Cope, 'Where the Sestigers Came Unstuck', in *Simposium oor die Sestigers*, pp. 149–51 (p. 149).

27 Similar questions are raised by a letter Coetzee had written on 26 May 1973 to none other than Jack Cope, then editor of *Contrast*: 'It would seem more natural to try to publish it [*Dusklands*] in South Africa. Should I translate it into Afrikaans and become a Sewentiger? The idea is absurd.' Quoted in Kannemeyer, *A Life in Writing*, pp. 240–1.

28 Between 1962 and 1972 alone, Brink translated no less than forty-six works into Afrikaans, ranging from *Don Quixote* and Colette's *La Vagabonde* to *Richard III* and Lewis Carroll's *Alice's Adventures in Wonderland*.

29 André P. Brink, *Die Ambassadeur* (Cape Town and Pretoria: Human & Rousseau, 1963). Published in Brink's own translation as André Brink, *File on a Diplomat* (London: Longmans, 1967). All references are to the latter edition and are given after quotations in the text.

30 André P. Brink, *Orgie* (Cape Town: John Malherbe, 1965). All further references are to this edition and are given after quotations in the text.

31 Brink, *Aspekte*, p. 127.

32 J. M. Coetzee, *In the Heart of the Country* (London: Secker and Warburg, 1977), South African edn (Johannesburg: Ravan Press, 1978). Subsequent references are to the Ravan edition and are given after quotations in the text, except where indicated.

33 Rimmon-Kenan, *Narrative Fiction*, p. 56.
34 Ibid., p. 57.
35 *Dust*, dir. by Marion Hänsel (20th Century Fox, 1985).
36 Genesis 3:19.
37 Asterisks are used here and elsewhere to indicate hypothetical variants of actually occurring phrases and clauses.
38 J. M. Coetzee, 'The First Sentence of Yvonne Burgess's *The Strike*', *English in Africa*, 3.1 (1976), 47–8.
39 Coetzee, 'Achterberg's "Ballade van de gasfitter"', p. 293.
40 Brink, *Aspekte*, p. 126.
41 J. M. Coetzee, 'Clouts, Sydney', in *English and South Africa*, ed. by Alan Lennox-Short (Cape Town: Nasou, 1973), p. 23.
42 The association of the Word with the True and the Rock is one with which readers of the Gospels will be familiar. See John 1:1 and Matthew 7:24–5.
43 Coetzee, 'Achterberg's "Ballade van de gasfitter"', p. 287, p. 295.
44 André P. Brink, 'Die konteks van Sestig: herkoms en situasie', in *Simposium oor die Sestigers*, pp. 15–31 (p. 19).
45 André P. Brink, 'André Brink', with Avril Herber, in *Conversations: Some People, Some Places, Some Time – South Africa*, ed. by Avril Herber (Johannesburg: Bataleur, 1979), pp. 10–15 (p. 10).
46 Brink, 'Die konteks van Sestig', pp. 18–23.
47 Rimmon-Kenan, *Narrative Fiction*, p. 57.

Chapter 3

1 J. M. Coetzee, 'Speaking: J. M. Coetzee', with Stephen Watson, *Speak*, 1.3 (1978), 21–4 (p. 24).
2 Coetzee draws on 'Dream Song 1', which begins 'Huffy Henry hid the day', and on 'Dream Song 29', the final stanza of which reads: 'But never did Henry, as he thought he did,/ end anyone and hacks her body up/ and hide the pieces, where they may be found. / He knows: he went over everyone, & nobody's missing. / Often he reckons, in the dawn, them up. / Nobody is ever missing'. John Berryman, *77 Dream Songs* (London: Faber and Faber, 1964).
3 Simon Featherstone, 'The Rhythms of Prose', in *Writing with Style*, ed. by Rebecca Stott and Simon Avery (Harlow: Pearson Education, 2001), pp. 86–104 (p. 87). Italics in original.
4 Jane Gardam, 'The Only Story', *Sunday Times*, 7 September 1986, p. 49.
5 J. M. Coetzee, 'Surreal Metaphors and Random Processes', *Journal of Literary Semantics*, 8.1 (1979), 22–30 (p. 22).
6 J. M. Coetzee, *Waiting for the Barbarians* (London: Secker & Warburg, 1980; Johannesburg: Ravan Press, 1981), p. 2. Subsequent references are given after quotations in the text, except where indicated.
7 Roberts, 'Not a Wasted Word', p. 7; Charles Larson, 'Anglophone Writing from Africa and Asia', *World Literature Today*, 52.2. (1978), 245–6 (p. 245).

8 Adam Piette, *Remembering and the Sound of Words: Mallarmé, Proust, Joyce, Beckett* (Oxford: Oxford University Press, 1996).

9 Tom Paulin, 'Incorrigibly Plural: Recent Fiction', *Encounter*, 49.4 (1977), 82–9 (p. 89).

10 Georg Lukács, *The Historical Novel*, trans. by Hannah Mitchell and Stanley Mitchell (Harmondsworth: Penguin, 1969), p. 103. It is in this sense that Lukács uses the term pejoratively of the novels of Joyce and Kafka.

11 Thomas Pringle, *Poems Illustrative of South Africa: African Sketches Part One*, ed. by John Robert Wahl (Cape Town: C. Struik, 1970), pp. 8–12.

12 The average for each passage is as follows: 26.8; 28.8; 25.4; 33.5; 41.8; 30.5; 24.2.

13 For a discussion of *scene, summary, slow-down, ellipsis* and *pause*, see Bal, *Narratology*, pp. 101–11.

14 Coetzee, 'The English Fiction of Samuel Beckett', p. 76, p. 95. Italics in original.

15 Coetzee, *Doubling the Point*, pp. 59–60. Italics in original.

16 J. M. Coetzee, 'Hero and Bad Mother in Epic, a Poem', *Staffrider*, 1.1 (1978), 36–7. Subsequent line references are given after quotations in the text.

17 Coetzee, 'Surreal Metaphors', pp. 22–3.

18 Ibid.

19 Wallace Stevens, 'The Paltry Nude Starts on a Spring Voyage', in *Harmonium* (London: Faber and Faber, 2001), p. 6. For further references to Stevens in Coetzee's work, see: Coetzee, 'Nabokov's *Pale Fire*', p. 5; Coetzee, 'Achterberg's "Ballade van de gasfitter"', p. 286.

20 John Berger, *Ways of Seeing* (London: Penguin, 1972), pp. 52–5.

21 Of the twenty-five nouns used in the first ten stanzas, eighteen have appeared already by the fourth stanza. Likewise, nine of the twenty adjectives have been encountered by this stage.

22 Fredric Jameson, *Brecht and Method* (London: Verso, 1998), p. 43.

23 Paull F. Baum, *The Other Harmony of Prose: An Essay in English Prose Rhythm* (Durham, NC: Duke University Press, 1952), p. 43.

24 Wightman, 'Something Familiar about the Barbarians', p. 6.

25 Lynne Bryer, 'Underlying Melancholy of a Doomed Way of Life', *Cape Times*, 4 March 1981, p. 8.

26 Jane Kramer, 'In the Garrison', *New York Review of Books*, 2 December 1982, pp. 8–12 (p. 8); Howe, 'A Stark Political Fable of South Africa', p. 1; Clayton, 'Coetzee Blends Fable with Harsh SA Reality', p. 8.

27 Coetzee Papers, Cambridge, MA, Houghton Library, Harvard College, MS STOR 343 *94M-85.

28 Coetzee, 'Achterberg's "Ballade van de gasfitter"', p. 293.

29 Coetzee, 'Clouts, Sydney', p. 23.

30 Mothobi Mutloatse, 'Introduction', in *Forced Landing: Africa South Contemporary Writings*, ed. by Mothobi Mutloatse (Johannesburg: Ravan Press, 1980), pp. 1–7 (p. 1).

31 'About *Staffrider*', *Staffrider*, 1.1 (1978), p. 1.

32 David Attwell, *Rewriting Modernity: Studies in Black South African Literary History* (Scottsville: University of KwaZulu-Natal Press, 2005), pp. 144–5, 155.

33 Ibid., p. 137.

34 Bertolt Brecht, *Brecht on Theatre: The Development of an Aesthetic*, ed. and trans. by John Willett (New York: Hill and Wang, 1978), p. 22, p. 87.

35 Sipho Sepamla, *A Ride on the Whirlwind* (Johannesburg: Ad. Donker, 1981), pp. 15–17, p. 25. Italics are mine.

36 Ibid., p. 31, p. 51, p. 56, p. 97, p. 103.

37 Mongane Serote, *To Every Birth Its Blood* (Johannesburg: Ravan Press, 1981), p. 28, p. 30, p. 269, p. 29, p. 54, p. 318, p. 326, p. 359.

38 Towards the novel's end, Tsi's voice does return in a few brief passages, but it is no less marked by an alienated individualism, albeit one induced by exile.

39 J. M. Coetzee, 'Grubbing for the Ideological Implications: A Clash (More or Less) with J. M. Coetzee', with Alan Thorold and Richard Wicksteed, *Sjambok* [1981], 3–5.

40 Coetzee, 'Speaking', p. 23; Coetzee, 'The Novels of Alex La Guma', pp. 19–20.

41 Coetzee, 'The First Sentence of Yvonne Burgess's *The Strike*', p. 48.

42 J. M. Coetzee, '*Staffrider*', *African Book Publishing Record*, 5.4 (1979), 235–6 (p. 235).

43 David Lindley, *Lyric* (London: Methuen, 1985), p. 23.

44 For a related point, though one made in the service of a Levinasian reading of Coetzee's 'linguistico-ethics', see Clarkson, *J. M. Coetzee: Countervoices*, pp. 56–64.

45 Nathalie Sarraute, 'Conversation and Sub-conversation', trans. by Maria Jolas, in *The Age of Suspicion: Essays on the Novel* (New York, George Braziller, 1963), pp. 77–117.

46 Claude Mauriac, *The Marquise Went Out at Five*, trans. by Richard Howard (New York: George Brazziler, 1962), p. 310.

47 Robbe-Grillet, *For a New Novel*, p. 58, p. 53. Italics in original.

48 Mauriac, *The Marquise Went Out at Five*, p. 311.

49 Robbe-Grillet, *For a New Novel*, p. 29, p. 24.

50 Coetzee, 'Speaking', p. 24.

51 Ibid.

52 Ibid.

Chapter 4

1 J. M. Coetzee, 'Blood, Flaw, Taint, Degeneration: The Case of Sarah Gertrude Millin', *English Studies in Africa*, 23.1 (1980), 41–58 (p. 47, p. 42).

2 J. M. Coetzee, 'Linguistics and Literature', in *An Introduction to Contemporary Literary Theory*, ed. by Rory Ryan and Susan van Zyl (Johannesburg: Ad. Donker, 1982), pp. 41–52 (p. 43).

3 J. M. Coetzee, 'Newton and the Ideal of a Transparent Scientific Language', *Journal of Literary Semantics*, 11.1 (1982), 3–13 (p. 11, p. 7).

4 Ibid., p. 10.
5 Richard Boyd, 'Metaphor and Theory Change: What is "Metaphor" a Metaphor For?', in *Metaphor and Thought*, ed. by Andrew Ortony, 2nd edn (Cambridge: Cambridge University Press, 1993), pp. 481–532 (p. 486). Italics in original.
6 Coetzee, 'Newton', pp. 10–11.
7 Ibid., p. 11.
8 George Lakoff and Mark Johnson, *Metaphors We Live By* (Chicago, IL: University of Chicago Press, 1980).
9 George Lakoff and Mark Turner, *More than Cool Reason: A Field Guide to Poetic Metaphor* (Chicago, IL: University of Chicago Press, 1989). The use of capitalized roman font is the convention adopted by Lakoff and his co-authors for stating a conceptual metaphor.
10 Ibid., p. 107, p. 113.
11 Ibid., p. 52. Coetzee makes a similar point about the 'poetry of high Modernism' in 'Linguistics and Literature', p. 41.
12 These connotations are surprisingly difficult to analyse. What, for example, is the difference between *life is a journey* and *life is like a journey*? Perhaps it is that the simile more obviously marks the metaphorical process and so may be used either when the mapping is uncertain or unfamiliar or when there is a desire to draw attention to the process. There is a great deal more to be said about this, but to do so would be to embark on a different project entirely.
13 J. M. Coetzee, *Life & Times of Michael K* (London: Secker & Warburg; Johannesburg: Ravan Press, 1983), p. 139, p. 158, p. 159, p. 216. Subsequent references are to this edition and are given after quotations in the text, except where indicated.
14 Coetzee, 'Blood, Flaw, Taint, Degeneration', p. 42.
15 Coetzee, 'Speaking', p. 22.
16 J. M. Coetzee, 'Michael Wade: *Nadine Gordimer*', *Research in African Literatures*, 11.2 (1980), 253–6.
17 J. M. Coetzee, 'J.-M. Coetzee: "Il n'est pas de texte qui ne soit politique"', with Sophie Mayoux, *La Quinzaine littéraire*, 357 (1981), 6.
18 J. M. Coetzee, 'The Great South African Novel', *Leadership SA*, 2.4 (1983), 74, 77, 79 (p. 74).
19 See, for example: Paul Rich, 'Tradition and Revolt in South African Fiction: The Novels of André Brink, Nadine Gordimer and J. M. Coetzee', *Journal of Southern African Studies*, 9.1 (1982), 54–73; Christopher Hope, 'The Political Novelist in South Africa', *English in Africa*, 12.1 (1985), 41–6; Sheila Roberts, 'A Questionable Future: The Vision of Revolution in White South African Writing', *Journal of Contemporary African Studies*, 4.1/2 (1985), 215–23.
20 Lukács, *The Historical Novel*.
21 J. M. Coetzee, 'Idleness in South Africa', *Social Dynamics*, 8.1 (1982), 1–13.
22 J. M. Coetzee, 'SA Authors Must Learn Modesty', *Die Vaderland*, 1 May 1981, p. 16.
23 Ibid.

24 Ibid. Italics in original.

25 Coetzee, 'Blood, Flaw, Taint, Degeneration', p. 57.

26 Ibid.

27 Ibid., p. 56.

28 Nadine Gordimer, *July's People* (London: Jonathan Cape, 1981).

29 Ibid., p. 73. Subsequent references are to this edition and are given after quotations in the text.

30 Lakoff and Turner, *More than Cool Reason*, p. 103.

31 Stephen R. Clingman, *The Novels of Nadine Gordimer: History from the Inside* (Johannesburg: Ravan Press, 1986), p. 8.

32 Nadine Gordimer, *The Black Interpreters: Notes on African Writing* (Johannesburg: Spro-Cas/Ravan, 1973), pp. 31–2.

33 Nadine Gordimer, 'Living in the Interregnum', in *The Essential Gesture: Writing, Politics and Places*, ed. by Stephen Clingman (London: Penguin, 1989), pp. 261–84 (pp. 277–8).

34 Georg Lukács, *The Theory of the Novel: A Historico-Philosophical Essay on the Forms of Great Epic Literature*, trans. by Anna Bostock (London: Merlin Press, 1971), p. 46.

35 Lukács, *The Historical Novel*, p. 103, p. 123, p. 154.

36 Ibid., p. 164, p. 290.

37 Ibid., p. 239, p. 149.

38 J. M. Coetzee, 'Die skrywer en die teorie', *SAVAL Papers* (1980), 155–61 (pp. 160–1). All translations of this text are my own. Italics in original.

39 Coetzee, 'Great South African Novel', p. 77.

40 Ibid., Italics in original.

41 Ibid., p. 74, p. 77.

42 Ibid., pp. 77–9.

43 Coetzee, 'Idleness in South Africa', p. 11. Italics in original.

44 Amongst the others who would like to know K's story, there are, for example, Robert (106–8); the military officer and his subordinate interrogator (167–8); and December, the man on the beach (239).

45 Aristotle, *De Anima (On the Soul)*, trans. by Hugh Lawson-Tancred (London: Penguin, 1986), p. 163.

46 Lakoff and Turner, *More than Cool Reason*, pp. 166–7. It is worth noting here that the analysis of the Great Chain of Being in fact originates with Arthur Lovejoy, *The Great Chain of Being: A Study of the History of an Idea* (Cambridge, MA: Harvard University Press, 1936); and E. M. W. Tillyard, *The Elizabethan World Picture* (London: Chatto & Windus, 1943).

47 Lakoff and Turner, *More than Cool Reason*, pp. 166–7.

Chapter 5

1 Lawrence A. Hamilton, *The Political Philosophy of Needs* (Cambridge: Cambridge University Press, 2003).

2 Coetzee, *Life & Times of Michael K*, p. 34.

3 J. M. Coetzee, *Foe* (London: Secker & Warburg; Johannesburg: Ravan Press, 1986), p. 6, p. 7, p. 8, p. 10, p. 10, p. 11. Subsequent references are to this edition and are given after quotations in the text.

4 The italics here are my own.

5 Enright, 'Visions and Revisions', p. 20.

6 Coetzee, *Dusklands*, p. 10.

7 Coetzee, *In the Heart of the Country*, p. 22.

8 Coetzee, *Dusklands*, p. 9, p. 100.

9 Coetzee, *Waiting for the Barbarians*, p. 5, p. 90, p. 96.

10 Coetzee, *Dusklands*, p. 13, p. 91, p. 93.

11 Coetzee, *Waiting for the Barbarians*, p. 101.

12 Ibid., p. 118.

13 Coetzee, *Dusklands*, p. 5, pp. 26–7.

14 Ibid., p. 111, p. 71, p. 90, p. 100.

15 Coetzee, *In the Heart of the Country*, pp. 134–5, p. 10, p. 42.

16 Ibid., p. 13, p. 36, p. 137.

17 Coetzee, *Life & Times of Michael K*, p. 151.

18 J. M. Coetzee, *Age of Iron* (London: Secker & Warburg, 1990), p. 92. Subsequent references are to this edition and are given after quotations in the text, except where indicated.

19 For Coetzee's own comments on the 'derided' authority of the classics and Mrs Curren's 'totally untenable historical position', see his near-contemporary interview with David Attwell, where he pauses on his use of *soul* and stops short of admitting *grace*, *Doubling the Point*, pp. 243–50 (p. 250).

20 J. M. Coetzee, *The Master of Petersburg* (London: Secker & Warburg, 1994), p. 4. Subsequent references are to this edition and are given after quotations in the text, except where indicated.

21 J. M. Coetzee, *Disgrace* (London: Secker & Warburg, 1999), pp. 51–2, p. 58. Subsequent references are to this edition and are given after quotations in the text.

22 J. M. Coetzee, 'Confession and Double Thoughts: Tolstoy, Rousseau, Dostoevsky', *Comparative Literature*, 37.3 (1985), 193–232 (p. 252). That Coetzee was working on the essay alongside *Foe* is confirmed in Kannemeyer, *A Life in Writing*, p. 400. Also noteworthy is Coetzee's comment to Attwell: 'more and more I see the essay on Tolstoy, Rousseau and Dostoevsky emerging as pivotal', *Doubling the Point*, p. 391.

23 Peter Trudgill, *A Glossary of Sociolinguistics* (Edinburgh: Edinburgh University Press, 2003), p. 110.

24 Adorno, *Aesthetic Theory*, p. 76.

25 Coetzee, *Age of Iron*, pp. 71–2; Coetzee, *The Master of Petersburg*, p. 196.

26 Coetzee, *The Master of Petersburg*, p. 43, p. 37, p. 112.

Conclusion

1 Stephen Mulhall, *The Wounded Animal: J.M. Coetzee & the Difficulty of Reality in Literature & Philosophy* (Princeton, NJ: Princeton University Press, 2009), p. 159, p. 216, p. 166.

Bibliography

'About *Staffrider*', *Staffrider*, 1.1 (1978), p. 1.

Abrahams, Lionel, 'Drama of Desperation', *Rand Daily Mail*, 15 May 1978, p. 6.

'Reflections in a Mirror', *Snarl*, 1.1 (1974), pp. 2–3.

Adorno, Theodor W., *Aesthetic Theory*, ed. by Gretel Adorno and Rolf Tiedemann, trans. by Robert Hullot-Kentor (London: Continuum, 2004).

    Notes to Literature, ed. by Rolf Tiedemann, trans. by Shierry Weber Nicholsen, 2 vols (New York: Columbia University Press, 1991).

    'Punctuation Marks', in *Notes to Literature*, ed. by Rolf Tiedemann, trans. by Shierry Weber Nicholsen, 2 vols (New York: Columbia University Press, 1991), I, pp. 91–7.

Adorno, Theodor W., and others, *Aesthetics and Politics* (London: Verso, 2007).

Agamben, Giorgio, *Homo Sacer: Sovereign Power and Bare Life*, trans. by Daniel Heller-Roazen (Stanford, CA: Stanford University Press, 1998).

Aristotle, *De Anima (On the Soul)*, trans. by Hugh Lawson-Tancred (London: Penguin, 1986).

Attridge, Derek, *J. M. Coetzee and the Ethics of Reading: Literature in the Event* (Chicago, IL: University of Chicago Press, 2005).

    The Singularity of Literature (London: Routledge, 2004).

Attwell, David, *J. M. Coetzee: South Africa and the Politics of Writing* (Berkeley: University of California Press, 1993).

    Rewriting Modernity: Studies in Black South African Literary History (Scotsville: University of KwaZulu-Natal Press, 2005).

Bailey, Richard W., 'Current Trends in the Analysis of Style', *Style*, 1.1 (1967), 1–14.

Bal, Mieke, *Narratology: Introduction to the Theory of Narrative*, 2nd edn (Toronto: University of Toronto Press, 1997).

Barnett, Ursula A., 'South Africa', *Books Abroad*, 50.2 (1976), 459–60.

Barry, Charles, 'Compassion Makes Memorable Work', *Star*, 28 October 1983, p. 12.

Barthes, Roland, *Writing Degree Zero*, trans. by Annette Lavers and Colin Smith (New York: Hill and Wang, 1968).

Baum, Paull F., *The Other Harmony of Prose: An Essay in English Prose Rhythm* (Durham, NC: Duke University Press, 1952).

Beckett, Samuel, *The Complete Short Prose, 1929–1989* (New York: Grove Press, 1995).

Imagination Dead Imagine (London: Calder & Boyars, 1965).

Lessness (London: Calder & Boyars, 1970).

Murphy (New York: Grove Press, 1957).

'Ping', in *The Complete Short Prose, 1929–1989* (New York: Grove Press, 1995), pp. 193–6.

Three Novels: Molloy, Malone Dies, The Unnamable (New York: Grove Press, 1965).

Berger, John, *Ways of Seeing* (London: Penguin, 1972).

Berryman, John, *77 Dream Songs* (London: Faber and Faber, 1964).

Bethlehem, Louise, *Skin Tight: Apartheid Literary Culture and Its Aftermath* (Pretoria: University of South Africa Press, 2006).

Boekkooi, Jaap, 'Injustice for "Society's Sake"', *Star*, 19 February 1981, p. 12.

Bourdieu, Pierre, *The Field of Cultural Production: Essays on Art and Literature*, ed. by Randal Johnson (Cambridge: Polity Press, 1993).

The Rules of Art: Genesis and Structure of the Literary Field, trans. by Susan Emanuel (Cambridge: Polity Press, 1996).

Bowers, Frances, 'First SA Modern Novel?', *Cape Times*, 5 June 1974, p. 8.

Boyd, Richard, 'Metaphor and Theory Change: What is "Metaphor" a Metaphor For?', in *Metaphor and Thought*, ed. by Andrew Ortony, 2nd edn (Cambridge: Cambridge University Press, 1993), 481–532.

Brecht, Bertolt, *Brecht on Theatre*, ed. by John Willett (New York: Hill and Wang, 1978).

'Popularity and Realism', in *Aesthetics and Politics*, Theodor W. Adorno and others (London: Verso, 2007), pp. 79–85.

Brink, André P., *Die Ambassadeur* (Cape Town and Pretoria: Human & Rousseau, 1963).

'André Brink', with Avril Herber, in *Conversations: Some People, Some Places, Some Time – South Africa*, ed. by Avril Herber (Johannesburg: Bataleur, 1979), pp. 10–15.

Aspekte van die nuwe prosa (Pretoria and Cape Town: Academica, 1967).

File on a Diplomat (London: Longmans, 1967).

'Is dié "Engelse Sestiger" 'n aanklag teen onsself?', *Rapport*, 19 May 1974, p. 9.

Kennis van die aand (Cape Town: Buren, 1973).

'Die konteks van Sestig: herkoms en situasie', in *Die verslag van die Simposium oor die Sestigers*, ed. by Jim Polley (Cape Town and Pretoria: Human & Rousseau, 1973), pp. 15–31.

'Kortsluiting in die kritiek?', *Sestiger*, 1.1 (1963), 11–16.

''n Oeserige jaar…', *Die Burger*, 2 December 1977, p. 6.

Orgie (Cape Town: John Malherbe, 1965).

'Verbysterende roman van Coetzee dring diep in die hart van die land', *Rapport*, 9 October 1977, pp. 14–15.

Brink, André P., and J. M. Coetzee, eds., *A Land Apart: A Contemporary South African Reader* (London: Faber and Faber, 1986).

Bryer, Lynne, 'Underlying Melancholy of a Doomed Way of Life', *Cape Times*, 4 March 1981, p. 8.

Buber, Martin, *I and Thou*, trans. by Walter Kaufmann (New York: Touchstone, 1970).

Cantor, Paul A., 'Happy Days in the Veld: Beckett and Coetzee's *In the Heart of the Country*', *South Atlantic Quarterly*, 93.1 (1994), 83–110.

Casanova, Pascale, *The World Republic of Letters*, trans. by M. B. DeBevoise (Cambridge, MA: Harvard University Press, 2004).

Clarkson, Carrol, *J. M. Coetzee: Countervoices* (Basingstoke: Palgrave Macmillan, 2009).

Clayton, Cherry, 'Coetzee Blends Fable with Harsh SA Reality', *Rand Daily Mail*, 2 March 1981, p. 8.

Cleary, Joe, 'Realism after Modernism and the Literary World-System', *Modern Language Quarterly*, 73.3 (2012), 255–68.

Clingman, Stephen R., *The Novels of Nadine Gordimer: History from the Inside* (Johannesburg: Ravan Press, 1986).

Coetzee, J. M., 'Achterberg's "Ballade van de gasfitter": The Mystery of I and You', *PMLA*, 92.2 (1977), 285–96.

Age of Iron (London: Secker & Warburg, 1990).

'The Agentless Sentence as Rhetorical Device', *Language and Style*, 13.1 (1980), 26–34.

'Alex La Guma and the Responsibilities of the South African Writer', *Journal of the New African Literature and the Arts*, 9/10 (1971), 5–11.

'Blood, Flaw, Taint, Degeneration: The Case of Sarah Gertrude Millin', *English Studies in Africa*, 23.1 (1980), 41–58.

Boyhood: Scenes from Provincial Life (London: Secker & Warburg, 1997).

'Captain America in American Mythology', *UCT Studies in English*, 6 (1976), 33–9.

The Childhood of Jesus (London: Harvill Secker, 2013).

'Clouts, Sydney', in *English and South Africa*, ed. by Alan Lennox-Short (Cape Town: Nasou, 1973), p. 23.

'The Comedy of Point of View in Beckett's *Murphy*', *Critique*, 12.2 (1970), 19–27.

'Confession and Double Thoughts: Tolstoy, Rousseau, Dostoevsky', *Comparative Literature*, 37.3 (1985), 193–232.

Diary of a Bad Year (London: Harvill Secker, 2007).

Disgrace (London: Secker & Warburg, 1999).

Doubling the Point: Essays and Interviews, ed. by David Attwell (Cambridge, MA: Harvard University Press, 1992).

Dusklands (Johannesburg: Ravan Press, 1974).

Elizabeth Costello (London: Secker & Warburg, 2003).

'The English Fiction of Samuel Beckett: An Essay in Stylistic Analysis' (unpublished doctoral dissertation, University of Texas at Austin, 1969).

''n Ernstige blik op 'n verdeelde psige', *Rapport*, 6 August 1978, p. 17.

'The First Sentence of Yvonne Burgess's *The Strike*', *English in Africa*, 3.1 (1976), 47–8.

Foe (London: Secker & Warburg; Johannesburg: Ravan Press, 1986).

'From *In the Heart of the Country*', *Standpunte*, 124 (1976), 9–16.

'Grubbing for the Ideological Implications: A Clash (More or Less) with J. M. Coetzee', with Alan Thorold and Richard Wicksteed, *Sjambok* [1981], 3–5.

'The Great South African Novel', *Leadership SA*, 2.4 (1983), 74, 77, 79.

'Hero and Bad Mother in Epic, a Poem', *Staffrider*, 1.1 (1978), 36–7.

'Idleness in South Africa', *Social Dynamics*, 8.1 (1982), 1–13.

'An Interview with J. M. Coetzee', with Jean Sévry, *Commonwealth: Essays and Studies*, 9.1 (1986), 1–7.

In the Heart of the Country (London: Secker & Warburg, 1977).

In the Heart of the Country, South African edn (Johannesburg: Ravan Press, 1978).

'J. M. Coetzee, "Il n'est pas de texte qui ne soit politique"', with Sophie Mayoux, *La Quinzaine littéraire*, 357 (1981), 6.

J. M. Coetzee Papers, Cambridge, MA, Houghton Library, Harvard College, MS STOR 343 *94M-85.

'La Guma, Alex', in *English and South Africa*, ed. by Alan Lennox-Short (Cape Town: Nasou, 1973), pp. 111–12.

Life & Times of Michael K (London: Secker & Warburg; Johannesburg: Ravan Press, 1983).

'Linguistics and Literature', in *An Introduction to Contemporary Literary Theory*, ed. by Rory Ryan and Susan van Zyl (Johannesburg: Ad. Donker, 1982), pp. 41–52.

'Lughartig, met erns', *Beeld*, 20 October 1975, p. 10.

'Man's Fate in the Novels of Alex La Guma', *Studies in Black Literature*, 5.1 [4.4] (1974), 16–23.

'The Manuscript Revisions of Beckett's *Watt*', *Journal of Modern Literature*, 2 (1972), 472–80.

The Master of Petersburg (London: Secker & Warburg, 1994).

'Michael Wade: *Nadine Gordimer*', *Research in African Literatures*, 11.2 (1980), 253–6.

'Nabokov's *Pale Fire* and the Primacy of Art', *UCT Studies in English*, 5 (1974), 1–7.

'Newton and the Ideal of a Transparent Scientific Language', *Journal of Literary Semantics*, 11.1 (1982), 3–13.

'The Novel Today', *Upstream*, 6.1 (1988), 2–5.

'Pauline Smith and the Afrikaans Language', *English in Africa*, 8.1 (1981), 25–32.

'The Rhetoric of the Passive in English', *Linguistics*, 18.3/4 (1980), 199–221.

'SA Authors Must Learn Modesty', *Die Vaderland*, 1 May 1981, p. 16.

'Samuel Beckett and the Temptations of Style', *Theoria*, 41 (1973), 45–50.

'Samuel Beckett's *Lessness*: An Exercise in Decomposition', *Computers and the Humanities*, 7.4 (1973), 195–8.

'Die skrywer en die teorie', *SAVAL Papers* (1980), 155–61.

Slow Man (London: Secker & Warburg, 2005).

'Speaking: J. M. Coetzee', with Stephen Watson, *Speak*, 1.3 (1978), 21–4.

'*Staffrider*', *African Book Publishing Record*, 5.4 (1979), 235–6.

'Statistical Indices of "Difficulty"', *Language and Style*, 2.3 (1969), 226–32.

Summertime: Scenes from Provincial Life (London: Harvill Secker, 2009).

'Surreal Metaphors and Random Processes', *Journal of Literary Semantics*, 8.1 (1979), 22–30.

Waiting for the Barbarians (London: Secker & Warburg, 1980; Johannesburg: Ravan Press, 1981).

'The White Man's Burden', *Speak*, 1.1 (1977), 4–7.

White Writing: On the Culture of Letters in South Africa (New Haven, CT: Yale University Press, 1988).

Youth (London: Secker & Warburg, 2002).

Cope, Jack, 'Where the Sestigers Came Unstuck', in *Die verslag van die Simposium oor die Sestigers*, ed. by Jim Polley (Cape Town and Pretoria: Human & Rousseau, 1973), pp. 149–51.

Crewe, Jonathan, '*Dusklands*', *Contrast*, 9.2 (1974), 90–5.

Darke, Neill, 'Coetzee Novel Bewildering and Tortuous', *Argus*, 23 October 1986, p. 29.

'Coetzee's Prize-Winning Novel Original, Compelling', *Argus*, 23 November 1983, p. 26.

Derrida, Jacques, *Of Grammatology*, trans. by Gayatri Chakravorty Spivak (Baltimore, MD: Johns Hopkins University Press, 1976).

De Villiers, G. E., ed., *Close to the Sun: Stories from Southern Africa* (Johannesburg: Macmillan South Africa, 1979).

Dust, dir. by Marion Hänsel (20th Century Fox, 1985).

Ekelund, Bo G., *In the Pathless Forest: John Gardner's Literary Project* (Uppsala: Uppsala University, 1995).

Emants, Marcellus, *A Posthumous Confession*, ed. by Egbert Krispyn, trans. by J. M. Coetzee (Boston, MA: Twayne, 1975).

Een nagelaten bekentenis (Amsterdam: Van Holkema & Warendorf, [1894]).

Enright, D. J., 'Visions and Revisions', *New York Review of Books*, 28 May 1987, pp. 18–20.

Esty, Jed and Colleen Lye, 'Peripheral Realisms Now', *Modern Language Quarterly*, 73.3 (2012), 269–88.

Etherington, Ben, 'What is Materialism's Material? Thoughts toward (actually against) a Materialism for "World Literature"', *Journal of Postcolonial Writing*, 48.5 (2012), 539–51.

Fanon, Frantz, *Black Skin, White Masks*, trans. by Richard Philcox (New York: Grove Press, 2008).

The Wretched of the Earth, trans. by Constance Farrington (New York: Grove Press, 1968).

Featherstone, Simon, 'The Rhythms of Prose', in *Writing with Style*, ed. by Rebecca Stott and Simon Avery (Harlow: Pearson Education, 2001), pp. 86–104.

Fish, Stanley, *Is There a Text in This Class? The Authority of Interpretive Communities* (Cambridge, MA: Harvard University Press, 1980).

Gardam, Jane, 'The Only Story', *Sunday Times*, 7 September 1986, p. 49.

Glendinning, Victoria, 'A Harsh Voice Crying in the Wilderness', *Sunday Times*, 23 January 1983, p. 45.

Gordimer, Nadine, *The Black Interpreters: Notes on African Writing* (Johannesburg: Spro-Cas/ Ravan, 1973).

   Burger's Daughter (London: Jonathan Cape, 1979).

   The Conservationist (London: Jonathan Cape, 1974).

   The Essential Gesture: Writing, Politics and Places, ed. by Stephen Clingman (London: Penguin, 1989).

   July's People (London: Jonathan Cape, 1981).

   'The Idea of Gardening', *New York Review of Books*, 2 February 1984, pp. 3, 6.

   'Living in the Interregnum', in *The Essential Gesture: Writing, Politics and Places*, ed. by Stephen Clingman (London: Penguin, 1989), pp. 261–84.

Gordimer, Nadine and Lionel Abrahams, eds., *South African Writing Today* (Harmondsworth: Penguin, 1967).

Gray, Rosemary, 'J. M. Coetzee's *Dusklands*: of War and War's Alarms', *Commonwealth: Essays and Studies*, 9.1 (1986), 32–43.

Gray, Stephen, *Southern African Literature: An Introduction* (Cape Town: David Philip; London: Rex Collings, 1979).

The Guest: An Episode in the Life of Eugene Marais, dir. by Ross Devenish (Athol Fugard Productions, 1977).

Hamilton, Lawrence A., *The Political Philosophy of Needs* (Cambridge: Cambridge University Press, 2003).

Harris, Peter, 'The Art of Being a Survivor', *Cape Times*, 30 November 1983, p. 14.

Harwood, Ronald, 'An Astonishing First Novel', *Sunday Times*, 12 June 1977, p. 41.

Hayes, Patrick, *J. M. Coetzee and the Novel: Writing and Politics after Beckett* (Oxford: Oxford University Press, 2010).

Hegel, G. W. F., *Aesthetics: Lectures on Fine Art*, trans. by T. M. Knox, 2 vols (Oxford: Clarendon Press, 1975).

   Phenomenology of the Spirit, trans. by A. V. Miller (Oxford: Clarendon Press, 1977).

Herber, Avril, ed., *Conversations: Some People, Some Places, Some Time – South Africa* (Johannesburg: Bataleur, 1979).

Heywood, Christopher, *A History of South African Literature* (Cambridge: Cambridge University Press, 2004).

Hofmeyr, Isabel, 'A Bewildering Parable', *Star*, 22 September 1986, p. 14.

Hope, Christopher. 'The Political Novelist in South Africa', *English in Africa*, 12.1 (1985), 41–6.

Howe, Irving, 'A Stark Political Fable of South Africa', *New York Times Book Review*, 18 April 1982, pp. 1, 36.

Iser, Wolfgang, *The Act of Reading: A Theory of Aesthetic Response* (Baltimore, MD: John Hopkins University Press, 1978).

Jameson, Fredric, *Brecht and Method* (London: Verso, 1998).

Jarvis, Simon, *Adorno: A Critical Introduction* (Cambridge: Polity Press, 1998).

Johnston, Alexander, 'Skilful Work on Many Levels', *Sunday Tribune*, 18 January 1987, Today section, p. 8.

'Triumphs of the Human Spirit', *Sunday Tribune*, 25 December 1983, Today section, p. 15.

Kannemeyer, J. C., *A Life in Writing*, trans. by Michiel Heyns (Johannesburg and Cape Town: Jonathan Ball, 2013).

'Die toekoms van die Afrikaanse Letterkunde', in *Die verslag van die Simposium oor die Sestigers*, ed. by Jim Polley (Cape Town and Pretoria: Human & Rousseau, 1973), pp. 181–4.

Kellman, Steven G., 'J. M. Coetzee and Samuel Beckett: The Translingual Link', *Comparative Literature Studies*, 33.2 (1996), 161–72.

Kramer, Jane, 'In the Garrison', *New York Review of Books*, 2 December 1982, pp. 8–12.

Kratz, Henry, Review of *Life & Times of Michael K*, *World Literature Today*, 58.3 (1984), 461–2.

La Guma, Alex, *And a Threefold Cord* (Berlin: Seven Seas, 1964).

In the Fog of the Seasons' End (London: Heinemann, 1972).

The Stone Country (Berlin: Seven Seas, 1967).

A Walk in the Night and Other Stories (Evanston, IL: Northwestern University Press, 1968).

Laing, R. D., *The Divided Self: An Existential Study in Sanity and Madness* (Harmondsworth: Penguin, 1965).

Lakoff, George, and Mark Johnson, *Metaphors We Live By* (Chicago, IL: University of Chicago Press, 1980).

Lakoff, George, and Mark Turner, *More than Cool Reason: A Field Guide to Poetic Metaphor* (Chicago, IL: University of Chicago Press, 1989).

Larson, Charles, 'Anglophone Writing from Africa and Asia', *World Literature Today*, 52.2. (1978), 245–6.

Leech, Geoffrey N., and Michael H. Short, *Style in Fiction: A Linguistic Introduction to English Fictional Prose* (Harlow: Longman, 1981).

Lennox-Short, Alan, ed., *English and South Africa* (Cape Town: Nasou, 1973).

Leroux, Etienne, 'Tegnieke, temas en toekomsplanne', in *Die verslag van die Simposium oor die Sestigers*, ed. by Jim Polley (Cape Town and Pretoria: Human & Rousseau, 1973), pp. 126–39.

To a Dubious Salvation: A Trilogy of Fantastic Novels, trans. by Charles Eglington and Amy Starke (Harmondsworth: Penguin, 1972).

'Vernuwing in die prosa', *Sestiger*, 2.4 (1965), 31–5.

Lindley, David, *Lyric* (London: Methuen, 1985).

Louw, N. P. van Wyk, 'Sestig, Sestiger, Sestigste', *Sestiger*, 1.3 (1964), 3–11.

Vernuwing in die prosa: grepe uit ons Afrikaanse ervaring, 3rd edn (Pretoria and Cape Town: Academica, 1970).

Lovejoy, Arthur, *The Great Chain of Being: A Study of the History of an Idea* (Cambridge, MA: Harvard University Press, 1936).

Lukács, Georg, *The Historical Novel*, trans. by Hannah Mitchell and Stanley Mitchell (Harmondsworth: Penguin, 1969).

The Theory of the Novel: A Historico-Philosophical Essay on the Forms of Great Epic Literature, trans. by Anna Bostock (London: Merlin Press, 1971).

Mackie, Heather, 'Consummate Literary Brilliance of Coetzee Emerges Again', *Cape Times*, 31 December 1986, p. 6.

Mauriac, Claude, *The Marquise Went Out at Five*, trans. by Richard Howard (New York: George Braziller, 1962).

Maus, Derek, 'Kneeling before the Father's Wand: Violence, Eroticism and Paternalism in Thomas Pynchon's *V.* and J. M. Coetzee's *Dusklands*', *Journal of Literary Studies*, 15.1/2 (1999), 195–217.

McDonald, Peter D., *British Literary Culture and Publishing Practice, 1880–1914* (Cambridge: Cambridge University Press, 1997).

The Literature Police: Apartheid Censorship and its Cultural Consequences (Oxford: Oxford University Press, 2009).

Miles, J. D., 'Om die nate te versit', in *Die verslag van die Simposium oor die Sestigers*, ed. by Jim Polley (Cape Town and Pretoria: Human & Rousseau, 1973), pp. 32–41.

Milic, Louis T., 'Against the Typology of Styles', in *Essays on the Languages of Literature*, eds. by Seymour Chatman and Samuel R. Levin (Boston, MA: Houghton Mifflin, 1967), pp. 442–50.

Mulhall, Stephen, *The Wounded Animal: J. M. Coetzee & the Difficulty of Reality in Literature and Philosophy* (Princeton, NJ: Princeton University Press, 2009).

Mutloatse, Mothobi, ed., *Forced Landing: Africa South Contemporary Writings* (Johannesburg: Ravan Press, 1980).

'Introduction', in *Forced Landing: Africa South Contemporary Writings*, ed. by Mothobi Mutloatse (Johannesburg: Ravan Press, 1980), pp. 1–7.

Nathan, Manfred, *South African Literature* (Cape Town and Johannesburg: Juta & Co, 1925).

Ortony, Andrew, ed., *Metaphor and Thought*, 2nd edn (Cambridge: Cambridge University Press, 1993).

Ozick, Cynthia, 'A Tale of Heroic Anonymity', *New York Times Book Review*, 11 December 1983, pp. 1, 26, 28.

Paulin, Tom, 'Incorrigibly Plural: Recent Fiction', *Encounter*, 49.4 (1977), 82–9.

Phelan, James, *Living to Tell about It: A Rhetoric and Ethics of Character Narration* (Ithaca, NY and London: Cornell University Press, 2005).

Piette, Adam, *Remembering and the Sound of Words: Mallarmé, Proust, Joyce, Beckett* (Oxford: Oxford University Press, 1996).

Pogrund, Anne, 'Survival against Odds Powerfully Portrayed', *Rand Daily Mail*, 12 December 1983, p. 12.

Polley, Jim, ed., *Die verslag van die Simposium oor die Sestigers* (Cape Town and Pretoria: Human & Rousseau, 1973).

Pringle, Thomas, *Poems Illustrative of South Africa: African Sketches Part One*, ed. by John Robert Wahl (Cape Town: C. Struik, 1970).

Rabie, Jan, *Die groot anders-maak* (Cape Town and Pretoria: Human & Rousseau, 1964).

'Nuwe bakens in Afrikaans', *Sestiger*, 1.1 (1963), 43–7.

Rich, Paul, 'Tradition and Revolt in South African Fiction: The Novels of André Brink, Nadine Gordimer and J. M. Coetzee', *Journal of Southern African Studies*, 9.1 (1982), 54–73.

Riffaterre, Michael, 'Describing Poetic Structures: Two Approaches to Baudelaire's "Les Chats"', *Yale French Studies*, 36/37 (1966), 200–42.

Rimmon-Kenan, Shlomith, *Narrative Fiction: Contemporary Poetics* (London: Routledge, 1989).

Robbe-Grillet, Alain, *For a New Novel: Essays on Fiction*, trans. by Richard Brown (Evanston, IL: Northwestern University Press, 1989).

The Erasers, trans. by Richard Howard (New York: Grove Press, 1964).

Jealousy, trans. by Richard Howard (New York: Grove Press, 1959).

Roberts, Beryl, 'Not a Wasted Word in this Major Work', *Sunday Times* [South Africa], 13 November 1983, Lifestyle section, p. 7.

Roberts, Sheila, 'A Questionable Future: The Vision of Revolution in White South African Writing', *Journal of Contemporary African Studies*, 4.1/2 (1985), 215–23.

Rouse, Blair, and James R. Bennett, 'Editorial', *Style*, 1.1 (1967), v–vii.

Ryan, Rory, and Susan van Zyl, eds., *An Introduction to Contemporary Literary Theory* (Johannesburg: Ad. Donker, 1982).

Sampson, Anthony, 'Introduction', in *South African Writing Today*, ed. by Nadine Gordimer and Lionel Abrahams (Harmondsworth: Penguin, 1967), pp. 11–15.

Sarraute, Nathalie, *The Age of Suspicion: Essays on the Novel*, trans. by Maria Jolas (New York: George Braziller, 1963).

Do You Hear Them?, trans. by Maria Jolas (New York: George Braziller, 1973).

The Planetarium, trans. by Maria Jolas (New York: George Braziller, 1960).

Sanders, Mark, *Complicities: The Intellectual and Apartheid* (Pietermaritzburg: University of Natal Press, 2002).

Schorer, Mark, 'Technique as Discovery', *Hudson Review*, 1.1 (1948), 67–87.

Searle, John R., *The Construction of Social Reality* (New York: Free Press, 1995).

Segal, Philip, 'On *Waiting for Godot*', in *Essays and Lectures: Selected Literary Criticism*, ed. by Marcia Leveson (Cape Town: David Philip, 1973), pp. 188–92.

Sepamla, Sipho, *A Ride on the Whirlwind* (Johannesburg: Ad. Donker, 1981).

Serote, Mongane Wally, *To Every Birth Its Blood* (Johannesburg: Ravan Press, 1981).

Shakespeare, Nicholas, 'Forever Blowing Bubbles', *The Times*, 13 January 1983, p. 8.

'A Slap Bang Farce Nipped in the Bud', *The Times*, 11 September 1986, p. 11.

Simpson, Paul, *Stylistics: A Resource Book for Students* (London: Routledge, 2004).

Stevens, Wallace, *Harmonium* (London: Faber and Faber, 2001).

Stott, Rebecca, and Simon Avery, eds., *Writing with Style* (Harlow: Pearson Education, 2001).

T. M., 'Exploring an Inner World', *Sunday Tribune*, 30 July 1978, Insight section, p. 3.

Temple, Peter, 'The Private World of a Major New SA Talent', *Star*, 14 June 1974, Literary Review section, p. 3.

Thompson, Garner, 'J. M. Coetzee's *Life and Times of Michael K* ... Not All Praise', *Weekend Argus*, 29 October 1983, p. 13.

Tillyard, E. M. W., *The Elizabethan World Picture* (London: Chatto & Windus, 1943).

Tomalin, Claire, 'The Magical Historical Shortlist', *Sunday Times*, 25 September 1983, p. 41.

Trudgill, Peter, *A Glossary of Sociolinguistics* (Edinburgh: Edinburgh University Press, 2003).

Van der Vlies, Andrew, *South African Textual Cultures: White, Black, Read All Over* (Manchester: Manchester University Press, 2007).

Watson, Stephen, 'Colonialism and the Novels of J. M. Coetzee', *Research in African Literatures*, 17.3 (1986), 370–92.

Wightman, Dave, 'Something Familiar about the Barbarians', *Sunday Tribune*, 22 February 1981, p. 6.

Wilhelm, Peter, 'Vietnam, SA Powerfully Linked', *Star*, 24 April 1974, p. 21.

Wittenberg, Hermann, 'Towards an Archaeology of *Dusklands*', *English in Africa*, 38.3 (2011), 71–89.

Wood, W. J. B., '*Dusklands* and "The Impregnable Stronghold of the Intellect"', *Theoria*, 54 (1980), 13–23.

Yeoh, Gilbert, 'J. M. Coetzee and Samuel Beckett: Ethics, Truth-Telling and Self-Deception', *Critique: Studies in Contemporary Fiction*, 44.4 (2003), 331–48.

Zimbler, Jarad, 'Under Local Eyes: The South African Publishing Context of J. M. Coetzee's *Foe*', *English Studies in Africa*, 47.1 (2004), 45–59.

Index